The Heart of the Matter

High-Intermediate Listening, Speaking, and Critical Thinking

Marjorie Vai
The New School for Social Research
New York

Teacher's Notes
by Robyn Vaccara
The New School for Social Research
New York

Heinle & Heinle Publishers
Boston, MA 02116

An International Thomson Publishing Company

This book is dedicated to my son, Daniel.

The publication of The Heart of the Matter was directed by members of the Newbury House ESL/EFL team at Heinle & Heinle:

Erik Gundersen, Editorial Director
Bruno Paul, Market Development Director
Maryellen Eschmann Killeen, Production Services Coordinator

Also participating in the publication of this program were:

Stanley J. Galek, Vice President and Publisher
Ken Pratt, Associate Editor
Mary Sutton, Associate Market Development Director
Mary Beth Hennebury, Manufacturing Coordinator
Heide Kaldenbach-Montemayor, Assistant Editor
Rollins Design and Production: interior design and production
Ha Nguyen Design: cover design
Donald Pharr, editorial consultant and copyeditor
Martha Friedman, photo researcher

Library of Congress Cataloging-in-Publication Data

Vai, Marjorie.
   The heart of the matter: high-intermediate listening, speaking, and critical thinking / Marjorie Vai
      p. cm.
   ISBN 0-8384-7857-3
   1. English language—textbooks for foreign speakers. 2. English language—spoken English—Problems, exercises, etc. 3. Critical thinking—problems, exercises, etc. 4. Listening—Problems, exercises, etc. I Title.
PE1128.V28   1997
428.3'4—dc21

CONTENTS

1   What Will I Do When They Find Out I'm Me? . . . Be Confident   2

Topic: Dealing with anxiety and becoming more confident

Listening 1
(Expert Opinion): A magazine publisher outlines seven rules that can help us all become more confident

Listening 2
(Personal Perspective): A story about the seven rules

Listening 3
(Other Voices): Three people apply the seven rules to their lives

Video
Television broadcast: "The Horatio Alger Awards Ceremony," profiles of three people who overcame great obstacles to succeed

2   Legacy of the Blues   12

Topic: The sound, feeling, and history of an American musical style: the blues

Listening 1
(Expert Opinion): A music historian describes the origin of the blues

Listening 2
(Personal Perspective): A Blues musician talks about jazz and the blues

Listening 3
(Other Voices): Two musical selections: Dinah Washington sings "Come Rain or Come Shine" and Muddy Waters performs "Mannish Boy"

Video
Short film: *Carolina Underground,* the story of a blues musician who plays in the subway

3   Food: Business & Pleasure   22

Topic: Doing what you love for a living (for example, starting a food business)

Listening 1
(Expert Opinion): The director of a culinary arts program talks about America's passion for food and gives an overview of food professions

Listening 2
(Personal Perspective): A successful food entrepreneur's story

Listening 3
(Other Voices): Two others who started successful food businesses talk about why they love what they do

Project
Researching and planning a business of one's own

ACKNOWLEDGMENTS

Each chapter of this book required a great deal of searching, discussing, and problem solving. I am grateful to a number of people for their help and encouragement.

First, I must acknowledge my association with the New School in general. Its culturally rich environment has infused the content of this book. Specifically I would like to thank the Dean of the New School, Elizabeth Dickey and Associate Deans, Elissa Tenny and Sandra Farganis for their support and encouragement.

I would like to thank Erik Gundersen of Heinle & Heinle for gently nudging me back into writing another book and for, in the end, supporting the notion that ESL/EFL students can and will rise to the challenge of tackling the sophisticated, authentic, and engaging listening materials collected for this book. I would also like to thank him for including Linda Lee in the developmental process, and, in turn, thanks to Linda Lee.

I would especially like to thank Robyn Vaccara who piloted the book and formally stepped into the project at a very important point in its development. Her perspective and support contributed a great deal to refining the project.

I would also like to acknowledge Richard Selden, who frequently served as a sounding board while I was developing ideas and instructed me on technical aspects of the blues and jazz.

I am grateful to Michael Curren who helped me mine the film and videos in the New School's Media Studies Department for the excellent examples of student and faculty work included in this book. And of course I am also very grateful to those who allowed their work to be included in this project.

I am greatly indebted to all of the subject matter specialists who generously agreed to be interviewed for this book. They are identified within each chapter.

Thanks to Fred Winston, director of the New School's Guitar Studies Center and Martin Meuller, Associate Director of the New School Jazz Program at Mannes College of Music for their advice and/or expert opinion in working on the Blues chapter and Mark Lipton of the Milano Graduate School for his help on the Work chapter.

A final thanks to Carole Rollins who expertly pulled together the production of this demanding project, under considerable time restraints.

To the Teacher

The Story of *The Heart of the Matter*

The Heart of the Matter provides the richest and most varied collection of listening materials available. Using a Sony Professional™, the recording device used by National Public Radio and other broadcasters, the author interviewed a wide array of musicians, artists, teachers, entrepreneurs, and other professionals on a host of intriguing topics. The most engaging segments recorded became the wellspring for creative listening, speaking, and critical thinking activities in this book. An interview with musician Junior Mance, playing blues on the piano for us, is one of many memorable listenings that serve as springboards for learning opportunities in *The Heart of the Matter.*

Audience

This book is designed for English as a second or foreign language (ESL/EFL) students at the high-intermediate level who wish to further develop their listening and speaking skills and bridge the gap between social and academic or professional uses of these skills.

Purpose and Goals of the Book

• Develop listening strategies and skills in an organized way using a variety of authentic listening samples.

• Spark intellectual curiosity. Listening subjects are intended to be compelling in that they contain information and activities reflecting universal concerns and interests, and yet are adaptable enough so that they can be discussed on a personal level.

• Develop conversation skills that grow naturally from the authentic listenings.

• Develop critical thinking and discussion skills that evolve from analyzing and synthesizing the information provided through the listenings, class discussion, and outside sources.

• Reinforce note-taking and summarizing skills that are built up from a series of focused, step-by-step tasks in each chapter.

• Build vocabulary. This is usually done "after the fact." That is, since this book reflects real world challenges, vocabulary activities are done after the listenings rather than before. Listening for explanations and inferring meaning from context are two skills that are encouraged in the vocabulary exercises.

• Introduce basic research skills. The goal here is to show students how to use other sources to build up a body of information on a specific topic.

Components

• Student Book (including a glossary, teacher's notes and tapescripts)

• Audio Cassette tape

• Videotape

Organization of the Book

Each chapter is organized around three listenings. Captured in one-on-one interviews using a Sony Professional™ recorder, these listenings are authentic in quality and structured in format. The colorful and engaging content of these listenings forms the heart and soul of the book. The final page of each chapter offers an extension activity that encourages students to consolidate and expand upon the material they have studied. In this final section, students either work through a video-based activity or tackle a research project.

Each chapter is 10 pages long and is organized as follows:

• **Listening 1** (Expert Opinion)

The first listening is usually a 3–4 minute "mini-lecture" on the topic. The first four pages of the chapter are concerned with this lecture and surrounding text which is used to expand on the topic. This listening will usually be somewhat formal in style. The activities in *Listening 1* ask students to listen for a general topic, listen for specific information, and develop notetaking skills.

• **Listening 2** (Personal Perspective)

This second listening deals with the topic on a more subjective level. For example, in the chapter called "Legacy of the Blues," the author speaks with a well-known jazz musician, while in the chapter called "Food: Business & Pleasure," she speaks with the creator and editor-in-chief of a food magazine.

The second listening may be longer but also less formal than the first. Here, students are provided with new perspectives on the chapter's topic, and further develop their notetaking skills. Various springboards for conversation and vocabulary development are also provided.

• **Listening 3** (Other Voices)

This final listening section offers students a more open-ended opportunity to hear about and discuss the topic at hand. Many of the segments in *Listening 3* are "person-on-the-street" interviews in which nonexperts provide reflections on the topic at hand. Students listen with more of a global purpose in mind here, and actively discuss and debate issues.

• **Video or Project**

The final page of each chapter provides a rich opportunity for students to consolidate the content knowledge, vocabulary sets, and listening skills they have learned through either a video-based activity or a research project.

TO THE STUDENT

The Heart of the Matter teaches listening, speaking, and critical thinking skills. Here are a few observations that will help you learn the most from this book.

Listening

Listening is one of the most difficult language skills to master, yet it is probably the least emphasized skill in the language learning classroom. Unlike reading and writing, you cannot take your time and look things up when listening. Of course when you are listening to someone you have some control because you can ask the other person to repeat or restate something you did not understand. However when at a movie, or listening to a lecture or the radio you have no control over the situation. The good news is . . . you can develop listening strategies that will help you in these situations.

In designing the goals for this book, it seemed helpful to focus on a few, very important listening strategies. You will be reminded of these strategies and tips through the use of "Listening Notes" that appear throughout the book. If at the end of the course you walk away remembering just these "Notes," you will have gone a long way in developing your listening skills.

Here are some listening tips to remember as you study with *The Heart of the Matter*:

1. You already know a lot. Use your knowledge! Predict. Guess. Take risks. Use what you already know to think about the subject beforehand and to fill in gaps while you're listening.

2. You don't need to get every idea the first time. Speakers usually repeat or restate important ideas. They do this for emphasis or to make the idea clearer to their audience. You will see this happen over and over again in the listenings in this book. In longer lectures and talks you will notice that speakers usually provide introductions and summaries which go over the main ideas they are talking about.

3. You don't need to get every word. Don't stop listening because you're worried about a word you've missed. You'll have a better chance of getting the meaning as a whole if you just keep listening.

Speaking

The best way to develop a natural conversational style in English is to pick up phrases, expressions, idioms, and vocabulary from native speakers of the language. This book shows you how to understand the expressions you hear and use them in your own discussions and conversations.

Critical Thinking Skills

Developing critical thinking is one of the key skills needed to succeed in your chosen profession. This book is filled with problem solving activities and opportunities to analyze and synthesize facts and information. These activities will help you develop valuable thinking and coping skills.

Good luck in your English studies!

What will I do when they find out I'm me?

Listening 1

A. Before You Listen

1. 👥 What makes people feel anxious and lose confidence? Read the statements below and study the chart. Then tell how anxious each event would make you feel. Check (✓) your answer.

   Fear is a reaction to a real danger. *When danger is removed, so is fear.*

   Anxiety is a reaction to an **imagined** danger. *Anxiety can last forever!*

Anxiety Level	High	Medium	Low
Going to a party alone			
Speaking English socially			
Starting a new class			
Going on a job interview			
Taking an exam			
Going on a first date			

2. 👥 Answer the following questions:
   a. What situations, other than the ones listed above, make you anxious?
   b. Do you think famous and successful people are always confident?
   c. What does it take to be confident?
   d. What is a high-anxiety experience? Give an example.

B. Who Will You Be Listening To?

Walter Anderson is the author of *The Confidence Course*™, a book based on a course he teaches at the New School. He is also the editor of *Parade* magazine.

   Anderson believes that if people are responsible and lead a good life, they will feel more confident. In this listening, he talks about the things one can do to lead this kind of life.

> **Culture Note**
>
> Many Americans speak openly about personal feelings such as fear and anxiety. They think it's good to speak openly and honestly about themselves.

...Be Confident

C. 🎭 Listening for a General Topic

🎧 What's the talk about? Listen and check (✓) the general topic.

_____ 1. The importance of fame

_____ 2. Seven rules to live by

_____ 3. Love and confidence

D. 👥 Listening for Specific Information/Notetaking

🔊 Listen to the first half of the talk again and write down Walter Anderson's "seven rules to live by."

1. I am _____responsible_____

2. Believe in _____

3. Practice _____

4. Be _____

5. _____ because you should know _____

6. Be _____

7. _____

Compare answers with a partner.

> **Listening/Notetaking Note**
> Because the seven rules are stated very simply, you may not be able to guess the meaning of unfamiliar words from the context. When this happens, write down the words that you don't understand and go on. Later, you can look them up or ask about them. Don't stop listening!

Jerry Lewis

Sylvester Stallone

E. 👥 Listening for Details

Read activities 1–3 below and try to fill in the blanks.

1. Walter Anderson says that he has met some important people. Who does he mention? Complete the list below.

   a. heads of _____nations_____

   b. people who've created great _____, great _____

   c. people who've run _____

   d. some of best _____ America has

   e. some of the greatest _____

   f. the most famous of _____ and _____

2. According to Walter Anderson, most people are afraid others will discover that they are inferior in some way. Check (✓) the five ways he mentions.

   ___ vulnerable   ___ able to be hurt

   ___ don't belong   ___ poor

   ___ lonely   ___ deserve to be rejected

   ___ nervous   ___ not quite good enough

3. Write the names of two famous Sylvester Stallone movie characters that Anderson mentions when he talks about courage.

   _____   _____

   Which one does he say is truly courageous?

   _____

4. 👥 Listen and check your answers.

F. 🎬 Vocabulary and Dictation

1. 👂🧍 Your teacher will read sentences and phrases from the listening. The words on the left below are from these sentences. Listen and match these words to their definitions on the right.

_D_ 1. decade   a. healthy in mind

____ 2. noble   b. bend the head down and up to show agreement

____ 3. phenomenal   c. easily hurt, sensitive

____ 4. ambitious   d. ten years

____ 5. nod   e. acceptance and respect

____ 6. sane   f. extraordinary

____ 7. vulnerable   g. showing qualities of high moral character

____ 8. rejected   h. refused acceptance, turned away

____ 9. tolerance   i. having a strong desire to succeed

2. 👂🧍 Listen to your teacher and write the sentences you hear. Then compare sentences with a partner.

G. Expanding Meaning

Complete each sentence with the correct form of a word from the list above.

> **Vocabulary Note**
> The prefix <u>in</u> means "not" when it is attached to an adjective. For example, the word <u>invulnerable</u> means "not vulnerable."
> **Examples:** intolerance
>   insane

1. To live in peace we must have _____tolerance_____ for the differences of others.

2. The bank _____ his request for credit because of his poor credit record.

3. He has been the president of the country for nineteen years—almost two _____!

4. His new business is a _____ success. In just two years he's opened five stores.

5. She is greatly respected and admired because of her _____ spirit.

6. He may act a bit crazy at times, but he's really quite _____ and reasonable.

7. The new manager is very _____. She wants to increase sales by 20% next year.

8. When I asked her if she would marry me, she just _____ her head.

9. Tom has just lost both his job and his girlfriend. He's feeling very _____.

Listening 2

A. Before You Listen

1. Walter Anderson uses stories to give life to the points he is making. He thinks that storytelling is a popular and effective way of communicating with people.

    Below is a story Anderson tells about someone else. Which of the seven rules are illustrated in this story?

    There was a woman in Detroit, in 1945, who had two sons. She was worried about them, especially the younger one, Ben, because he was particularly poor in school. Kids in his class called him a "dummy" and made fun of him because he seemed so slow.
    The mother decided that she would, herself, have to get her sons to do better in school. She told them to go to the Detroit Public Library to read a book a week and do a book report for her.
    One day, in Ben's class, the teacher held up a rock and asked if anyone recognized it. Ben raised his hand and the teacher called on him. "Why did Ben raise his hand?" they wondered. He was so dumb; what could he possibly want to say?
    Well, Ben not only recognized the rock; he explained its chemical composition, he named other rocks in its group and even knew where the teacher had found it. The teacher and the students were amazed. Ben had learned all this from doing one of his book reports.
    Ben gained confidence and went on to the top of his class. When he graduated high school, he went to Yale University and eventually became one of the most respected pediatric brain surgeons in the United States. He is best known for successfully separating a set of Siamese twins at the brain.
    After Ben had grown up, he learned something about his mother that he did not know as a child.
    She, herself, had never learned how to read.

2. Answer the questions below.
    a. What role does storytelling play in your culture?
    b. Do you prefer personal stories or folk stories? Can you give an example of a story that you particularly like?

B. Who Will You Be Listening To?

In his teens, Walter Anderson lived in a neighborhood that was poor and fairly rough. In this listening, he tells a short but very powerful story about an event that changed his life.

C. Understanding the Rhythm of English

1. Read Anderson's story on the next page and put a [/] where you think he will pause.

    Pauses: Speakers usually pause when they complete a thought or a meaningful phrase.

Example:

I was raised in a tenement/and one night my mother asked me to go across the street to the telephone booth/(we had no telephone in our apartment)/and call my brother.

Listen to the story and check your work.

2. Listen to the story again and read along as you draw a line under the words that are stressed.

    Stress: The important words in a story are stressed in English.

Example:

I was raised in a <u>tenement</u> and one <u>night</u> my <u>mother</u> <u>asked</u> me to <u>go</u> <u>across</u> the street to the <u>telephone</u> <u>booth</u> (we had <u>no</u> <u>telephone</u> in our <u>apartment</u>) and <u>call</u> my <u>brother</u>.

Listen to the story and check your work.

3. Listen to the story again and read along as you listen. Use a [‿] to connect the words you think the speaker connects.

    Linking: In English, speakers connect words to maintain rhythm. Two words are usually connected when the second word begins with a vowel.

Example:

I was raised in‿a‿tenement‿and one night my mother asked me to go across the street to the telephone booth‿(we had no telephone‿in‿our apartment)‿and call my brother.

Listen to the story and check your work.

Pronunciation Note

Rhythm is very important in English. If you pronounce all the sounds correctly but have serious problems with rhythm, you will probably not be understood. However, if you get some sounds wrong but your rhythm is right, you probably will be understood. Stressing the wrong syllable in a word can change its meaning. For example, reCORD = to tape something, like music or a movie (verb). RECord = a disk with recorded material on it, usually music (noun).

I was raised in a tenement, and one night my mother asked me to go across the street to the telephone booth, (we had no telephone in our apartment), and call my brother. Now I don't remember what the telephone call was about but I'll remember that as long as I live because when I hung the receiver back up my hand had blood on it, and I reached up and touched my face . . . my face had blood on it. Whoever had used the telephone before me had been either hurt or wounded, which was not unusual in the neighborhood I grew up. And I opened the bifold doors and I looked to my left, I looked to my right, and I ran across the street, and I ran up the steps to the tenement, went into our apartment. I washed the blood off my face and hands before my mother could see it.

A little later I went back down stairs and I sat on the stoop . . . now it's never quiet, really, in New York, but it was relatively quiet . . . the sounds of the city around, and I was alone. And I started to think about this mysterious person whose blood I had worn, and I became angry, I became enraged, and I vowed "I'm getting out of here," and I meant it.

It was in that moment that I first began to accept responsibility for my own life.

4. ♪ *Tempo:* Listen to the story one last time and notice some of the things that Anderson does to hold the interest of the listener. When and why does he speak very quickly? When and why does he speak slowly?

5. Read the story to your partner. Try to tell it the way Walter Anderson does.

D. 👥 Telling a Story

Below is a list of phrases and markers used in the story. Use some or all of them to build a story, real or imaginary, about your childhood or someone else's. First write down some notes. Then prepare to tell your story to the group.

I was raised . . .

One night (day) my mother (father, teacher, etc.) asked me to . . .

Now I don't remember . . . but I'll remember as long as I live that . . .

E. Expanding Knowledge—Other Resources

1. Can a person learn to be confident? Read this description of Walter Anderson's *The Confidence Course*™. Would you like to take a course like this? How could it help make you more confident?

> **Culture Note**
> The idea that people can improve themselves is very popular in the United States. Self-help books, tapes, CDs, courses, and workshops are available to help people.

THE CONFIDENCE COURSE™
7 sessions., Tues., 7:45–9:30 p.m.
Walter Anderson

"What will I do when they find out I'm me?" Anxiety can be either the enemy or the friend of effective speaking, writing, leadership, and living. To help students grow in self-confidence, this workshop begins by exploring the nature of self-doubt, anxiety, risk-taking, and courage. An analysis of communication techniques and interpersonal skills follows. In-class exercises and at-home assignments are designed to help students overcome a negative self-image. More than a public speaking course, this is a lesson plan for life.

2. Look at the cover (see page 3) and table of contents (below) of the book *The Confidence Course*™. Would this book be more or less helpful than the course itself? Why?

Table of Contents

Listening 3

A. 👥 Who Will You Be Listening To?

You will hear three people comment on Walter Anderson's seven rules. One is a native speaker, and two are ESL students. Their names are given below.

B. Before You Listen

Each speaker was asked these two questions:

1. Which of these rules do you think you now live by?
2. Which rule do you think is important but difficult to live by?

Before you listen, think about how you would answer these questions.

C. Listening for Specific Information/Notetaking

1. 👂 Fill in the chart below as you listen.
2. 👥 Use your notes and your memory of what was said to answer the questions below.

	Lives By	Finds Difficult to Live By
Johanna		
Rista Luna		
Metta		

a. Which rule was mentioned most?
b. Which rule seems hardest to achieve?
c. Johanna said that she had a problem with a word used in one of the rules. Which word was it? Does it have a negative meaning in your native culture or language as well? If so, what English word would you use instead?

D. Personal Reflection

👥 Take turns answering the questions in section B above.

REMINDER: THE 7 RULES

1. I AM RESPONSIBLE.
2. BELIEVE IN SOMETHING BIG.
3. PRACTICE TOLERANCE.
4. BE BRAVE.
5. LOVE SOMEONE.
6. BE AMBITIOUS.
7. SMILE.

Listening Tip

Two of the speakers are not native speakers. It may be difficult to understand them. Don't worry about getting every word. Just try to understand the general meaning.

Video

A. What Will You Be Watching?

The video selections that you will see are from a Horatio Alger Awards Ceremony.

Horatio Alger was an American author who lived from 1834 to 1899. The main characters in his books are heroes who become successful and lead admirable lives in spite of the poverty and problems they face. The Horatio Alger Awards honor Americans who have succeeded in spite of great difficulties in their lives. These people have also contributed to society in special ways.

Walter Anderson, Dorothy Brown, and Ben Carson are three of the people who have received Horatio Alger Awards. These video segments give you some idea of the lives and contributions of these people.

> **Listening Note**
>
> You can get a lot of help from the visual clues in this video. Use them to help you understand what is being said.

B. 🎬 Notetaking

Read the questions in the chart below. Then watch the video and take notes.

	Walter Anderson	Dorothy Brown	Ben Carson
What problems did they face growing up?			
How did they overcome their problems?			
Did they get help?			
What do they do now?			
How do they give back to society?			

C. 👥 Analysis and Synthesis

Decide which of the seven rules are illustrated in the stories of these three people. Then present your group's ideas to the class.

LEGACY OF THE *Blues*

Louis Armstrong

Listening 1

A. Before You Listen

1. 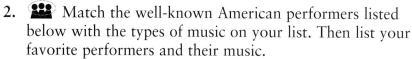 What kinds of American music are you familiar with? List them below.

   rhythm and blues

   _____   _____

   _____   _____

   _____   _____

Madonna

2. 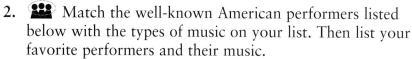 Match the well-known American performers listed below with the types of music on your list. Then list your favorite performers and their music.

Performers	Type(s) of Music
Madonna	rock 'n' roll
Louis Armstrong	_____
Billy Joel	_____
Whitney Houston	_____
_____	_____
_____	_____

Whitney Houston

*R*ock 'n' roll *began in the 1950s. Jazz began even earlier. Where did these forms of music come from? How have they developed and evolved?*

Robert Johnson

3. Read these definitions and answer the questions below.

blues /bluz/ *n. pl.* **1.** a feeling of sadness: *I've got the blues today.* **2.** a style of music that developed from southern Black American secular songs.

legacy /'legəsi/ *n.* something passed on or left from an ancestor or from an earlier generation.

a. Do you think the two definitions of *blues* are related? If so, how?

b. Look at the pictures on these two pages. Which of the two definitions of *blues* will you discuss in this chapter?

c. Look at the definition of *legacy*. What do you think the title "Legacy of the Blues" means in this chapter?

Historical Perspective

Look at this time line of important events in the United States. Pay attention to the order of events, especially those around the time of the Civil War between the North and the South. How were the lives of many Black Americans changed?

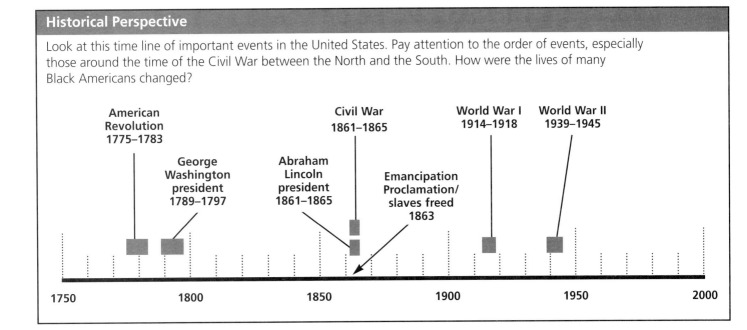

B. Who Will You Be Listening To?

Stephen Tarshis teaches a course called "Blues Power: The History, Meaning and Significance of the Blues" at the Guitar Studies Center at the New School. He is also the author of several books on music, including *The Real Jimi Hendrix*.

Steve Tarshis

Culture Note

Today many people prefer the term "African American" to "Black." The term "African American" recognizes cultural background as well as race. It is OK to say either Black or African American.

Listening Note

There will be a few words in this lecture that you will not understand. Don't worry! You will see that you can understand the lecture without them.

C. Listening for a General Topic

🎧 What's the talk about? Listen and check (✔) the general topic.

_____ 1. The connection between blues and rock 'n' roll
_____ 2. The origin and heritage of the blues
_____ 3. The roots of blues in European classical music

D. Listening for Specific Information/Notetaking

1. 🎧 Read the questions below and use them as a guide for taking notes on the listening. Listen and write your notes on a separate piece of paper.
   a. What is the blues?
   b. When and where did the blues originate?
   c. What are the elements that make up the blues?
   d. Who was Robert Johnson?
   e. Why is the blues so important?

2. Use your notes to write a summary below.

Summary Writing Note

A summary should be short and contain the main ideas of the listening. Do not include details in the summary.

Summary: _____

_____

_____

_____

_____

_____

_____

E. 🎬 Listening for Details

🔊 There is a mistake in each sentence below. Listen again and correct the mistakes.

1. Bach, Beethoven, and Brahms were ~~American~~ European composers.

2. Blacks emigrated to the Mississippi Delta after World War I.

3. Blacks went to the Mississippi Delta mainly to build roads.

4. Robert Johnson was a rock 'n' roll singer.

5. Jazz and rock are not related to the blues.

Vocabulary Note

Steve Tarshis uses the term "in other words" twice in this lecture. He does this to tell you that he will define the word or term that he is using. The term "that is" can also be used in this way.

F. 🎬 Vocabulary and Dictation

1. 🔊👤 Your teacher will read phrases from the listening twice each. Listen and match these words from the sentences to the definitions on the right.

_c_	1. heritage	a.	begin
___	2. originate	b.	a wild area of land
___	3. emigrate	c.	a tradition or legacy
___	4. wilderness	d.	to begin to have city-like qualities
___	5. generation	e.	a separate unit (or group)
___	6. entity	f.	the time it takes to become an adult (25–30 years)
___	7. chord	g.	to leave one place or region for another
___	8. urbanize	h.	three or more musical tones or notes sounded at the same time

2. Listen to your teacher and write the sentences you hear. Then compare sentences with a partner.

Listening 2

A. 👥 Before You Listen

1. What do the following music terms mean? Look them up in the glossary or ask someone in or outside of class to explain them to you. If possible, listen to examples of the music.

rhythm and blues

free jazz

boogie woogie

rock and roll

SOUL

bebop

Dizzy Gillespie

Aretha Franklin

Playing "Bop" is like playing Scrabble with all the vowels missing.   —Duke Ellington (1899–1974), American jazz composer

2. 👂 Listen and write the number of each music sample next to a type of music in the list below. Pay attention to the sound or meaning of each term. If you are not sure, guess.

_____ **rhythm and blues**, Ray Charles _____

_____ **boogie woogie**, Meade Lux Lewis _____

  1   **bebop**, Dizzy Gillespie _____

_____ **rock 'n' roll**, Chuck Berry _____

_____ **free jazz**, Ornette Coleman _____

_____ **soul**, Aretha Franklin _____

3. 👂 Listen again. What words come to mind when you listen to each type of music? Write your ideas on the lines above, and then compare ideas with your classmates.

Junior Mance

B. Who Will You Be Listening To?

This second listening is an interview with the internationally respected jazz pianist Junior Mance, who is known to be a jazz man with a very "bluesy" feeling to his work. Mance has been playing professionally for more than fifty years. He played with legendary performers such as Dizzy Gillespie, Coleman Hawkins, Charlie Parker, Dinah Washington, Aretha Franklin, and Cannonball Adderley.

He now teaches in the New School Jazz Program at Mannes College of Music.

It's a highly emotional feeling. . . . It's the hardest thing to teach the Blues. . . .
—Junior Mance

C. 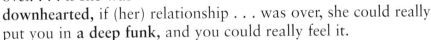 Listening for Specific Information/Notetaking

1. Before listening, read these sentences from the interview. Use the context to guess the meaning of the boldfaced words.

    a. My mother was very **partial to** the blues.

    b. (Dinah) **put** so much **feeling into it,** but it was always that bluesy **feeling.** If she had a good man . . . oh, she would sing songs about that and give you a good feeling when the song was over. . . . if she was **downhearted,** if (her) relationship . . . was over, she could really put you in **a deep funk,** and you could really feel it.

    c. I don't have to **get into** any certain kind of **mood** to have to play the blues.

2. 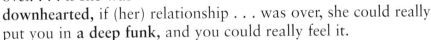 Read the questions below. Then listen for the answers and take notes.

    a. What does Junior Mance say about the blues?

    b. How does he feel about the way Dinah Washington sang the blues?

    c. How does he feel about being a blues/jazz performer?

Compare answers with your classmates. Then listen to the interview again.

D. 🖎 Interviewing

1. Get together with a partner and ask the questions below.

   a. What's your favorite kind of music? How does it make you feel?

   b. Who is one of your favorite musicians? Why?

   c. Do you like the kinds of music discussed in this chapter? Do you like music from your culture? Compare the two.

2. Get together with another pair. Tell them about your partner's interest in music.

E. Speaking Styles

Junior Mance's style of speaking is quite different from that of Steve Tarshis. Who is more formal in his speaking style—Junior Mance or Steven Tarshis? How do you know?

Charlie Parker

F. 🖎 Making Inferences

🎧 Read the following quotations from famous American performers. Then listen to the Junior Mance interview again. Would he agree or disagree? Check (✔) yes or no (X) and explain why.

Music is your own experience, your own thoughts, your own wisdom. If you don't live it, it won't come out of your horn.   —Charlie Parker (1920–1955), U.S. jazz musician

Agree? _____ Yes _____ No
Why? _____

_____

W. E. B. Du Bois

[Blues] is the music of an unhappy people, of the children of disappointment; they tell of death and suffering and unvoiced longing toward a truer world. . . .
     —W. E. B. Du Bois (1868–1963), U.S. civil rights leader and author

Agree? _____ Yes _____ No
Why? _____

_____

You can't lose with the blues.
     —Ray Charles (b. 1930), U.S. rhythm and blues performer and composer

Agree? _____ Yes _____ No
Why? _____

_____

Ray Charles

Jazz is the big brother of the Blues. If a guy's playing Blues like we play, he's in high school. When he starts playing Jazz it's like going on to college, to a school of higher learning.

—B.B. King (b. 1925), U.S. blues guitarist

Agree? _____ Yes _____ No

Why? _____

_____

_____

_____

B. B. King

Share ideas with your classmates.

Bonus Listening

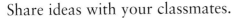 Here's an additional listening from Junior Mance. He plays some samples of the kinds of music he's talked about and/or the music discussed on page 16. Some of what he talks about is historical; some is musical. Just listen.

WEST AFRICA
AND THE BLUES

As Steve Tarshis has said, the blues began when the work songs "that probably had their origins in African music met the harmonies that were introduced by the Europeans to Black people in America." Here are three qualities that you can find in West African music that influenced the blues:

- *Repetition is used to organize the music into patterns.*
- *The musicians improvise on these patterns.*
- *Singing styles include great freedom of vocal color.*

Can you give examples of how these features are used in modern American music like jazz and rock? See if you can find any of these characteristics in the music you hear in this chapter.

Listening 3

A. 👥 What Will You Be Listening To?

In this section you will listen to two full-length pieces of music.

B. Listening for Specific Information

1. Read the words listed below. Look up any you don't understand in the glossary, or ask your teacher about them.

rough	playful	fast	easy	complicated
emotional	joyful	jumpy	mellow	simple
smooth	wild	rhythmic	slow	sophisticated
passionate	screaming	throbbing	soft	loud

. . . and remember West Africa . . . repetitive   improvised   vocally colorful

2. Use these words and/or your own words to describe each piece of music you hear on a separate piece of paper.

Dinah Washington

a. 👂 Dinah Washington, one of America's most critically acclaimed jazz singers, was known as the Queen of the Blues. As Junior Mance said in his interview, "her singing always had a blues tinge to it." In this classic tune, "Come Rain or Come Shine," Washington is accompanied by Junior Mance.

b. 👂 Muddy Waters is a key figure in the development of the blues; he helped create the music style known as rhythm and blues. He inspired many musicians as far apart as Bob Dylan and Elvis Presley. Unfortunately, he never achieved the level of commercial success of many of his imitators. Here he sings a piece called "Mannish Boy."

C. 👥 Analysis and Synthesis

1. "Mannish Boy" consists of only one chord. Musically speaking, it is a rather simple song. Discuss Muddy Waters' singing in terms of the following quotation:

Blues is easy to play, but hard to feel.
—Jimi Hendrix (1942–1970), U.S. rock musician

2. Do you like this music? Which piece did you like more? Why? Discuss.

Muddy Waters

Video

A. What Will You Be Watching?

In the early days of the blues, there were no blues records or blues clubs. Performers like Robert Johnson traveled alone with their guitars, mostly around the South, and played on the streets.

This video is about a New York blues performer, Elija "Carolina Slim" Staley. He is originally from South Carolina. He went to New York after the Korean War, got married, and has been there for almost forty years now.

I play mostly . . . the everyday street man type of blues.

—Carolina Slim

B. Listening for Specific Information

Before watching the video, read the questions below. Then watch the video and listen for answers.

1. In this video, Carolina Slim talks about his experiences singing the blues underground in the New York subway. Does he like singing in the subway? Why or why not?

2. Carolina Slim also talks about his background. Why did he become a musician?

3. What does Carolina Slim say about the blues that is similar to what Junior Mance says?

C. Comparison and Contrast

Talk about Carolina Slim's music, using the words on page 20. Compare his blues style to that of Muddy Waters.

FOOD:

Most people need to work for a living. Some people love their work, while others hate working. In this unit you will hear about some people who started businesses in the food industry and love what they do.

Preparation Note

At the end of this chapter you will work on a project related to planning a business of your own. It might help to keep a journal of your thoughts and ideas on this subject as you go through the chapter.

Listening 1

A. Before You Listen

1. The chart below lists things a large number of people are interested in. Follow the instructions to complete the chart.

	A	B
Movies		
Travel		
Music		
Sports		
Fashion		
Food		

a. Together, as a class, add four more items to the chart.

b. On your own, rank the items in the chart from most interesting (1) to least interesting (10). Write the numbers in column A.

c. Ask a partner to write his or her answers in column B. Are your thoughts similar to his or hers?.

Business & *Pleasure*

3

Culture Note

A self-made person is someone who starts with little or nothing and creates his or her own profitable occupation. This is most commonly done by starting a small business. Starting your own business is generally encouraged in the United States, and many people immigrate to the U.S. for this opportunity.

2. This chapter focuses on something that a lot of people find interesting: food. Which of the things below motivates you to eat? Rank them from most important (1) to least important (9). Then compare ideas in your group.

_____ taste	_____ socializing	_____ comfort
_____ health	_____ escape	_____ adventure
_____ fun	_____ boredom	_____ hunger

3. List the top three places you like to eat (e.g., at home, diners, Chinese restaurants, fancy restaurants). Discuss why.

1. _____

2. _____

3. _____

4. To the list below, add five jobs related to food. Which job would be the most interesting to you? The least interesting? Why?

chef   nutritionist

restaurant reviewer   _____   _____

_____   _____   _____

B. Who Will You Be Listening To?

Gary Goldberg is the Executive Director of the New School Culinary Arts Program. Over 150 courses are offered each semester on such topics as cooking, baking, restaurant management, food and wine tasting, cookbook writing, and food styling.

Gary Goldberg

23

C. Listening for a General Topic

What's the talk about? Listen and check (✔) the general topic.

_____ 1. Healthy eating

_____ 2. America's love affair with food

_____ 3. The food business

D. ♟ Listening for Specific Information/Notetaking

1. Read the outline below. Then listen and take notes on the opening statement, the two main ideas, and the closing statement. Write your notes on a separate piece of paper.

2. Work with your partner to summarize the opening statement, main ideas, and closing statement on the appropriate lines below. An example is given.

3. Listen again and check your answers.

> ### Listening/Notetaking Tips
>
> 1. Remember your goal each time you listen. Take notes on the items you are looking for, and take notes on other details only if you have time.
> 2. If you don't know a word, just write it down as best you can and fin the definition later. You can often understand what's being said from the context.
> 3. Details or examples will sometimes help you recognize the main ide This is particularly true in this listening. If you think that you misse the main idea, keep listening and try to figure it out from the deta and examples.

Opening Statement: _____

Details: ___ There are many gourmet shops.

___ There's an explosion of cooking schools.

_1_ There are many restaurants of every type.

___ There are dozens of food magazines/cookbooks.

Main Idea: _____

Details: ___ People love it.

___ There are many jobs available.

_1_ It's a wonderful career.

Main Idea: People study culinary arts as an avocation or hobby.

Details: _1_ They cook for themselves.

___ It's ephemeral.

___ It involves all the senses.

___ It has immediate gratification.

_2_ Cooking is fun.

___ It's creative.

_3_ They cook to entertain.

Closing Statement: _____

CULINARY CENTER OF NEW YORK, INC.

100 GREENWICH AVENUE
NEW YORK, NY 10011
(212) 255-4141

GARY A. GOLDBERG

E. Listening for Details

The details in the outline above are not in order. Listen again and number the details in the correct order.

F. 👥 Vocabulary and Dictation

1. 👂👤 Your teacher will read sentences and phrases from the listening twice each. Listen and match the words on the left to their definitions on the right.

_F_	1. **proliferation**	a.	one's work, occupation
____	2. **gourmet**	b.	an activity one does for enjoyment
____	3. **produce**	c.	lasting for only a very short time
____	4. **avocation**	d.	fancy, special (regarding food)
____	5. **vocation**	e.	fruits and vegetables
____	6. **motive**	f.	rapid or great growth
____	7. **ephemeral**	g.	reason or need to do something

Gary Goldberg and his students

> ### Vocabulary Note
>
> Gary mentions that his "enrollments tripled" in the last six years. This means that they are three times larger than they were. For example, if they went from 1,500 to 4,500, they tripled. If they were only twice as large, they would have doubled. If they were four times as large, they would have quadrupled.

2. Fill in each blank with one of the vocabulary words above.

   a. The beauty of flowers is ___ephemeral___, lasting only two or three days.

   b. Art is his _____ and banking his _____. He paints because he loves it and works in the bank to make a living.

   c. Fresh _____ is much healthier for you than canned foods.

   d. I'm not sure what her _____ was for buying that car. It's so impractical!

   e. There's been a _____ of bad TV talk shows. There seems to be a new one every day.

   f. _____ foods are more expensive, but they're usually more delicious as well.

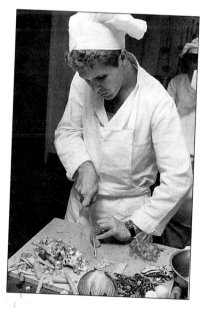

3. 👂👤 Listen to your teacher and write the sentences you hear. Then compare sentences with a partner.

Listening 2

A. 👥 Before You Listen

1. Choose one of the questions below to discuss in your group. Have one person take notes and report your group's ideas to the class.

   - Is starting your own business a romantic idea or a practical one?
   - What are the pros and cons of working for someone else?
   - What are the pros and cons of being in business for yourself?

2. There are two important stages in starting your own business: the idea stage and the planning stage. Below are some questions you need to answer at each stage. Which question comes first in the planning stage? Second? Number these questions from 1 to 4.

Questions to answer at the idea stage:

<u> 2 </u> Do I have the ability and experience to succeed?

<u> 1 </u> What is the product or service?

Questions to answer at the planning stage:

_____ How will I package the product or service to make it appealing?

_____ What is the market? (Are there enough customers out there interested in the product or service?) What is the competition?

_____ How will I market the product or service? (How will I advertise and promote it?)

_____ How will I support the business financially until it begins making profits?

B. Who Will You Be Listening To?

Emel Basdoğan (pronounced: Bash-do-an) is co-owner and editor-in-chief of Turkey's first food magazine, *Mutfak Rehberi*, which means "Kitchen Guide" in English. In this interview she tells her success story.

Emel Basdoğan (center)

Listening Note

In Chapter 1, we focused on the rhythm used by native speakers of American English. In "real life," you will be listening to non-native speakers of English as well.

All non-native speakers of English bring with them the rhythm and pronunciation traits of their native languages. So, in these cases, you must try to adjust to the unique patterns of the individual. In this listening, the speaker is Turkish. Her English is quite good. However, she has a strong Turkish accent.

Listen and try to adjust to her way of speaking and her accent.

Capsouto Frères
RESTAURANT

Charles Tutino
Chef

451 Washington St.
NY • NY • 10013
212 • 966 • 4900

C. 👥 Listening for a Sequence of Events

In this interview Emel Basdoğan talks about the sequence of events that led to her success.

1. Below is an outline of the stages that she went through in building up her business. Listen and briefly describe each step in the chart below. Then compare what you've done with your group.

2. 👂 Listen again and check your answers.

Listening Tip

Look for surrounding information that will help you understand what is being said. The interviewer's questions will help you guess what to expect.

I	Interest	passion for food
D	The product	
E	Experience	
A	Ambition	
P	Identifying the market	
L	Financial support	
A	Packaging	
N	Marketing	

the NEW PROSPECT
brings good taste home

Michael Gross • Catering Direct[or]

52 Seventh Avenue • Brooklyn, NY 11217 • 718 230 8900 • Fax 718 230 9[...]

CAROL GILLOT
E. 11TH ST., NY, NY 10003
212 353-1174

(717) 296-8094
Reservations Requested

Le Gorille

a country restaurant

RR 2, Box 2051
Twin Lakes Road
Shohola, PA 18458

Chef Peter Daniel
Sharon Berliner-Daniel
Proprietors

IACP's Chairwoman of CORCO
212–580–8172

RHONDA STIEGLITZ
CULINARY TROUBLESHOOTER
172 WEST 79th ST., SUITE 2D
NEW YORK, NY 10024
Have Blades, Will Travel
[Re]cipe Testing/Development/Styling

WALTER LUQUE
Pastry Chef / Master Baker
(718) 297-7304

Cafe VIVA

2578 BROADWAY AT 97th STREET
(212) 663-VIVA

CHO SUN OK *Restaurant*
조선옥
KOREAN FOOD. JAPANESE SUSHI. CHINESE STYLE.
136-73 Roosevelt Ave. Flushing, N.Y. 11354
Tel. (718) 762-8960, 762-8964

D. 👥 Ordering a Sequence of Events

When people tell stories, they use special words to sequence events. The story below tells how Gary Goldberg began a culinary arts school. Underline the words used to sequence the events.

The Idea

Gary Goldberg grew up with great cooking, and so he loves food. <u>When</u> he was in college, he worked as a waiter and learned how to run a dining room for catering events. He graduated college, went to graduate school for education, and <u>then</u> got a job writing and producing educational films. He also had a part-time catering business. He was in his mid-twenties when he realized that he enjoyed his part-time work more than his day job, so he went back to college to get a certificate in food management. But he soon realized that the courses would not help him do what he wanted to do—open and run a restaurant. That's when he came up with the idea of starting a school of his own.

The Plan

Gary began to plan what he would do. He already knew there was a market for a school like this because he knew quite a few other students in the same situation. The first thing he had to do was figure out how to finance the school until it was making money on its own. This was a problem since it is very difficult to get a loan for a food business. Gary took out a personal loan and decided to support the school by running a catering business out of the school. Next he needed to find a place to house the school that would be appealing to students. He found an 1832 townhouse in the historic section of Greenwich Village with a beautiful garden and fixed it up. Finally, he needed to find a way to market the school. This was a problem since he could not afford advertising. He had heard that the New School might be interested in starting a new culinary

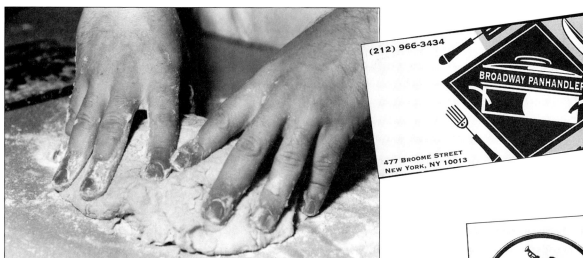

arts school, so he approached them with a proposal. This was good for Gary because he gained prestige being associated with a large university and was able to promote the courses through the New School's bulletins and advertising. The school benefited because the number of students who took courses grew from 750 the first semester to 6,000 per year today.

E. 🖾 Telling a Story

Below is a list of the connectors, transition words, and time markers used to sequence the events in Gary's story. Use some or all of them to retell Emel's story, using the notes in your chart. Take turns with your partner.

1. When . . .

   then . . .

   also . . .

   So . . .

   Soon . . .

   But . . .

   That's when . . .

2. (He) began . . .

   The first thing . . .

   Until . . .

   Next . . .

   Finally . . .

   In the end . . .

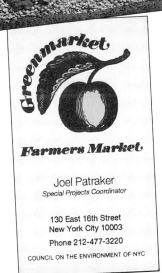

F. 🏛 Telling Your Own Story

Take turns telling a success story—your own or someone else's. Use the words above whenever possible.

Listening 3

A. 👥 Who Will You Be Listening To?

You will hear two short interviews. Irene Khin Wong is a Southeast Asian food specialist. She is a consultant to people who are opening restaurants, a caterer, and an organizer of culinary tours to Asia for Americans.

John Massachio owns two Northern Italian restaurants in Manhattan, both called La Dolce Vita. John was a social worker for seventeen years before he went into the restaurant business.

B. 👥 Listening for Specific Information

👂 Read the questions below. Then listen and write the answers.

1. **Irene**

   a. What did she do before she was in the food business?

   _____

   b. What was the first thing she did in the food industry?

   _____

   c. Why did she change what she was doing within the food industry?

   _____

   _____

Irene Khin Wong

John Massachio

2. **John**

   a. What was his first job in the food industry?

   _____

   b. What did he do once he decided that he wanted to open a restaurant?

   _____

   _____

C. 👥 Analysis and Synthesis

Work together to answer the questions below. Choose one person in your group to take notes and report your group's answers to the class.

1. John's story is similar to someone else's in this chapter. Whose? Discuss the similarities and the differences of the two.

2. Irene and John were asked how they felt about their work. Talk about their responses. What do they both feel is one of the great benefits of their profession apart from food?

3. In one way or another, all of the people in this chapter—Gary, Emel, Irene, and John—talked about why food is so appealing. What did they say? How has working on this chapter changed the way you think about food?

Project

A. What Will You Be Doing?

In this project you will have the opportunity to think about, research, and plan a business of your own.

B. 👥 Brainstorming

Together, choose an area of interest (e.g., food, sports, clothing). Brainstorm in your group to decide on a specific goal. Will you produce a product? Will you offer a service?

C. 👥 Researching

Follow the steps below to interview a successful self-employed person.

1. Interview Questions

In your group, make up a set of interview questions for your area of interest. Base your questions on these models, but make them more specific:

The idea
- How did you get the idea to start (this business)? Do you like what you do? Why or why not?

Identifying the market
- How did you know people would be interested in buying your (product or service)?
- How did you know the market was big enough for you to succeed?
- Is there a lot of competition in (this business)? Can you give me some examples?
- How do you stay ahead of the competition?

Financial support
- What were your basic expenses in starting up a new business (in this area)?
- How could you afford to start a new business? How did you get start-up money?

Packaging
- What do you do to make (your product or service) appealing to your customers?

Marketing
- How do people find you? Do you advertise? How do you promote (your product or service)?

Problems
- Did problems come up along the way? If so, how did you solve them?

2. The Interview

Find someone to interview who has either started a business or who knows something about starting a business. Ask him or her the questions you developed, and take notes.

D. 👥 Planning

Think about your area of interest, look over your interview, and write a basic plan for your business. Follow the organization of the questions listed above. Present your idea and plan to the class. When explaining the steps of the plan, use examples from the experience of the person you interviewed.

Us and THEM:

Language plays a key role in helping us understand the world and how it works. When we can name things or groups of people, we feel that we know them because we can call to mind a description of them. For example, think of the different images these groups call to mind: Australians, university professors, ten-year-old boys. How can the naming of people be helpful? How can it be harmful?

Listening 1

A. Before You Listen

1. The words below can be used to describe people. Look up any unfamiliar words in the Glossary at the back of the book.

inventive	untrustworthy
unfriendly	lazy
practical	open-minded
open	cultured
conservative	materialistic
loud	talkative
generous	unattractive
avaricious	reserved
courteous	impractical
impolite	emotional
attractive	individualistic
ambitious	sociable

2. Use the words above to describe the American and the British people. Fill in the chart on page 33 and then compare ideas with your partner.

3. Descriptive words are not usually neutral; we tend to think of them as either negative or positive in value. Look at each word in the list above. If the word describes something negative, write (–) before the word. If it describes something positive, write (+). Are any of the traits neutral? Compare ideas with other members of your group.

Creating the Other

British	Americans

4. On a separate piece of paper, write the name of a group to which you belong (for example, nationality, religion, profession). Then list some words that other people use to describe your group. Are the words an accurate description of your group? Explain.

5. How did you develop the opinions you have about the British and the Americans? What role do family, the media, and history play in forming your ideas?

6. What would it be like if everyone were the same? How would things be better? How would they be worse?

B. Who Will You Be Listening To?

John Mayher is professor of education at New York University and the author of a textbook on education called *Uncommon Sense*.

C. 🖐 Listening for a General Topic

👂 What's the talk about? Listen and check (✔) the general topic.

_____ 1. Human nature and war

_____ 2. Fighting negative stereotyping, living together in peace

_____ 3. Human ignorance

D. Listening for Main Ideas

👂 Four important ideas from the listening are listed below, but each idea has been broken into two parts. With your partner, try to match one part from the left with one part from the right. Then listen and check your answers.

Culture Note

"Multiculturalism" has become an important focus in American schools. In a multicultural approach, students learn about ideas that come from many different countries, races, and religions. Multiculturalism is generally viewed as a positive and necessary element of education that will promote greater understanding among people in a country with a diverse population.

_____ 1. The human mind seems to need to categorize things into groups when

    a. negative stereotyping, which in turn leads to thinking of people in another group as "the other."

_____ 2. Categorizing into groups may have been important for human survival tens of thousands of years ago, but in the modern world, grouping people often leads to

    b. but we can try not to attach negative values to the differences in others.

_____ 3. There is not much that we can do about the way our mind tends to categorize things,

    c. we can live together rather than kill each other.

_____ 4. If we realize that human beings are more alike than they are different,

    d. trying to understand how the world works.

E. 👥 Listening for Specific Information/Notetaking

👂 John Mayher uses examples to clarify or emphasize the points he is making. Below are sentences from his talk. Fill in the blanks as you listen.

> **Listening/Notetaking Strategy**
>
> If you don't understand a word, write it down the way it sounds and continue listening. Later, you can compare notes with your partner or find the word in the Glossary. Don't stop listening!

1. Starting as very little children, we begin to categorize things into good and bad, ___hot and cold___, ___sweet and sour___, or ___edible and inedible___.

2. They teach us who's in our family and who's not. Who's in our _____ , and who's not. Who's in our _____ and who's not, who are strangers and who are _____.

3. They are other than we and we don't understand them. They eat differently, _____ different, and so they somehow are frightening to us. And so we want to keep them away, keep them _____, and we give them _____ traits.

4. We can think about people belonging to different groups and learn to value them, to say Ah! They aren't like my family, they aren't like _____, but that's an _____ tribe.

5. We're much more alike than we are different, and yet we do have different color _____ and different color _____ and different color skins.

6. We have historically killed people because they had different religion, because they had different _____, because they belonged to a _____, or because they spoke a diffcrent _____.

F. 👥 Vocabulary and Dictation

1. 👂🧑 Your teacher will read phrases from the listening twice each. Listen and match the words on the left with the definitions on the right.

_____ 1. fascinating	a.	thinking of a person as an example of a general type, often in a negative way
_____ 2. categorizing	b.	qualities or features of someone/something
_____ 3. species	c.	very interesting
_____ 4. tribe	d.	very unfriendly
_____ 5. counterproductive	e.	a group of plants or animals of the same kind
_____ 6. characterization	f.	a group of people of the same race, beliefs, language, etc., and led by a chief of some sort
_____ 7. stereotypical	g.	organizing or placing into groups
_____ 8. traits	h.	not useful or helpful
_____ 9. dilemma	i.	description of one's character or personality
_____ 10. hostile	j.	difficulty, problem

2. 👂🧑 Listen to your teacher and write the sentences you hear. Then compare sentences with a partner.

Listening 2

A. 👥 Before You Listen

> ___: you can't live with them, and
> you can't live without them!
> —American saying

> *Vive la différence!*
> —French saying

1. There are many ways to group or categorize people. In the chart below, list four more categories and give examples.

Category	Examples
profession	teacher, actor, shopkeeper...
race	

2. Look over your list and rank the categories from most important (1) to least important (6). For example, if a person were described as being male, American, black, and a doctor, which characteristic would be most important? When you are done, compare what you've done with your group.

3. The American saying at the top of the page is very common. "Them" refers to the largest "other" group in the world. What group do you think it is? The popular French saying above is more positive but expresses a similar idea. Is there a saying in your culture that expresses this idea? If so, translate it for the class and discuss.

4. Split into two groups, men in one and women in the other. The group of women should create a list of men's traits. The men should create a list of women's traits. When you have completed the lists, remain in your groups and exchange lists. Do you agree or disagree with the list the other group created? Present your group's reaction to the class.

chael Barrett

Linda Farhood-Karasava

A. Who Will You Be Listening To?

Michael Barrett and Linda Farhood-Karasava are English language teachers. Linda is trying to understand a communication problem she is having with a male friend, so she decided to ask another "guy" about it.

B. 👫 Listening for Opinions/Summarizing

1. 👂 Read the questions below and then listen and take notes. Compare notes with your partner. Finally, summarize your notes into a one-sentence answer to each question.

   a. According to Michael, how do men solve problems?

   _____

   _____

   b. According to Linda, how do women solve problems?

   _____

   _____

> **Thinking Strategy**
>
> Read the statements in the chart below very carefully, and think about the positions that Michael and Linda took. Don't assume anything.

2. Read the statements in the chart below. In the spaces provided, indicate whether Michael and Linda agree (use ✔) or disagree (use X) with the statement. If you can't tell, use a question mark (?).

Statements	Michael	Linda
Men don't talk about their problems.		
Women talk about their problems.		
Talking about problems doesn't solve anything.		
Women's approach to solving problems doesn't work.		
Men don't care about problems; they ignore them.		
The video Linda saw is a good example of the differences in the ways men and women deal with problems.		

3. 👂 Compare what you've done with your partner, and then listen and check your answers.

C. 👥 Speaking Styles/Perspectives

On each line below, show where Michael and Linda belong. Write M for Michael and L for Linda.

	1	2	3	4	5	
FORMAL>						<INFORMAL
HUMOROUS>						<SERIOUS
OPEN-MINDED>						<CLOSED-MINDED
OBJECTIVE>						<SUBJECTIVE

D. 👥 Comparing and Contrasting

1. 👂 Read the statements below and decide who you think said them. Write M for Michael or L for Linda. Then listen again and check your answers.

   ___ a. . . . little girls and little boys problem solve differently.

   ___ b. . . . there must be different mechanisms for dealing with problems . . . that boys and girls have.

   ___ c. if a man was going to talk about something, he wants to talk about it because he has a problem and he wants to get a solution to it. Whereas if you talk to a woman they just want to talk about how they feel about things and sort of work through it that way. . . .

   ___ d. I suppose you could look at it as being a guy thing, but . . . it's the way that men and women talk about things that's different.

   ___ e. The girls talked their way through, and about how they feel and you did it and trying to problem solve and all that kind of thing, and it takes some time and they reach their solution . . . the boys just went BAM! You know . . . they just solved the problem right away without talking about it.

   ___ f. Is this a guy thing? If this were a woman, there would be no problem talking.

   ___ g. I think men and women both have a spectrum of things; there's the emotional part of them, and there's the problem-solving part of them. . . . I think women tend to go more toward revealing their feelings and talking. . . .

2. Choose one of the topics below or another related topic.

   a. Discuss the difference between men and women in dealing with one of the following: work, family, friends, free time, marriage, children.

   b. Compare and contrast two cultures and the way they deal with one of the following: work, family, friends, free time, marriage, children.

Through the Eyes of Children

3. Look at the cartoon at the right. How is the perspective of the children different from that of the adults? What happens to us between early childhood and adulthood that changes the way we see others? As parents and teachers, what can we do to teach children tolerance and respect for others?

Dr. Seuss and the "Other"

E. Bonus Listening

Dr. Seuss is one of America's most beloved children's story writers. He wrote *The Butter Battle Book* to teach children about the absurdity of war. The excerpt below is from the beginning of the book. An old man is telling his grandson why their group, the Yooks, are at war with the Zooks. Read the excerpt; then listen as Daniel, age 11, reads it as well. Discuss it in terms of what we've covered in this chapter.

On the last day of summer,
ten hours before fall . . .
    . . . My grandfather took me
out to the Wall. . . .
"As you know on this side of the Wall
we are Yooks.
On the other side of this Wall
live the Zooks."
Then my grandfather said,
"It's high time that you knew
of the terribly horrible thing that Zooks do.
In every Zook house and in every Zook town
*Every Zook eats his bread
with the butter side down!*

But we Yooks, as you know,
when we breakfast or sup,
spread our bread," Grandpa said
"with the butter side *up.*
That's the right, honest way!"
Grandpa gritted his teeth.
"So you can't trust a Zook who spreads
bread underneath!
Every Zook must be watched!
He has kinks in his soul!
That's why as a youth I made watching my goal.
Watching Zooks for the Zook-Watching
border patrol!"

Listening 3

A. 👥 Who Will You Be Listening To?

The Democrats and the Republicans are the two major political groups in the United States. When a voter feels that he or she is not a strong supporter of either party, the voter can register as an Independent. Independents do not belong to any political party. You will hear one speaker from each of these three groups.

B. Before You Listen

> **Culture Note**
>
> **The American Political Picture—The Parties and Where They Stand**
>
> The United States has a two-party system, now called the Democrats and the Republicans. Though there are other political parties, none of them is big enough to elect one of its candidates to the presidency. However, they do try! The chart below outlines the relative positions of the two parties. Look up any words you don't understand.
>
> Left   Right
>
>   DEMOCRATS   REPUBLICANS
>
> Radicals   <   Liberals   <   Moderates / Moderates   >   Conservatives   >   Reactionaries
>
> ←———————— I N D E P E N D E N T S ————————→

C. Notetaking

👂 We asked three people if they could explain the differences between the Democratic and Republican parties. Take notes on their responses in the chart below. When you are done, work with your group to predict their answers to the second question: "Are you a Republican, a Democrat, or an Independent?"

	Democrats	Republicans
Neal		
Thomas		
Stephen		

D. Analysis

How objective were the three speakers in answering the first question? In your opinion, who was the most objective? Why do you think this is so?

Video

A. 👥 **What Will You Be Watching?**

A group of foreign students is complaining about two different but related difficulties they face in the United States.

B. **Notetaking**

👂 Watch the video and answer the questions.

1. Have you had any experiences like these students?
2. Do you think people have experiences like these when visiting your country of origin?

C. 👥 **Notetaking/Role-playing**

👂 Break into four groups and follow the instructions below.

1. Each group should pick one of the following characters and take notes on that person only: the second Italian woman, the woman from Kenya, the Indian man, the Spanish woman.

2. Compare notes in your group and come to an agreement on what was said.

3. Choose one person from your group to represent the person you took notes on. This person should role-play a conversation with the representatives from the other three groups. Include things they actually said, but also add additional comments to show how these people feel about the way they are perceived.

D. 👥 **Map Reading**

Look at the box above. It lists the names of the students in the video and the countries they are from.

On the world map below, the first eight countries are in dark gray, and the additional countries are filled in with black. Write the number of the country listed in the box on the corresponding line on the map. Compare your answers with those of other groups.

Country	Student
1. Italy	Luisa, Mariarosi, Francesco
2. Greece	Sofia
3. India	Seth
4. Kenya	Kagendo
5. Spain	Olga
6. Korea	Young Man Khan
7. Argentina	Ana
Additional Countries	
8. Vietnam	
9. Afghanistan	
10. Iraq	
11. Zaire	
12. Columbia	
13. Algeria	
14. Guatamala	

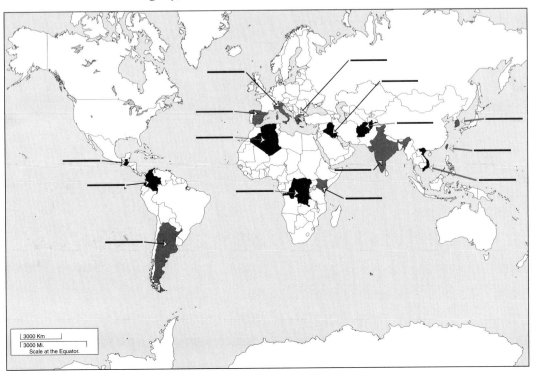

```
3000 Km
3000 Mi.
Scale at the Equator.
```

Michelangelo (Italian), *David* (detail), 1501–04, marble, 13' 5", height. *Academy, Florence. Alinari/Art Resource, NY.*

ART, SOCIETY,

AND THE

ARTIST

WHAT IS THE PURPOSE OF ART?

IS ART A REFLECTION OF SOMETHING? IF SO, WHAT? THE SPIRITUAL IN US? NATURE? SOCIETY? WEALTH? OR JUST THE ARTIST'S PERSONAL VIEW?

Shunsho, Katsukawa (Japanese), *The Actor Ichikawa Danjuro IV in a Shibaraku Role*, c. 1770, woodblock print, 26 x 38.3 cm. *Clarence Buckingham Collection, 1925.2365. Photograph © 1997, The Art Institute of Chicago. All rights reserved.*

Listening 1

A.  Before You Listen

1. Discuss the following questions.

    a. Is art important to you? If so, why?

    b. Which of these works of art do you like? Which do you dislike? Why?

Kollwitz, Kathë (German), *Never Again War (Nie Wieder Krieg)*, 1924, black crayon and charcoal on two sheets of attached trans paper. *National Gallery of Art, Washington. Rosenwald Collectic*

(Greek) Poseidon, bronze, 1.95 m., height. National Archaeological Museum, Athens. Photograph © by Erich Lessing/Art Resource.

Ch'eng, Li *(Att.)* (Chinese), *A Solitary Temple Amid Clearing Peaks,* hanging scroll, ink and slight color on silk. 44" x 22" (111.8 x 56.0 cm.). Northern Sung Dynasty (960–1127). *The Nelson-Atkins Museum of Art, Kansas City, MO (Purchase: Nelson Trust).*

2. The words below can be used to describe the art in this chapter. Look up any words that you don't understand. Then use these words and your own to describe the pictures on these two pages.

dark	harmonious	spiritual
simple	balanced	controlled
primitive	decorative	beautiful
light	modern	earthy
complex	reasoned	emotional
sophisticated	free	strong
peaceful	organized	subjective

(Ancient Peru), *Mohica. From the collection of Nathan Cumming, Chicago. Giraudon/Art Resource, NY.*

Picasso, Pablo (Spanish), *Girl Before a Mirror,* March 1932, Boisgeloup, 64 x 51-1/4 in., (162.3 x 130.2 cm.), oil on canvas. *The Museum of Modern Art, New York. Gift of Mrs. Simon Guggenheim. Photograph © 1997 The Museum of Modern Art, New York.*

Charles Olton

B. Who Will You Be Listening To?

The speaker is Dean Charles Olton of Parsons School of Design in New York City. Parsons is the largest art and design school in the United States.

C. 👫 Listening for a General Topic

What's the talk about? Listen and check (✔) the general topic.

_____ 1. The history of art _____ 2. Art in context _____ 3. Painting

D. 👫 Listening for Main Ideas

Read the items below. Then listen and check (✔) the two main ideas in the listening.

_____ Renaissance art rejected the mystical themes of Medieval art.

_____ Modern design reflects modern needs.

_____ Art reflects its own traditions. This is one of the contexts.

_____ Graffiti art reflects the economic conditions of its time.

_____ Social, historical, political, and economic conditions are part of the context of art.

> **Listening Note**
>
> There are only two main ideas in this listening. The speaker spends most of his time giving examples to support these main ideas. Use the examples to help you find the main ideas.

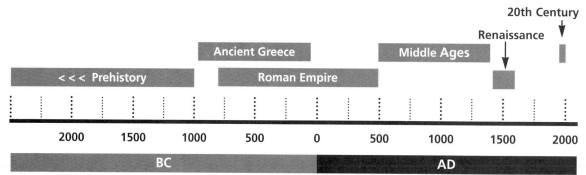

Historical Perspective

When looking and talking about art, it is important to have a historical perspective. Look at the time line below. Notice the order of the periods mentioned in the talk: prehistoric times, classical Greece and Rome, the Medieval period, the Renaissance, and today. What was happening in your country during these periods?

20th Century

Renaissance

Ancient Greece · Middle Ages

<<< Prehistory · Roman Empire

2000 · 1500 · 1000 · 500 · 0 · 500 · 1000 · 1500 · 2000

BC · AD

E. 👫 Listening for Details

Dean Olton talks about the contexts of two art periods by comparing each to an older period.

1. In the charts on page 45, fill in as many details as you can remember from the listening.

2. Listen again and complete the details in the charts on the next page. Then compare your answers with your partner.

*Note: Two examples of Renaissance art are Michelangelo's *David* on page 42 and da Vinci's *Portrait Sketches of Cesare Borgia* on page 50. A good example of art from the Middle Ages is the column shown on the right.

Nave, 6th North Pillar, West Capital: *Battle of Demons* (from North-West), Vezelay, Sainte-Madelaine, France. *Marburg/Art Resource, NY.*

Middle Ages/Renaissance

The social, historical, political, and economic contexts:

- the _end_ of the Medieval period
- the decline of Medieval _____ organizations
- the decline of Christian church _____
- the rise of the nation _____
- The increase of capitalism and _____
- the discovery of the New _____

The artistic contexts:

- a rejection of Gothic _forms_
- a return to the Classicism of ancient Greece and _____ , which artists believed was more rational, had a greater clarity of _____ , and which focused on more universal concepts of _____

Prehistory/Today

The social, historical, political, and economic contexts:

- In the ancient times, prehistoric man painted their experiences, their _____, their angers, their _____ on the walls of caves.
- Today, modern graffiti artists express the _____ conditions in which they live, _____ poverty, anger, protest.
- They are political and _____ outcasts often, and they express their ideas in this way.

The artistic contexts:

- Graffiti art reflects an artistic rejection of the traditional _____ of art, of paint and _____.
- Instead, graffiti artists use spray _____, and they paint on the _____ environment itself.

Lascaux cave painting, Perigord, Bordogne, France. _Giraudon/Art Resource, NY._

Artist unknown, graffiti art, Boston, MA. _J. Berndt/Stock, Boston._

F. 👫 🎧 Vocabulary and Dictation

1. Your teacher will read sentences from the listening. Listen and match these words from the sentences to the definitions on the right.

_c_	1. **context**	a.	dropout, exile
___	2. **graffiti**	b.	object to, challenge
___	3. **prehistoric**	c.	conditions in which an event occurs
___	4. **economic**	d.	before recorded history
___	5. **urban**	e.	related to money, trade, and business
___	6. **protest**	f.	of the city
___	7. **outcast**	g.	drawings, writing on the wall

2. Listen to your teacher and write the sentences you hear. Then compare sentences with a partner.

Listening 2

A. Before You Listen

1. Write down two or three words describing each image below. Then write a sentence describing how the painting makes you feel (e.g., **happy, lonely, depressed**) and why.

1. _____
2. _____
3. _____

This painting makes
me feel . . .
because . . .
_____
_____

Magritte, René (French), *La Reproduction Interdite (Portrait of Edward James)*, 1937, oil, 32" x 25-5/8". *Museum Boymans van Beuningen, Rotterdam, The Netherlands. Giraudon/Art Resource. © 1998 C. Herscovici, Brussels/Artists Rights Society (ARS), New York.*

1. _____
2. _____
3. _____

_____
_____
_____
_____
_____
_____

Warhol, Andy (American), *Marilyn Monroe*, 1967, screenprint, 36" x 36". *The Andy Warhol Foundation, Inc./Art Resource, NY. ©1998 Andy Warhol Foundation for the Visual Arts/ARS, New York.*

1. _____
2. _____
3. _____

_____
_____
_____
_____

Malevich, Kasimir (Russian), *Suprematist Composition: Airplane Flying*, 1915 (dated 1914), oil on canvas, 22 7/8 x 19" (58.1 x 48.3 cm.). *The Museum of Modern Art, New York. Purchase. Photograph © 1997 The Museum of Modern Art, New York.*

1. _____
2. _____
3. _____

_____
_____
_____
_____

Severini, Gino (Italian), *Armored Train in Action (Train blindé en action)*, 1915, oil on canvas, 45 5/8" x 34 7/8" (115.8 x 88.5 cm.). *The Museum of Modern Art, New York. Gift of Richard S. Zeisler. Photograph © 1997 The Museum of Modern Art, New York. ©1998 Artists Rights Society (ARS), New York/ADAGP, Paris*

2. 👥 Compare ideas with your group.

3. Read the four descriptions of artistic movements on the next page. Match each description to an image on this page. Write the name of the artist in the space provided.

a. _Severini_____ **Futurism:** Futurist artists celebrated the sounds and movements of the technological future. Their art frequently represents speed and movement by breaking up and repeating forms.

b. _____ **Suprematism:** Suprematist artists were revolutionary artists—Russian revolutionary artists. They were strongly supported by the new political leaders who led the revolution in 1917 because they too were revolutionaries—artistic revolutionaries. They completely rejected forms that, in any way, looked like something in the real world.

c. _____ **Surrealism:** The Surrealists were strongly influenced by Sigmund Freud's work on the unconscious mind (see page 82). They intended to explore people's inner world. Dreams and dreamlike images became an important means of doing this.

d. _____ **Pop Art:** Pop artists worked in the 1950s and 1960s, emphasizing the values of these times as they saw them. They transformed the temporary, common, everyday images around them into art.

4. Compare ideas in your group. What was your reason for matching each artistic movement to the appropriate picture?

B. Who Will You Be Listening To?

Brian Brooks is the director of educational programs at the Brooklyn Museum of Art in New York City. It is his job to help visitors enjoy and appreciate the art they see. In this interview, Brooks talks about the two works of art shown on page 48. The first is a carved wooden Luba chief's stool from Africa. The second piece is a Cubist painting of a woman.

Brian Brooks

C. Looking, Listening, and Notetaking

1. Before listening, look on the next page at the two works Brooks will be describing. Write a short description of each one on the lines below.

a. _____
   _____
   _____

b. _____
   _____
   _____

Listening Note

Look carefully at the art while you are listening. Try to see what Brooks is describing. If you understand what you see, you will be able to write notes in your own words.

Luba people (Zaire), *Royal Marriage Stool*, late 19th or early 20th century, wood, 15" x 19" (38.0 x 23.8 cm.). *Brooklyn Museum of Art, Gift of A. and P. Peralta-Ramos. 56.6-92.*

Villon, Jacques (French), *Le Philosphe*, 1930, oil, 39 5/8" x 31 7/8". *Brooklyn Museum of Art, Gift of Gerda Stein. 34.1000.*

2. 👂 For each piece of art, listen and write two things about its social context and its artistic context in the chart below.

Luba Chief's Stool	Cubist Painting
Social Context The stool was used by the chief to assert his powers.	**Social Context**
Artistic Context	**Artistic Context**

3. 🎬 How did Brooks's explanation affect the way you saw the works? Did the information help you understand each work? Did it help you appreciate the work? Discuss your answers in your group.

Close, Chuck (American), *Phil/Fingerprint II*, drawing, stamp pad ink and pencil on paper, 29 3/4 x 22 1/4 in. (75.6 x 56.5 cm.). *Purchase, with funds from Peggy and Richard Danziger. Collection of Whitney Museum of American Art, New York. Photograph Copyright © 1997 Whitney Museum of American Art, New York.*

D. Language—Visual Description

When describing a work of art, two parts of speech are especially important: adjectives and verbs. In his talk Brooks emphasizes the role of the artist by using more verbs than adjectives. Notice that he uses the historical present tense rather than the past to emphasize the artist's actions and his role. He also explains what the forms are doing by using verbs. Here are some examples:

For the Luba stool:

- The artist **uses** the image of a woman.
- The artist **exaggerates** the size of the head.
- The artist **plays down** the role of the fingers . . . toes . . . feet.
- The rings **are . . . lined up.**
- Rings . . . **emerge** from the trunk of the tree.

For the Cubist painting:

- [Things **are**] **broken up** . . . **deemphasized** . . . **emphasized.**

1. Look at the drawings on this page and try to describe them by using similar techniques.

2. Add to your descriptions, using appropriate adjectives. Use the adjectives on page 43 and your own words.

Munch, Edvard (Norwegian), *Attraction I*, 1896, lithograph.© *1998 The Munch Museum, Oslo. The Munch Museum, Oslo/The Munch-Ellingsen Group/Artists Rights Society (ARS), New York. Photo: Munch Museum/Sidsel de Jong.*

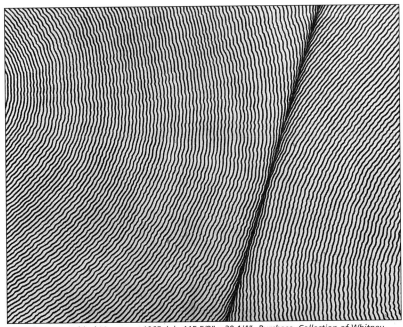

Pearson, Henry, *Ethical Movement,* 1965, ink, 115 5/8" x 20 1/4". *Purchase. Collection of Whitney Museum of American Art, New York. Photograph Copyright © 1997 Whitney Museum of American Art, New York.*

👥 *Listening 3*

A. Who Will You Be Listening To?

Since the purpose of art seems to be such a controversial issue, we should see what the experts had to say. You will hear quotations from seven famous artists.

B. Before You Listen

The works of six of the artists in the listening are represented in this chapter. Review the chapter to become familiar with the artists' work. This will help you to complete the following activities.

C. Notetaking

1. 🎧 👥 Listen to the seven quotations. Most of them are very short. For each quotation, write down a few key words on a separate piece of paper. As a group, try to match the quotations to the names of the artists below.

_____ 1. Paul Klee (1879–1940), Swiss

_____ 2. Pablo Picasso (1881–1973), Spanish

_____ 3. Diego Rivera (1886–1957), Mexican

_____ 4. Gino Severini (1883–1966), Italian

_____ 5. *Shih-T'ao (1641–c. 1717), Chinese

_____ 6. Paul Gauguin (1848–1903), French

_____ 7. Leonardo da Vinci (1452–1519), Italian

*Note: For a good example of Chinese painting, look at the painting by Li Ch'eng on page 43.

2. 🎧 Check with your teacher for the correct answers. Then, listen again and try to understand each artist's statement in relation to his artwork.

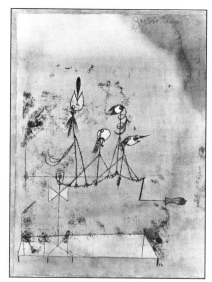

Klee, Paul (Swiss), *Twittering Machine (Zwitscher-Maschine)*, 1922, watercolor, and pen and ink on oil, transfer drawing on paper, mounted on cardboard, 25 1/4" x 19" (63.8 x 48.1 cm.). *The Museum of Modern Art, New York. Purchase. Photograph © 1997 The Museum of Modern Art, New York. © 1998 Artists Rights Society (ARS), New York/VG Bild-Kunst, Bonn.*

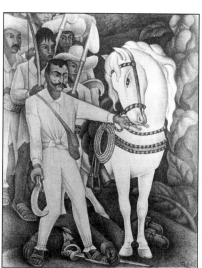

Rivera, Diego (Mexican), *Emiliano Zapata*, 1932, lithograph. *Giraudon/Art Resource, Inc.*

da Vinci, Leonardo (Italian), *Portrait Sketches of Cesare Borgia*. Palazzo Reale, Turin, Italy, *Alinari/Art Resource, NY.*

Gauguin, Paul (French), *Nirvana: Portrait of Meyer de Haan*, oil, turpentine, silk. 1943.445. *Wadsworth Atheneum, Hartford, CT, The Ella Gallup Sumner and Mary Catlin Sumner Collection Fund.*

Video

A. What Will You Be Watching?

The filmmaker Reiko Tahara deals with many kinds of images from Japan, America, her family, and the media. Although the film may sometimes look like a documentary, it is not one. A documentary film presents facts in an objective way. Tahara presents a very personal vision through the use of special artistic techniques. She hopes that these techniques will communicate her personal thoughts and feelings.

1. 🎧 What impressions and feelings do you have about this film? Compare your ideas with members of your group.

2. Why do you think Tahara called her film *remnants*?

B. 👥 Identifying Themes

🎧 In this video Reiko Tahara has several concerns that she wants to present. Read the list below and watch the video again. Then check (✔) the main themes of the video. Discuss your answers with the group.

_____	The conflict between tradition and modernization in Japan	_____	Tahara's own identity: self and others
_____	The effect of modern toys on Japanese children	_____	The way Tahara's family deals with issues of tradition and modernization
_____	Education in Japan	_____	Homesickness

C. Analysis and Synthesis

Discuss or write about the following:

1. **Art in Context:** How are social, political, and economic concerns expressed in the film?

2. **Artistic Tradition:** From your experience watching films, do you think Reiko Tahara is following the artistic traditions of the past or rejecting them? Compare this film with another film you've seen.

3. **Visual Description:**
   a. Describe the visual effects of the film. Why do you think Tahara used certain effects? Try to give specific examples.
   b. Compare the film to the art movements you have studied in this chapter. Which one(s) does it remind you of?

4. **The Purpose of the Film:**
   a. Why do you think Tahara made the film?
   b. What purpose does this film serve for those who watch it?

SMARTS!

Listening 1

A.  Before You Listen

1. Read the information below and then answer the questions.

In 1984, Harvard professor Howard Gardner published a book about human intelligence called *Frames of Mind.* He begins the book by talking about I.Q. tests, which are relied on around the world to test the intelligence of children. Although these tests may predict how well students do in school subjects, they do not predict how well they will do in life!

a. Do you think that someone who is successful in school is guaranteed to be successful in life? Why or why not?

b. Does a person who is successful in school have a better chance at being successful in life? Why or why not?

2. Read the definition of *intelligence* below and then answer the questions.

An intelligence is the ability to solve problems, or to create products, that are valued within one or more cultural settings. . . . —Howard Gardner, *Frames of Mind*

a. Do you agree with this definition of *intelligence*? Why or why not?

b. I.Q. tests usually measure linguistic and mathematical intelligence. How well do you think I.Q. tests measure the kind of intelligence Professor Gardner is talking about?

3. Howard Gardner has identified seven different intelligences. Scan this chapter to find their names.

1. __linguistic intelligence__   5. _____
2. _____   6. _____
3. _____   7. _____
4. _____

Preparation Note

At the end of this chapter, you will work on a project. The first step will be to assess your strengths and weaknesses as they relate to multiple intelligences. It may help to keep a journal of your thoughts on this subject as you go through the chapter.

It's not how smart you are; it's how you're smart!

Linguistic Intelligence

✔
- ❏ Love reading books, poetry, newspapers
- ❏ Enjoy writing
- ❏ Keep a journal or diary
- ❏ Have an excellent vocabulary
- ❏ Speak easily and well
- ❏ Prefer language-related subjects in school—for example, history, literature
- ❏ Like word games
- ❏ Good at verbal humor, jokes

4. 👥 The boxes at the right list some of the characteristics of linguistic intelligence and mathematical/logical intelligence. These are very important if you want to get a high score on an I.Q. test. Read the information in the boxes and then answer the questions below.

   a. Which of the terms on these lists describe you? Check (✔) them off.

   b. If your linguistic skills are weak, how might that affect your success in school? In learning English? In life?

   c. If you're not strong in mathematical/logical intelligence, how might it affect your success in business? In organizing your financial affairs? In organizing your life?

You will see more boxes like these throughout the chapter. Check (✔) the items as you've done here. Once you've heard Listening 1, you'll know why.

Mathematical/ Logical Intelligence

✔
- ❏ Can double or triple numbers and measurements in head
- ❏ Like to outline, organize, categorize things
- ❏ Prefer math/science to language subjects in school
- ❏ Enjoy strategy games like chess
- ❏ Enjoy learning how things work
- ❏ Tend to look for logical explanations for things
- ❏ Find problem solving interesting and challenging

B. Who Will You Be Listening To?

Mara Krechevsky

Mara Krechevsky is an educational researcher at Project Zero at the Harvard Graduate School of Education. Project Zero is a research group that looks at educational development issues in children. Howard Gardner co-directed Project Zero for many years.

C. Listening for a General Topic

🦻 What is the talk about? Listen and check (✔) the general topic.

_____ **1.** Multiple intelligence theory

_____ **2.** I.Q. tests and intelligence

_____ **3.** The importance of linguistic and mathematical intelligence

D. 👥 Listening for Specific Information

1. a. 🦻 The speaker discusses eight intelligences. Listen again and, on the spaces provided, number the intelligences in the order you hear them.

Interpersonal	Musical	Intrapersonal	Linguistic
Physical/Bodily	Spatial/Visual	Naturalistic	Mathematical/Logical

1. _____   _4_   a. Perceive visual or spatial information and, perhaps, transform this information

2. _____   ____   b. Sensitive to the natural and physical world

3. _____   ____   c. Use all or parts of your body, like your hands or your mouth, to create products or solve problems

4. ___spatial___   ____   d. Use an understanding of yourself, your strengths and weaknesses, to be effective in the world

5. _____   ____   e. Use an understanding of other people to interact with them effectively

6. _____   ____   f. Create, communicate, and understand meanings made out of sound

7. _____   ____   g. Appreciate abstract relations

8. *_____   ____   h. Communicate easily through language

> ### Culture Note
>
> In the United States, most students are educated in public schools. In a number of schools, there are two programs for a minority of students with special needs. "Gifted and talented" programs have been created for students who score very high on I.Q. tests. On the other hand, "special education" programs have been created to answer the needs of students who score below normal on I.Q. tests or who face special emotional, developmental, or other challenges.

* Note: this eighth intelligence has not been included in the rest of the work in the chapter because it is "new."

b. Now match each word above to a description in the column on the right. Write the letter of the description in front of the word.

E. 👥 Vocabulary and Dictation

1. 👂🧑 Your teacher will read sentences and phrases from the listening.
   There are two synonyms for each vocabulary word below. Listen
   and check (✔) them.

a. **entity**	✔ thing	___ image	✔ item
b. **notion**	___ dream	___ belief	___ idea
c. **devised**	___ planned	___ developed	___ invented
d. **multiple**	___ many	___ several	___ two
e. **criteria**	___ lists	___ requirements	___ rules
f. **determine**	___ discover	___ say	___ find
g. **core**	___ central	___ basic	___ outside
h. **capacities**	___ abilities	___ centers	___ capabilities
i. **valued**	___ spent	___ appreciated	___ respected
j. **based**	___ built	___ developed	___ with
k. **currently**	___ quickly	___ now	___ at the moment

2. 👂🧑 Your teacher will now read a quotation from the listening.
   Write down what you hear and then check what you've done with
   another student.

Spatial/Visual Test Samples

Here are two examples of the types of activities used to test spatial intelligence.

Top left: Circle the form on the right
that matches the form on the left.

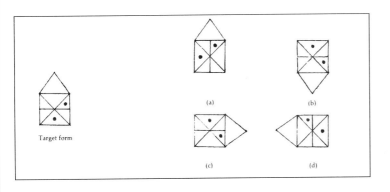

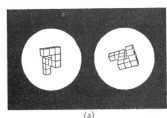

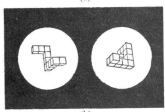

Right: Write in the letters of the two pairs of
forms that are the same but shown from different
angles. The third pair does not match at all.

_____   _____

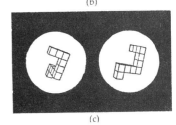

Listening 2

A. 👥 Before You Listen

Read the following and then answer the questions:

> **theory** /'θieri, 'θiri/ *n.* reasoned argument intended to explain
> something; an idea that has not yet been proved to be true.

MI (multiple intelligences) theory is an explanation that Howard
Gardner and others developed after a great deal of study on
intelligence. But it is not something that you can prove. Because of
this, people may not agree with such a theory. This excerpt from a
New York Observer editorial makes fun of some aspects of MI
theory but praises others.

> While the seven M.I.s make for fun guessing games among adults
> ("You're definitely spatial!"; "My body is smarter than your
> body!"), the place where M.I. will be most useful is in education.
> Dr. Gardner believes M.I. can be an effective teaching tool from
> kindergarten through college. . . . The best argument for M.I. is
> that it makes intuitive sense.

> Some of the M.I.-friendly techniques being used in one inner-city
> school in Indianapolis are dance, painting and staging plays.
> Instead of memorizing textbook versions of a famous scientific
> breakthrough, students are encouraged to write, direct and act out
> skits of the same. . . . If you lean toward bodily intelligence, for
> example, you will have a hard time learning about music from a
> book or record; but if you are allowed to move to the music, you'll
> learn it.

1. What do you think the writer means when he says M.I. theory
   makes intuitive sense?
2. Do you think that the techniques used in Indianapolis help
   students learn? Would you like to learn this way? How can these
   techniques be applied to language learning?
3. What kinds of tasks and activities help you the most in learning
   a language?
4. What do you think are the characteristics of a good
   language learner?

B. Who Will You Be Listening To?

Victoria Kimbrough and Marjorie Vai are English language
teachers. Here they are having a discussion about how an
awareness of the seven intelligences might help students with
their language learning.

Culture Note

The United States has a
long tradition of
progressive education and
educational reform. New
approaches for educating
children are always being
tried. Because there is no
national curriculum in the
U.S., different states have
had the freedom to
experiment with new
approaches to teaching
and learning.

Listening Strategy

This is the longest
listening in this book.
However, you will find
that the language used
is straightforward and
may be similar to the
language your teacher
uses in class. Focus on
your goal—that is, to
write down the
suggestions the
speakers give you.

Marjorie Vai (l) and Victoria Kimbrough (r)

C. 👥 Listening to a Brainstorming Session on Language Learning/Notetaking

1. In this listening, the speakers are brainstorming ways that students can become better English language learners. Read the information in the chart and think about what the speakers might say about the other intelligences. For example: *Mathematical/logical probably likes grammar charts.*

2. 👂 Listen and note two important ideas for each intelligence. Then compare notes with a partner.

Intelligence	Notes
Linguistic	1. Naturally good with language and therefore has an advantage in language learning. 2.
Mathematical/Logical	1. 2.
Spatial/Visual	1. 2.
Musical	1. Naturally good at the sound or "music" of language, pronunciation, stress, etc. Should use music, songs to help learn vocabulary and language. 2.
Physical/Bodily	1. 2.
Interpersonal	1. Try to get in as many situations as possible where you can talk with others in the language . . . parties, classes, meetings, etc. 2.
Intrapersonal	1. 2.

 # Spatial/Visual Intelligence

✔

- ❑ Frequently imagine things in clear visual images
- ❑ Sensitive to color
- ❑ Enjoy visual puzzles and games
- ❑ Have strongly visual dreams at night

- ❑ Like to paint or draw
- ❑ Like geometry more than other math subjects
- ❑ Can imagine what a solid object looks like from different angles
- ❑ Enjoy looking at visual patterns and designs

D. Language—Brainstorming/ Discussing Possibilities

1. Although the speakers are authors and professionals in English language teaching, they are not experts on MI theory. They each come up with ideas and possibilities they want to try out with the other. They do not speak in definite terms. Rather, they infer and make suggestions, using modals, conditionals, and special phrases when speaking. Look at these examples from their conversation.

a. <u>Modals</u>
- People . . . **might** use
- Students **might** want to pay attention to
- This type of person **might** want to use
- You **might** come up with
- People **might** be drawn to
- Pictures **would** help this kind of person
- That **would** be helpful
- They **would** hear what was going on
- People who . . . **would** like writing plays

Physical Intelligence

✔
- ❑ Regularly take part in physical activities
- ❑ Find it difficult to sit for a long time
- ❑ Enjoy working with hands
- ❑ Enjoy being outdoors
- ❑ Use hand gestures and body language
- ❑ Physically well-coordinated
- ❑ Prefer doing things rather than just reading about how to do them
- ❑ Enjoy acting, mime, role-playing designs

- They **could** look back and see
- People **could** watch television
- You **could** make a little line drawing

b. <u>Conditionals</u>
- If you are a reflective person it **would** help to
- If someone is motivated to read something . . . they are **going to**
- If you go after something you like . . . you **might be** more absorbed with

c. <u>Phrases</u>
- I think
- I guess
- What other . . . do you think?
- My understanding is that

2.  Listen again and check (✔) the words or phrases above as you hear them.

Musical Intelligence

✔
- ❑ Enjoy singing
- ❑ Play a musical instrument
- ❑ Know when a note is off-key
- ❑ Frequently listen to music
- ❑ Often hear a tune in head
- ❑ Like to tap out the beat when listening to music
- ❑ Can usually remember a tune heard once or twice
- ❑ Could not imagine a world without music

3.  Below are the stories of three people who need to succeed in studying English. Each of them has problems to overcome. Review your notes on pages 54 and 57 before beginning. Then choose one of these people and use the language on page 58 as well as your own words to brainstorm within your group. What might each person do to successfully learn English?

> **INTERpersonal Intelligence**
>
> ✔
>
> ❑ Thought of as a good advisor
> ❑ Prefer group sports to individual sports
> ❑ Prefer to talk out problems with others rather than working them out alone
> ❑ Have several close friends
> ❑ Prefer playing games with people rather than alone
> ❑ Enjoy teaching others
> ❑ Enjoy parties and social events
> ❑ Feel comfortable in a crowd

a. **Jan** has a growing manufacturing business in Warsaw. He knows that he must focus on the European market and consequently must work seriously on his English. He really likes studying English, but his problem is that he doesn't have much time to study. He now takes a class two hours a week, but that's not enough. He spends two hours a day in his car. He also loves music, plays the saxophone in a jazz band, and enjoys singing in the car. What can he do on his own to improve his English?

b. **Miki** is a high school student in Osaka. She is a talented artist and wants to study fashion design in New York. She is not close to getting the 550 TOEFL score she needs to get into the design school she wants to attend. She's very frustrated because she feels she's not good at learning languages—so she has not done well in English classes. As a matter of fact, she's always done better in art and math classes than in any of her language-related classes. She's also rather shy and doesn't like to share her problems with others. What could she do both in and out of class that would help her?

c. **Yolanda** is studying English at a community college in Illinois. She wants to be a nurse because it is a good job and because she has always liked science. In fact, when she lived in Colombia she wanted to study either math or science when she got to college. She has been in the States only one year, and she knows she has a long way to go before her English is good enough for nursing school. She works during the day and enjoys socializing with her Colombian friends when possible. She also likes to take walks and play sports. She really enjoys being physically active, but at both her job and at school she is sitting all the time. She needs to improve her English. What can she do?

INTRApersonal Intelligence

Need to spend a good amount of time alone to think or reflect
Strong-willed and independent
Think a lot about life and the future
Enjoy spending days at a time alone
Keep a personal journal
Self-employed or would like to be

Listening 3

A. Who Will You Be Listening To?

In this chapter, you have looked at how learning about yourself, about your strengths and weaknesses, can help you be a better learner. In this listening, you will hear about how this knowledge might help in another important area of your life—work. You will hear three people talking about their strengths and weaknesses.

B. Listening for Specific Information/Notetaking

1. 👂 Listen and complete the chart below.

	Strengths	How They Relate to Work
Karen		
George		
Robert		

Karen

George

Robert

2. 👥 Compare charts with your classmates.

C. Brainstorming—Working with Your Strengths

The speakers above talk about their situations differently. Brainstorm in groups about the kinds of work situations that would best match your strengths and skills.

Project

A. What Will You Be Doing?

In this project you will apply what you've learned about multiple intelligences. First, you will make a plan to help yourself become a better language learner. You will then reflect on how this plan could affect other areas of your life.

B. Self-Assessment

Work alone for this part of the project. If you have been writing down your thoughts on multiple intelligences, you may already have a good sense of your strengths and weaknesses.

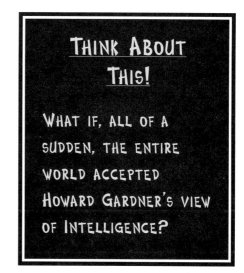

THINK ABOUT THIS!

WHAT IF, ALL OF A SUDDEN, THE ENTIRE WORLD ACCEPTED HOWARD GARDNER'S VIEW OF INTELLIGENCE?

1. Outline your general strengths and weaknesses on a piece of paper. You may want to divide the paper into two columns to do this.

2. On a second piece of paper, list your *language learning* strengths and weaknesses. What do you like about learning a new language? What do you dislike? What's easy for you? What's difficult?

C. 👥 Brainstorming with a Group

Share your language learning strengths and weaknesses with the group. Then take turns suggesting ways to learn English that emphasize or maximize each person's strengths. For example, the person who has strong visual skills but has a hard time remembering the meaning of vocabulary words could create a visual diary of vocabulary with pictures and/or drawings that relate to the words. The goal of your group is to develop a list of activities for each person that fits his or her personal strengths and skills. This personal list of activities should help each person take more control of and improve his or her language learning.

D. Presentation

1. Spend time on your own to see if you can add to the list you developed in your group.

2. Summarize your new approach to language learning and present it to the class.

E. Applying This Knowledge to Other Things

Discuss how this new knowledge about yourself can improve other areas of your life: other areas of learning, your personal life, special interests, work plans, etc.

AS

CRIME Entertainment

Listening 1

A. Before You Listen

1. Read the following quotation. How does it support the idea that "crime sells"?

If it bleeds, it leads. For those unfamiliar with this old TV maxim, it means that a juicy bit of violence . . . is a sure-fire candidate to top the late evening news.
—Clyde Haberman
The New York Times, May 3, 1996

2. Read the following statements. Check (✔) the ones you agree with and then compare ideas in your group.

_____ Sensational crime is interesting to most people.

_____ People are naturally attracted to scenes of violence.

_____ Interest in sensational crime is a sign of illness in society.

_____ Violence is as pervasive in movies, TV, and print in other countries as it is in the United States.

Poster design by Alphonse Mucha for the French production of the ancient Greek play *Medea.*

CRIME, violence, and sensationalism are pervasive themes in modern society. They are everywhere—in television news, newspapers, books, movies, magazines, video games, TV programs, and sports. Crime entertains. Crime sells!

gar Allen Poe (1809–1849), American poet
d short story writer.

Illustration from "The Pit and the Pendulum" from Edgar Allen Poe's *Poe: Prose Tales of Mystery and the Imagination.* Printed in New York in 1903, Howard W. Bell, publisher.

Culture Note

Edgar Allan Poe (1809–1849) was one of America's most brilliant writers. He was a poet, short story writer, editor, and critic. However, he is also remembered for his crime and horror stories, such as "The Murders in the Rue Morgue" and "The Pit and the Pendulum." He is considered the father of the modern detective story.

Robert Polito

B. Who Will You Be Listening To?

Robert Polito, director of the M.F.A. Program in Creative Writing at the New School, recently won the National Critic's Book Award for *Savage Art,* his biography of crime novelist Jim Thompson. Thompson wrote some of America's most innovative and most violent crime fiction.

In this listening, Robert Polito talks about crime in literature. Based on the information on these two pages, what do you think he might say? Write down one idea and then share it with your classmates.

C. Listening for a General Topic

What's the talk about? Listen and check (✔) the general topic.

_____ 1. Crime as Entertainment: A Sign of Our Time

_____ 2. Crime as Entertainment: A Classic Theme

_____ 3. Crime as Entertainment: The End of Order
and Peace

D. Listening for Specific Information

Read the following paraphrased main ideas and supporting details. Then listen to the tape again and organize the information in the outline below.

Main Ideas

• Our interest in murder is quite serious.

Supporting Details

• Shakespeare exploded a real cannon to add shock value to his play *Henry VIII*.

• Murder forces us to look at our basic beliefs about how the world works, about justice, and about ourselves.

• In ancient Greece, Shakespeare's time, and today, murder has been the theme of much great literature.

Outline

I. **Introduction:** Although detective fiction begins in the United States with Edgar Allan Poe, one could say that crime fiction began with the first American novel, Charles Brockton Brown's *Wieland* (1798).

II. **Main idea:** People who criticize today's entertainment for its focus on violence and shock forget about the violence in great literature of the past.

    a. Shakespeare exploded a real cannon to add shock value to his play Henry VIII.

    b. _____

       _____

III. **Main idea:** _____

    a. _____

       _____

IV. **Conclusion:** Modern media make violence so easy to see and understand that it seems to surround us all of the time. But violence for audiences of the past was just as real a concern as it is today.

E. 📽 Listening for Specific Information

👂 The statements below are incorrect. Read them first and then listen to the tape again and correct them.

                    America
1. Detective fiction in ~~England~~ begins with the short stories of Edgar Allan Poe.
2. The crime novel *Wieland* was published in 1898.
3. The Globe Theater was knocked down when a cannonball landed on the roof.
4. Television crime shows and tragedies are forms of modern media.
5. Gangsta rap is a type of video game.

F. 📽 Vocabulary and Dictation

1. 👂👤 Your teacher will read five sentences or phrases from the listening. There are two synonyms for each vocabulary word below. Listen and check them.

a.	fiction	✔ invention	✔ fantasy	___ truth
	character	___ writer	___ person	___ individual
b.	condemn	___ criticize	___ hate	___ attack
	contemporary	___ classical	___ modern	___ new
	reliance	___ need	___ dependence	___ harm
c.	universe	___ earth	___ cosmos	___ heavens
	crucial	___ common	___ important	___ significant
	ethical	___ moral	___ evil	___ virtuous
	ignore	___ see	___ overlook	___ disregard

2. 👂👤 📽 Your teacher will now read part of Robert Polito's talk. Write down what you hear and then check what you've done with another student.

Listening 2

A. 👥 Before You Listen

History/Culture Note:
The First Amendment and Freedom of Speech

The First Amendment of the U.S. Constitution will be mentioned more than once in this chapter. Read the following and answer the questions below.

The Bill of Rights was added to the U.S. Constitution in 1791 to provide guarantees of individual liberties to the American people. The First Amendment guarantees freedom of worship, of speech, of press, of assembly, and to petition the government. Americans take these freedoms very seriously, and the First Amendment is frequently mentioned in arguments against censorship.

- Do you agree with the right of freedom of speech?
- Can freedom of speech ever be harmful to a society?
- Can not having freedom of speech hurt a society?

1. Read the movie description below and study the ad for the movie. Would you like to see *Natural Born Killers*? Do you like movies like this in general?

One of the strangest and most violent American crime films ever produced was *Natural Born Killers,* directed by Oliver Stone. It is the story of two young lovers who travel around the country killing, it seems, everyone in their path—52 people by the time they're caught. Then they kill another 50 or so during their escape from prison. All of this killing makes them famous. In the end they are free, have children, and live happily ever after.

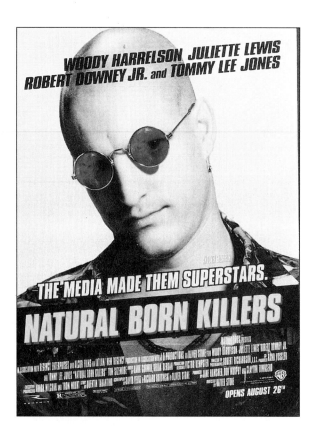

2. **a.** 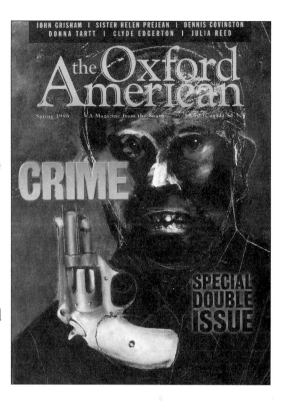 Read the following:

In a special "Crime" issue of *The Oxford American* magazine, its publisher, John Grisham, criticizes Oliver Stone's movie *Natural Born Killers*. Grisham is a well-known author of several crime novels, including *The Firm*.

    In the article, Grisham tells the story of a real-life young couple who traveled through the South, also killing people along the way. When the couple was caught, the girl said that seeing *Natural Born Killers* influenced them to begin killing on their own. Grisham criticizes *Natural Born Killers* and movies like it.

b. Now read the specific points Grisham makes, and Oliver Stone's replies to these points. For each point below do you agree with Grisham or Stone? Why?

John Grisham speaks out:	Oliver Stone's replies:
1. The couple had no history of violence. The movie glorified crime and killing and encouraged them to kill people. Other young people claim that the movie inspired them to kill too.	The lovers were disturbed young people and would probably have killed people whether or not they had seen the film.
2. Neither Oliver Stone nor the studios that make these movies think about these consequences. Instead, "Hollywood hides behind . . . First Amendment arguments . . . and the necessities of artistic freedom of expression."	Grisham is too sophisticated to speak up against the First Amendment and ask for censorship, so instead he suggests that the creators be sued. You might as well sue Shakespeare for writing *Hamlet* if your father is murdered.
3. Movies should be treated like products so that the makers can be sued if the movies influence people to commit crimes.	Artists don't create crime and violence. Their works of art just reflect things that already exist in society. This movie is a satire on the media's glorification of violence.

B. Who Will You Be Listening To?

Robyn Vaccara and David Rogers are Americans in their 20's. Robyn feels strongly that too much exposure to scenes of crime and violence is damaging to people. David saw *Natural Born Killers* and "thought it was cool." You will hear them discuss the film.

C. Listening for Main Ideas/Notetaking

1. 👂 Listen and write down two points that each speaker makes.

David	Robyn
1.	1.
2.	2.

2. 👥 Compare notes with a partner. Then listen again and add to your notes. Do you agree more with David or Robyn? Why?

D. Recognizing Fillers in Spoken English

👂 Read the Language Note. Then listen to the tape again and raise your hand each time you hear someone use a filler.

E. 👥 The Language of Disagreeing

In the spaces provided, mark XX when the phrase can be used to disagree directly (i.e., strongly) and X for phrases used to disagree indirectly (i.e., softly). Then discuss your choices with the group.

> **Language Note**
>
> "Fillers" are words that we use to fill in gaps between thoughts when speaking. They do not carry meaning. David uses fillers such as "like," "totally," and "I mean." Once you learn to recognize fillers, you will be able to ignore them and just focus on the main points the speaker is making.

__X__ I agree, but

____ I don't know

____ I disagree

____ I partly agree, but

____ I'm not so sure

__XX__ How can you feel that way when

____ I certainly understand, but

____ (But) by the same token

____ (But) don't you think?

____ I wish I could agree with you, but

____ But there needs to be

____ (But) I think

____ I don't think so

____ That may be true, but

____ How can you say that!

F. Debating an Issue

1. 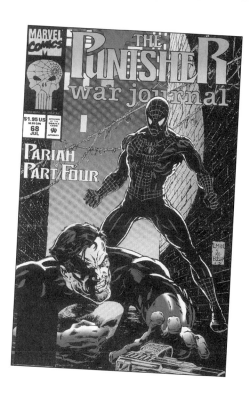 In two large groups, review and discuss the points that you noted on page 68.

2. Your group should now split in two. Half of the group should prepare an argument for crime in entertainment. The other half should prepare an argument against it. List your ideas in the appropriate column below. Use a separate piece of paper if necessary.

3. Each person in your half of the group should pair up with someone who has an opposing point of view. The pairs then argue and discuss their opinions.

Against Crime and Violence in Entertainment	Defending Crime and Violence in Entertainment
Criminals say that they have killed people under the influence of violent crime movies.	Crime and violence in books and literature have been around for thousands of years.

4. Discuss how effective the debates were. Has this activity changed your opinion of the role of crime in entertainment? If so, discuss why.

Listening 3

A. Who Will You Be Listening To?

The two speakers in this listening have professional perspectives on the issue of crime as entertainment. John Douglas is part owner of a bookstore called Partners & Crime. Laura Morgan teaches a university course called The History of Cinema.

B. 👥 Comparing Two Perspectives on an Issue/Notetaking

Laura Morgan

1. The speakers were asked to respond to this question: "Why are people attracted to crime and violence in entertainment?" Read the quotations below, then complete the sentences.

   People want to have an understanding about the roots of injustice and even the cause of death.   —John Douglas

   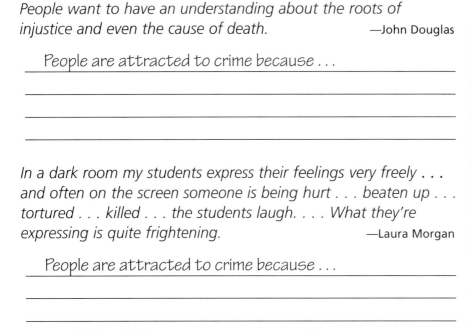

   People are attracted to crime because . . .

   _____

   _____

   _____

   In a dark room my students express their feelings very freely . . . and often on the screen someone is being hurt . . . beaten up . . . tortured . . . killed . . . the students laugh. . . . What they're expressing is quite frightening.   —Laura Morgan

John Douglas

   People are attracted to crime because . . .

   _____

   _____

   _____

2. 👂 Listen and note the two to three most important points that John and Laura make. Then compare notes with a partner.

C. 👥 Personal Perspective

Discuss the following questions in your group:

a. How do you respond when viewing a movie? Do you feel that you are in the movie in some way, or can you remain objective, always aware that it's not real?

b. Do you respond differently to scenes of violence in books than you do when watching them in movies? If so, why?

Video

A. What Will You Be Watching?

This video is a crime mystery, created by Christina Pallacio. Peter Montgomery (PM) is in prison on Death Row. His defense lawyers are trying to save him. When Peter killed the victim, Carlos Ramos (CR), he was sleepwalking. Therefore, his lawyers say, he was not in his right mind and should not die for the crime. See what you think.

B. Watching for Specific Information

1. 🎧 The facts below, when put in the correct order, describe the crime. Watch the first part of the video and number the events in the correct order.

_____ A witness saw PM walking towards the parking lot in his pajamas.

_____ PM left the parking lot in a silver car.

_____ A security camera videotaped PM entering the parking lot.

__1__ PM got up from bed, walked to the kitchen, and picked up the murder weapon.

_____ The silver car was found in front of PM's apartment on February 15.

_____ CR was found dead.

2. 🎧 The box at the right lists the speakers in the videotape. Watch the rest of the video and follow the outline. Put a check (✔) next to each speaker who says something in favor of Peter.

3. 🎧 Choose one of the ten speakers in the video. Watch the video again and take notes on what your character says.

4. 🎧 Watch the tape again and check your notes.

C. 🔁 Role-Playing

Play the role of the speaker you have chosen. Imagine you are being interviewed by a television reporter (your partner). Tell the story from your point of view. For example: *In my opinion, Peter is innocent because . . . .*

D. 👥 Analysis and Synthesis

Is Peter Montgomery guilty or innocent? Discuss your decision with the class.

VIDEO OUTLINE

1. Peter Miller, Defense Lawyer ✔
2. Geoffrey Scott, Psychiatrist ✔

Video Reconstruction

3. Peter Montgomery, the Accused
4. Mrs. Montgomery, Peter's Mother
5. Mrs. Ramos, the Victim's Mother
6. Margaret Harris, Prosecuting Lawyer
7. Sandra Reinhart, Psychiatrist

Can He Be Innocent?

8. Peter Montgomery
9. Sandra Reinhart
10. Geoffrey Scott

Security Video

11. Margaret Harris
12. Peter Miller
13. Mrs. Montgomery
14. Peter Montgomery

New Evidence

15. Anthony Koppeloff, Detective
16. Margaret Harris
17. Peter Miller
18. Geoffrey Scott
19. Witness

Security Video

20. Mrs. Ramos
21. Peter Montgomery

And What If...?

22. Psychic Reader (w/Mrs. Ramos)
23. Peter Miller
24. Margaret Harris
25. Mrs. Ramos
26. Anthony Koppeloff

Security Video

27. Peter Miller
28. Peter Montgomery

WORK in the 21ST CENTURY

Listening 1

A.  Before You Listen

1. How is the world of work different now than it was for your grandparents? How might it be different in the future?

2. When the economy is weak, the quickest way for a company to save money is to fire its employees.

   a. How does the fear of being fired affect people's working lives?

   b. How does it affect their personal lives?

3. Technology is changing so quickly that it's almost impossible to keep up with.

   a. How has technology changed your life in the past five years? Give examples.

   b. How does technology change the way we work and do business? Give specific examples.

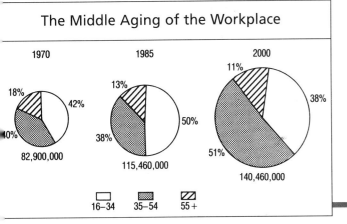

The Middle Aging of the Workplace

| 1970 | 1985 | 2000 |

1970: 18%, 42%, 40%, 82,900,000

1985: 13%, 50%, 38%, 115,460,000

2000: 11%, 38%, 51%, 140,460,000

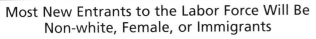

16–34 35–54 55+

Most New Entrants to the Labor Force Will Be Non-white, Female, or Immigrants

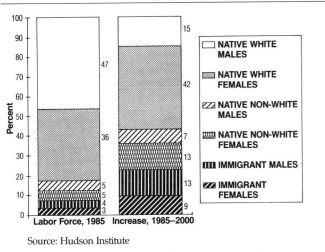

Labor Force, 1985   Increase, 1985–2000

- NATIVE WHITE MALES
- NATIVE WHITE FEMALES
- NATIVE NON-WHITE MALES
- NATIVE NON-WHITE FEMALES
- IMMIGRANT MALES
- IMMIGRANT FEMALES

Source: Hudson Institute

4. In the future, there will be more women, older adults, and minorities in the American workplace, especially from groups whose first language is not English.

   a. Look at the charts on the left. Compare the difference in the percent of men and women in the workforce in 1970 and 2000.

   b. How has the workforce changed since 1985?

   c. How will these changes affect society and business in the United States?

1. Singapore	6. United States	11. Switzerland	16. France
2. Denmark	7. Austria	12. Australia	17. Canada
3. Germany	8. Sweden	13. New Zealand	18. Hong Kong
4. Japan	9. Netherlands	14. Belgium/Lux.	19. Taiwan
5. Norway	10. Finland	15. Ireland	20. Korea

Workers of the World . . . GET TRAINING!

Who has the most qualified workforce? In a ranking combining quality of public education, levels of secondary schooling and on-the-job training, computer literacy, and worker motivation, these are the top 20 countries, in descending order.

Source: *Business Week.* Data: *World Competitiveness Report* (World Economic Forum and Lausanne Institute of Management Development).

5. The world has truly become a "global village." Business must be concerned with international markets to survive.

   a. How many Asian countries are listed above? How many European countries?

   b. How have changes in technology and telecommunications helped international business?

B. Who Will You Be Listening To?

Vivian Eyre (pronounced: Ā-er) is the founder of Partners for Women's Growth, Inc. By coaching women on current individual workplace issues, Eyre helps women advance and achieve their goals. She also teaches Managing Workforce 2000 at the Milano Graduate School.

Vivian Eyre

C. 👥 Listening for a General Topic

🎧 What's the talk about? Listen and check (✔) the general topic.

_____ 1. Preparing for work in the twenty-first century

_____ 2. U.S. corporations in the twenty-first century

_____ 3. Globalization and the changing workforce

Listening/ Notetaking Tip

Look at the list in section D. Think about what you already know before you listen again.

D. 🤼 Listening for Main Ideas/Notetaking

1. 🎧 Listen again for information to complete the list of main ideas below.

The Hudson Institute's study, Workforce 2000, showed three important changes in business:

___e___ 1. 33% of the workforce will be minorities, with major growth in Asian and Hispanic communities.

_____ 2. _____

_____

_____

_____ 3. _____

_____

_____

2. Look at the sentences listed below, then find one that is similar in meaning to the main ideas in the left-hand column. Write the letter of the corresponding main idea in the space provided. The first one has been completed for you.

a. Businesspeople will have to speak foreign languages.

b. Every worker will have to deal with some form of technology at work.

c. All workers will have their own computers.

d. Business will have to pay attention to international influences.

e. One third of the workforce will be from minority groups.

E. 🤼 Listening for Specific Information/Making Inferences

1. Based on what Vivian Eyre said, how do you think she would react to the following?

✔ = agree (two statements)   X = disagree (two
? = can't tell (two statements)   statements)

___X___ a. The number of minorities in the workforce will decrease.

_____ b. Workers can depend on employers to take care of them and help them succeed.

_____ c. People need to study foreign languages if they hope to succeed in a global market.

_____ d. Workers need skills in technology, reading, math, and critical thinking.

_____ e. People entering the workforce in the year 2000 can expect to have ten jobs by the time they retire.

_____ f. People must never stop looking for another job.

Listening Note

Notice that you are asked to base your answers on what Eyre has said. Answer (✔) or (X) only if she has made it clear how she thinks. If she hasn't, answer (?).

Critical Thinking Note:

An inference is a logical guess based on some information.

2. 🎧 Listen and check your answers. Then compare your answers with a partner.

F. Vocabulary and Dictation

1. 🎧🧍 Your teacher will read statements from the listening. Match these words from the sentences to their definitions on the right.

__f__	1. **minority**	a. to study and judge
_____	2. **expand**	b. weakness
_____	3. **evaluate**	c. analytical
_____	4. **liability**	d. to increase, to make larger
_____	5. **retire**	e. to stop working
_____	6. **critical**	f. group of a different race, ethnic background, or religion than the larger population

2. Fill in the blanks with the correct vocabulary words from the activity above.

   a. In order to solve a difficult problem, one must first _evaluate_ the problem. To do this well, you will need to use _____ thinking.

   b. My parents want to live in Florida when they _____ .

   c. Poor writing skills are a _____ in the business world.

   d. Lynne is hoping to _____ her business and open offices in other states.

   e. Hispanics are the largest growing _____ in the United States.

3. 🎧🧍 🧑‍🤝‍🧑 Listen to your teacher and write the sentences you hear. Then compare sentences with a partner.

4. Match the underlined terms with the meanings on the right.

__g__	1. age will no longer <u>determine</u>	a. internationalization
_____	2. understand . . . and <u>cope with</u> changes	b. groups of buyers, customers
_____	3. <u>globalization</u> of business	c. whatever
_____	4. expand to foreign <u>markets</u>	d. handle and manage
_____	5. held a <u>traditional</u> view in the past	e. of an older way of thinking
_____	6. <u>regardless of</u> the job	f. working or professional direction
_____	7. once we get in that <u>career path</u>	g. decide

G. 👥 Critical Thinking and Analysis

Work together to answer the question below, giving reasons to support your answer. Try to use some of the words and phrases you have learned in this chapter.

Is [a company's] first loyalty to its employment of Americans . . . or does the company serve the country better by maximizing its profits worldwide so that ultimately it can hire more workers, even if the price of global expansion is shipping some jobs abroad?
                                                                —The New York Times

Listening 2

A. 👥 Before You Listen

1. Read the four statements below. These statements are advice to educators on how they can help people deal with the new workplace. Why do you think each of these points is important?

   - Teach higher level skills such as critical thinking, problem solving, and interpersonal skills.
   - Encourage people to pursue work experiences as part of their education.
   - Prepare students to take control of their own careers by expecting and planning for change.
   - Cultivate the idea that learning is a lifelong pursuit.

2. Answer the questions below.

   a. How might students "pursue work experiences as part of their education"? Give examples.

   b. How might an educator help people take charge of their own careers? Give examples.

   c. What is lifelong learning? Can you imagine yourself being a lifelong learner?

> **Culture Note**
>
> Many American universities set up internship programs in cooperation with companies. This benefits students because they get on-the-job training. It benefits companies because they get inexpensive help and eventually may be able to hire graduates with some work experience.

The Occupations of the Future Will Require More Education	Current Jobs	New Jobs
Total	100%	100%
8 years or less	6%	4%
1–3 years of high school	12%	10%
4 years of high school	40%	35%
Median years of school	12.8	13.5

Source: Bureau of Labor Statistics; Hudson Institute.

   d. Discuss the chart above. Compare the difference in educational levels in current jobs and new jobs.

   e. All of the information above comes from reports paid for by the U.S. government. Is it important for a government to support projects like these? Why?

B. Who Will You Be Listening To?

Vivian Eyre has worked in the field of human resources, hiring and managing workers for over twenty-five years.

> **Listening Strategy**
>
> Before listening, think about what you've heard, read, discussed, and thought about so far in this chapter. This should help prepare you for some of the things Eyre will talk about.

C. 👥 Notetaking and Summarizing

1. 🎧 In this listening, Eyre gives five tips for success. Listen and note them on a separate piece of paper.

2. 🎧 Listen again and check your notes. Then compare notes with a partner.

3. Summarize the five tips on the lines below.

    1. _____
       _____

    2. _____
       _____

    3. _____
       _____

    4. _____
       _____

    5. _____
       _____

D. 👥 Making Inferences

Based on what Eyre has said, how do you think she would react to the following?

✔ = agree (six statements)   X = disagree (three statements)
? = can't tell (three statements)

___?___ 1. Buy a home computer.

_____ 2. Finish college.

_____ 3. Believe in and trust the company you work for.

_____ 4. Take as many vacations as you can and relax.

_____ 5. Continue studying after you finish college.

_____ 6. Invite your boss to dinner whenever possible.

_____ 7. Keep up with what's new in your field.

_____ 8. Look for an advisor at work who has more experience than you.

_____ 9. Ask for a raise in salary once a year.

_____10. Try to understand the company's special culture and way of doing things.

_____11. Play it safe! Always try to avoid problems and obstacles.

_____12. Learn how to speak up in front of decision makers in your company.

E. 👥 Problem Solving and Giving Advice

In this listening, Eyre is giving advice. Notice the language she uses for this:

find	learn about	speak up about
take charge	If you can	it's so important to
ask yourself	remember	cultivate
is no longer going to be enough	it's important to remember	persevere

Imagine that you are a job counselor. Give advice in the following situations. Try to use some of the language Eyre has used. (There are no right or wrong answers.)

1. Paul has been in the same job for ten years. He's fairly good at what he does, but he's not very interested in his work. His wife thinks that he should be doing something he's more interested in, but Paul feels the job is fairly secure, and he has a family to support. On the other hand, he's noticed that a couple of his friends who thought they had secure jobs have lost them in the last year. What should Paul do?

2. Theresa is an honors student in her last year of high school. She has applied to two colleges. She has been accepted into a good local state college and received a tuition scholarship. She has also gotten a full scholarship, including living expenses, to an excellent college in another state, but if she takes it she must agree not to work. She feels this is a problem because her mother is alone, doesn't make much money, and has two other children to raise. Her mother wants Theresa to do what's best for her. What should Theresa do?

3. Susan is forty-seven. She has worked as a secretary for a lawyer for more than twenty years and makes a fairly good salary. Her children are grown now, and she has saved enough so that she could take a year or more off if she wanted to. She sometimes dreams about going to graduate school so that she could get a degree and later a job in a field she is really interested in. But she feels she is too old, and, anyway, the need for people in the new field is not as great as the need for legal secretaries. Also, salaries are lower in the new field. What should Susan do?

F. 👥 Vocabulary—Crossword Puzzle

NOTE:

abbr. = abbreviation; *acronym* = letters used to represent a name—for example, IBM = International Business Machines

Across

1. Good outcome, achievement.
4. Diagrams or graphs with information.
8. Two of the same thing. A _____ of shoes.
9. That is, *abbr.* (from the Latin *id est)*
10. Request. _____ for a job.
12. 3rd person singular pronoun. _____ 's a dog.
13. Ready, prepared. Get _____ to go.
14. Writing instrument. Felt tip_____ .
15. Extraterrestrial, *abbr.*
16. The world as a small community (2 words).
20. European Community, *abbr.*
21. Mother (short form).
22. Preferences, prejudices.
24. Not/Applicable, *abbr.*
25. The publisher of this book, *abbr.* (See book cover.)
26. Point. A pen with a felt _____ .
27. Money borrowed from an individual or a bank.
28. Company, *abbr.*
30. Mother (short form).
31. The system of producing, distributing, and consuming a government's wealth and resources.
35. Unknown amount. Would you like _____ coffee?
36. 1st person singular of the verb *to be*. I _____ a student.
38. Rumors or talk about others' lives. I don't want to hear _____ .
40. Preposition, *abbr.*
41. A type of vine. _____ covered walls.
42. Internet, *abbr.* Surf the _____.
43. Opposite of *out.*
44. Ventilator (short form). The air conditioning _____ .
46. Happening. A sports _____ .
47. To solve a problem or remove an obstacle.
48. Located in. She lives _____ 9 West Street.

Down

1. Therefore. I was hungry, _____ I ate.
2. Becoming different, variable.
3. A person who collects secret information. He's an enemy _____ .
4. Analytical, insightful. _____ thinking helps with problem solving.
5. Time between midnight and noon. It's 5 _____ .
6. Necktie (short version).
7. See 13 across.
11. Professional (short form).
13. Strength and endurance.
14. A difficulty, an obstacle.
15. Numbers like 2, 4, 10, 20.
17. A type of work. She is in the fashion _____ .
18. Get, *past tense.*
19. Occupation, job paying salary.
23. Estimated Time of Arrival, acronym.
28. To try to win or do something better than another.
29. 1.
30. Belonging to me, possessive pronoun. _____ room.
32. Metal piece of money.
33. Group of people who want to buy things. Foreign _____ .
34. One who loves.
37. Memorandum (short form).
38. To hand over. _____ someone a gift.
39. Synchronization (short form). In _____ .
43. Incorporated, *abbr.*
45. Toward, preposition. Go _____ Paris.

Listening 3

A. 🎮 Who Will You Be Listening To?

You will be listening to three people: Mary Esther, Marcello, and David. None of them is settled in a career, but each has career plans.

B. Notetaking

1. 👂 What are the speakers doing now? Listen and take notes.

	Now	The Future
Mary Esther		
Marcello		
David		

2. 👂 What are the speakers planning to do in the future? Listen again and take notes.

C. 🎮 Analysis

1. Are each person's plans in line with the advice Vivian Eyre gives? If so, indicate how below.

   Mary Esther _____

   _____

   _____

   Marcello _____

   _____

   _____

   David _____

   _____

   _____

2. Do you identify with any of the speakers in particular? Which one? Explain why to your partner.

D. 🎮 Practical Applications

Describe your career plans. Has listening to these three speakers been helpful to you? If so, how?

Project

For this project, you will interview people outside of class.

A. 👥 Planning an Interview

1. Work in groups of three. Each group should choose one of the following interview topics:
   * Being self-employed
   * Working for someone else
   * Planning for the future

2. Each group should write a set of eight to ten questions for the topic it has chosen. Think about some of the following issues as you write your questions:
   * Financial advantages/disadvantages
   * Job security
   * Qualifications
   * Career development
   * Job satisfaction
   * Fringe benefits (for example: medical/dental insurance, pension plans, etc.)

B. Conducting the Interview

Each person in the group should interview two or three people, in English if possible. Then each student should write a summary of the interview findings. In the summary, write each question followed by one or two sentences describing the responses you heard.

C. Summarizing

In class, each group should work together to review each person's findings. Then write a general group summary to present to the class. This summary should also list the eight to ten questions your group asked, followed by a short statement of your general findings. An example is provided in the chart below.

Questions:	Answers:
1 Are you very satisfied with your job, somewhat satisfied, or not satisfied? Why?	1 Two people were very satisfied, three were somewhat satisfied,:The "very satisfied people told us…The somewhat satisfied people…
2.	2.

The Dreaming Self

Listening 1

A. Before You Listen

1. 👥 Some people think dreams predict the future. Some believe they are messages from God or from people who have died. Others believe they bring good or bad luck. What do you think dreams are for? Share your ideas in your group.

2. 👥 Read the selection below and the quotation from Italo Calvino on the next page. When you are done, list three important things you learned about the unconscious.

The conscious mind is the part of our mental life that we are aware of. The unconscious is the part of our mind where repressed or "forgotten" memories, experiences, and desires are kept. They are repressed because they are either too painful to remember or, in the case of desires, seem out of reach or forbidden. Frequently this unconscious mind controls us. It responds to our repressed inner thoughts and can cause problems for us by making us do things we may not want to do, such as fail at something we want to succeed at or hurt someone we love.

Sigmund Freud (1856–1939) was the first person to scientifically study the unconscious mind. He believed that through psychoanalysis we can explore unconscious actions and anxieties and deal with our problems. For Freud, dream analysis was a key to understanding the unconscious. His book *The Interpretation of Dreams* is considered his greatest work.

Sigmund Freud

All of us dream... all the time. Why?

Do you remember your dreams?

Do you find your dreams interesting?

Do you understand your dreams?

Does dreaming help you in any way?

Does it ever cause problems?

9

Culture Note

Psychotherapy is more common in the United States than it is in many other countries. One reason for this may be that many Americans think it is good to be open about feelings because this can lead to a greater understanding of oneself and others.

The unconscious mind is the ocean of the unsayable, of what has been expelled from the land of language, removed as a result of ancient prohibitions. —Italo Calvino (1923–1985), Italian author and critic

3. One key to analyzing our dreams is understanding what the symbols in dreams may mean. Match these symbols with their possible meanings below.

1. Store Items   2. House   3. Mirror   4. Examination   5. Police

_____ c. This symbol can represent protection and safety, or punishing and dangerous forces, depending on the dreamer's state of mind.

__2__ a. This symbol often represents the dreamer. Parts of it may symbolize the mind or body of the dreamer. Upstairs/downstairs, for example, can refer to the conscious/unconscious levels of the mind.

_____ d. These symbolize the good things in life or in the self. If unattainable, these could also represent frustration over being kept from attaining success.

_____ b. This symbol often represents anxiety. It may also symbolize success or failure in our lives. Ask yourself this question: What am I anxious about?

_____ e. This symbol reflects the dreamer's identity. An unfamiliar face may mean that an unknown part of the self wants to be seen.

Throughout the chapter you will see boxes with more examples of dream symbols and their meanings. These should help you later on when we analyze dreams.

B. Who Will You Be Listening To?

Patricia Simko is a psychotherapist specializing in dream analysis. She teaches courses that focus on the development of the self.

Patricia Simko

C. Listening for a General Topic

What's the talk about? Listen and check (✔) the general topic.

_____ 1. Interpreting dreams   _____ 2. Why we dream   _____ 3. Freud's dreams

D. 👥 Listening for Specific Information

Nine important ideas from Simko's talk are listed below, with choices given for key words. Read the ideas first and circle the correct word. Then listen to check your answers.

1. Dreaming is universal. **Everybody/few people** dream(s) a lot.
2. Dreams are **direct/indirect** messages from our unconscious.
3. The unconscious mind is **difficult/easy** to access.
4. The unconscious is the seat of our identity and all **creation/thinking** and the storehouse of all of our memories.
5. It's the **conscious/unconscious** mind that greatly runs us and determines who we are.
6. We can decline to accept the **gift/problem** that a dream gives us, but the dream will come back again and again until we pay attention to it.
7. Dreams will never fool us. They are painfully **honest/dishonest,** but they are also highly disguised. They are told symbolically.
8. Dreams bypass all the functions of our **conscious/unconscious** brain that tend to fool us.
9. Dreams are a mechanism used to help resolve inner conflicts. They can be a very powerful **tool/difficulty** in our own growth.

E. 👥 Listening for Details

1. Read the following details carefully and fill in the blanks with one of these words: **dream(s), conscious, unconscious.**

a. All people ___dream___, even those who do not remember their dreams.

b. It was in fact with dreams that Freud originally came up with the idea of the _____.

c. Two ways we can access messages from the _____ mind are through slips of the tongue and unintended behaviors.

d. The unconscious is where we put all the information that we can't or don't have time to deal with on a _____ level.

e. The _____ tells us who we are want to be, how we interact, think, rela what we create, and what our defenses are.

f. So we need to know the tools of worki with our _____ in order to get the truth of what lies at the heart of ou being.

g. Defense mechanisms, editing, and concepts of social desirability are tricks our _____ mind uses to fool us

h. _____ paint a picture of a struggle in progress, and help us resolve it.

2. Listen and check your answers.

F. 🙌 Vocabulary and Dictation

1. 🔊 Your teacher will read sentences from the listening. Listen and match these words from the sentences to the definitions on the right.

___f___ 1. psychic   a. Be similar to

_____ 2. consciousness   b. Entrance

_____ 3. access   c. Go around

_____ 4. unconscious   d. Infinite

_____ 5. limitless   e. Awareness

_____ 6. repository   f. Related to the mind in general

_____ 7. bypass   g. That part of the mind that we are usually not aware of

_____ 8. correspond   h. Place where things are kept

2. 🔊 Listen to your teacher and write the sentences you hear. Then compare sentences with a partner.

G. 👥 Analysis and Synthesis

1. In the first listening Patricia Simko said, "In a way you could say that your unconscious mind runs you." What does she mean?

2. Read the situations below. Why can't these people get what they want or need?

> **Vocabulary Note**
>
> A "Freudian slip" is a verbal mistake that seems to reveal an unconscious thought or emotion, usually a thought or emotion one does not want to reveal.

a. David loves Gina and wants her in his life. He would be terribly upset if they broke up. Yet he constantly does things to push her away. Sometimes he's just nasty, and sometimes he's too critical. Gina loves David, but she's beginning to pull away from him because she's tired of being treated badly. Why is David acting this way?

b. Carlos got an interview for the "perfect" job. He would be great for the job because he's qualified and enthusiastic. He's very nervous about the interview. He mismanages his morning and is almost a half hour late for the interview. This makes him even more nervous, and he doesn't get the job. Why wasn't Carlos more careful about being on time?

c. Laura is a talented artist. Even though art critics like her work and her paintings sell, she worries that her work is not good enough. A lot of the time she is unable or afraid to paint. The gallery that sells her work has scheduled a show for her. She can't make the deadline. Why is she missing the deadline?

Listening 2

A. Before You Listen

1. Read the following quotation. What does it say about dreams and the unconscious?

   The interpretation of dreams is the royal road to a knowledge of the unconscious activities of the mind.
   —Sigmund Freud, *The Interpretation of Dreams*

2. Freud believed that unconscious memories and experiences sometimes make us do things we do not really want to do. If we can bring these unconscious memories, experiences, and anxieties up to a conscious level, we may be able to understand and deal with them. Analyzing our dreams is one of the best ways to do this. Below are six things that Freud believed about dreams. Fill in the blanks with one of these words:

   analyzed
   socially
   desires
   symbols
   personality
   unconscious

   a. Dreams are disguised thoughts from the _____ mind that contain meaningful messages.

   b. Dreams express unfulfilled wishes and _____.

   c. Dreams contain hidden messages about _____ unacceptable desires for things such as sex or violence.

   d. Dreams frequently contain _____ instead of real-life images.

   e. Dreams tell us a great deal about a person's _____.

   f. Dreams can be _____ and interpreted.

B. Who Will You Be Listening To?

In this listening, Patricia Simko describes the process of analyzing a dream. To illustrate the process, she uses the dream of a person named Jane. Jane's dream is as follows:

I am in my car stopped at a curb. I want to pull out, but another car stops next to me, blocking my movement. Two of my co-workers are in this car. After a time they leave, and I can move my car again. Now I am driving along the road, but my car won't go. It starts to putter, and finally it stops totally.

C. 🎬 Listening to a Process

1. 👂 Listen and fill in the steps in the chart below.

2. 👂 Listen again and add more details to the chart.

How Can You Analyze a Dream?

Steps	Details
1. Tell the story.	Jane is stuck . . . can't move forward; her co-workers are blocking her. But even when they disappear, she still can't make progress.
2.	Jane had been at work and hadn't been able to . . .
3.	Jane and . . .
4.	Jane felt anxious when her progress was blocked and . . .
5.	People . . . Objects . . .
6. Speak about the meaning to her inner self.	When Jane speaks as the car, she feels . . . This dream gets to the heart of Jane's uneasiness with . . . Now . . . In early life . . .

D. Language—Describing a Process

1. When describing a process, it is helpful to the listener if you mark the steps in some way. Below are markers that you can use to describe a process.

2. Use the notes in your chart on page 87 and the markers below to explain how to analyze Jane's dream.

Patricia Simko's markers:

1. We start with the first step, which is . . .

2. In step two . . .

3. In step three . . .

4. Step four describes . . .

5. In step five . . .
   a. First . . .
   b. Next . . .
   c. Then . . .

Other markers:

1. Firstly . . . , We'll start with . . . , In (at) the first stage . . . , First . . . , One . . .

2. Secondly . . . , At (in) the second (next) stage . . . , Second . . . , Two . . .

3. Thirdly . . . , At (in) the third stage . . . , Thirdly . . . , Three . . . , Next . . .

4. At (in) the fourth stage . . . , Fourth . . . , Four . . . , after the . . . , we . . .

5. At (in) the fifth and final stage . . . , Fifth . . . , Five . . . , Lastly . . . , And finally . . . , The final stage . . . , At last . . .

Dream Symbols and Their Meanings

- Flying usually symbolizes something that is thrilling, an escape from the physical world, or freedom.

- Drowning often symbolizes being overpowered or "flooded" by feelings or situations that are too difficult to handle.

- A boat voyage often symbolizes a journey into the deep waters of the unconscious mind. This dream is often about the mother.

- Trying to run is common in dreams. Finding that your legs won't move leads to this question: What's holding me back?

Feminine Symbols

- The ocean is the symbol of the vast unconscious as well as of the mother.

- A cat is the symbol of intuitive female wisdom. It also represents the innocent and vulnerable part of the dreamer.

- A purse, because it can be opened and closed and contains riches, is a classic female sexual symbol.

- A cup is a classic female sexual symbol because of its capacity to hold and contain.

Masculine Symbols

- Mountains are a symbol of the masculine and may represent the power of the father. Climbing a mountain may also represent danger or self-determination.

- A knife is frequently a male sexual symbol. It represents the ability to penetrate, as well as violence and aggression.

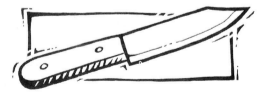

- Fire can represent conscious positive energy. It can also represent angry, destructive forces that are out of control.

Listening 3

A. Who Will You Be Listening To?

You will be listening to two people, Bill and Robyn, talk about their dreams. Their dreams contain some of the symbols you've read about in this chapter. Before listening, go through the chapter and read the descriptions of the symbols again.

B. ⛉ Notetaking

1. 👂 Bill describes two recurring dreams. First listen and identify the symbols in his dreams. Then listen again and note the important details.

Bill

Symbols	Descriptions
a. Can't run	Bill is being pursued by something that's getting closer and closer. He cannot run, and his feet feel like lead.
b.	

Compare charts with a partner.

2. 👂 Robyn had this dream a few days after her grandmother died. When she woke up, she felt very bad about something she and her mother had done in the dream. First listen and identify the symbols in her dream. Then listen again and write down the important details. Compare notes with your partner when you are done.

Robyn

Symbols	Descriptions
a.	
b.	

Project—Analyzing Your Dreams

A. 👥 What Will You Be Doing?

At last! It's time to analyze your dreams! Who knows what you may discover about yourself or your classmates? If you have not written down one of your own dreams, you can work on someone else's dream or use Robyn's dream from Listening 3.

B. 👥 Following the Steps in a Process

Follow the eight steps below to analyze a dream. (You should have already done the first two.) Write down notes for each step. Then present your dream to a partner.

1. **Remembering:** When you wake up, lie very still and try to remember your dream. You might remember only a detail. Take this detail and try to connect it with what may have come before or after it. Follow the dream as far as you can.

2. **Writing in Your Dream Journal:** Write your dream down. Write freely. Do not leave things out. Do not add things that were not in the actual dream. Give your dream a name.

3. **The Story:** Start by telling the story in terms of a theme. If it is a long dream, summarize it in two or three sentences.

4. **Day's Events:** Did something special happen the day before that led to the dream?

5. **Characters:** Who are the characters in the dream? What is important about them? What is their sex? Age? How are they important to you? What memories or thoughts do you have of them?

6. **Feelings:** What is the feeling of the dream? How did you feel? Was it similar to any feelings in a real-life situation?

7. **Symbols:** You have read explanations for several common dream symbols in this chapter. They should be helpful. However, the symbols in your dreams may have very personal meanings as well. Remember that dreams can have more than one meaning. Are the people in your dream people you know, or are they symbols for something (for example, the police)? Pay careful attention to the objects in your dreams. What does an object symbolize? What is it used for? Let your mind wander, and see what it comes up with.

8. **Inner Self:** What part of you do the people and things in your dream represent? Pick an object or person from the dream. "Become" that object or person. Start by saying, for example, "I am the car . . . " or "I am the curb, and. . . ." Fill in these sentences and speak as the object. In this way you can begin to see what part of you is represented by the object.

GLOSSARY

A

Abandon: *(v.)* stop doing s.t. or leave s.o. or s.t.

Ablaze: *(adj.)* on fire, burning.

Abroad: *(adv.)* out of the country.

Abstract: *(adj.)* related to ideas; theoretical (not concrete).

Absurdity: *(n.)* foolishness, stupidity.

Access: *(v.)* get into s.t., enter.

According to: *(prep.)* as stated by.

Accurate: *(adj.)* exact, correct.

Achieve: *(v.)* accomplish.

Acknowledged: *(adj.)* recognized.

Acoustic: *(adj.)* relating to a musical instrument whose sound is not electronically changed.

Acquaintance: *(n.)* a person whom one knows, but not well.

Active: *(adj.)* busy, *(syn.)* involved.

Admire: *(v.)* respect, approve of.

Adulthood: *(n.)* fully grown stage of human development.

Advance: *(v.)* improve, progress.

Adventure: *(n.)* an exciting event, *(syn.)* an exploit.

Adversarial: *(adj.)* against s.o., opposing.

Affair: *(n.)* 1. a relationship, usu. sexual or romantic in nature, between two people. 2. personal business, personal matter.

Afford: *(v.)* be able to pay for s.t. without difficulty.

Aggression: *(n.)* unfriendly or harmful action against s.o.

Amazing: *(adj.)* very surprising.

Ambitious: *(adj.)* wanting success, *(syn.)* driven.

Amendment: *(n.)* a formal change or addition to a document such as a constitution.

Amnesia: *(n.)* loss of memory, usually from shock or injury.

Analysis: *(n.)* a process by which s.t. is studied in detail.

Ancestor: *(n.)* a person from whom one is descended.

Angle: *(n.)* perspective, position from which a object is seen.

Annoyed: *(adj.)* irritated, bothered, mildly angered.

Anxiety: *(n.)* worry, nervous fear about the future.

Anxious: *(adj.)* worried, nervous.

Appealing: *(adj.)* attractive, having a pleasing aspect or quality.

Approach: *(v.)* begin to handle a situation or work on s.t.

Architectural: *(adj.)* related to a style of design and construction.

Arouse: *(v.)* excite.

Artful: *(adj.)* showing art or skill.

Asian: *(adj.)* related to Asia.

Aspect: *(n.)* a feature, part of s.t.

Assembly: *(n.)* a grouping of people, gathering.

Assessment: *(n.)* an evaluation, analysis.

Associate: *(v.)* connect or join together in one's own mind.

Attack: *(v.)* to make a serious attempt to do s.t., to undertake.

Attain: *(v.)* achieve, reach.

Attractive: *(adj.)* pleasing to the eye.

Autistic: *(adj.)* a medical condition in which one is abnormally introverted and accepting of fantasy rather than reality.

Avaricious: *(adj.)* desiring money, *(syn.)* greedy.

Average: *(adj.)* ordinary, common, neither very good nor very bad.

Avocation: *(n.)* a hobby.

Awareness: *(n.)* consciousness of or alertness to.

B

Balanced: *(adj.)* equal in strength, weight, etc.

Banking: *(n.)* the business of holding money for the purpose of savings or commercial business.

Bar: *(n.)* a public place where liquor is served, *(syn.)* a pub.

Base: *(v.)* use as a reason for doing s.t.

Basis: *(n.)* the main reason(s) for s.t., foundation.

Bebop: *(n.)* a style of jazz music with fast tempos in which a small group of players improvises, one after the other, on a short melody played at the beginning.

Beloved: *(n.)* (s.o. or s.t. that is) highly loved.

Benefit: *(n.)* gain, positive result.

Bias: *(n.)* prejudice, a point of view for or against s.o. or s.t.

Bill of Rights: *(n.)* in the USA, rights or privileges given by law, such as freedom of speech and freedom to meet publicly.

Biography: *(n.)* the history of a person's life.

Blare: *(n.)* a loud, continuous, unpleasant noise.

Block: *(v.)* prevent s.t. from happening.

Bog down: *(v.)* have too much work, be overburdened.

Boogie woogie: *(n.)* jazz piano music with a short, sharply accented base pattern played over and over by the left hand while the right hand plays freely using a variety of rhythms.

Book report: *(n.)* a summary of a book.

Boom: *(n.)* rapid or prosperous growth (an economy, industry).

Border Patrol: *(n.)* a group of people who guard the boundary between two countries.

Boredom: *(n.)* lack of interest in or weariness with s.t.

Botanist: *(n.)* a scientist who studies plant life.

Brainstorm: *(v.)* think of or suggest as many ideas as possible as quickly as possible.

Branch: *(n.)* a tree limb.

Brand new: *(adj.)* new and never used before.

Break up: *(phrasal v.)* separate into pieces.

Breakthrough: *(n.)* the act, result, or place of pushing past s.t. that blocks one's way.

Bulletin: *(n.)* a small periodical publication, *(syn.)* newsletter.

Burmese: Coming from or related to Mynamar (formally Burma), a country in Southeast Asia.

By the same token: *(adv.)* similarly.

Bypass: *(v.)* find a way around s.t.

By-product: *(n.)* s.t. that is produced as a result of s.t. else.

C

Calling: *(n.)* one's life's work or one's direction or purpose in life.

Candidate: *(n.)* person who runs for elected office or is nominated to run.

Capacity: *(n.)* 1. the ability to contain or to hold. 2. the ability to learn and remember knowledge, *(syn.)* mental ability.

Capital: *(n.)* wealth, such as money, land, or buildings, owned by a person, business, or institution (church, government); money put into a business by its owners or outside stockholders.

Career: *(n.)* a life's work, esp. in business or in a profession.

Carpentry: *(n.)* making and building things with wood.

Cartoon: *(n.)* a picture or group of pictures, often with words, drawn to make people laugh or to make fun of s.o. or s.t.

Case: *(n.)* convincing arguments or proof, (in law) a good cause or reason for an official action.

Cast: *(v.)* give or put a quality of one thing onto another.

Categorize: *(v.)* classify by placing things, ideas, etc. into groups based on similarities.

Caterer: *(n.)* a business or person who provides food and beverages for parties.

Cathartic: *(adj.)* releasing emotion and tensions and creating a good, purifying effect.

Caveman: *(n.)* (old usage) humans as they first lived before being civilized.

Censorship: *(adj.)* the official banning or removal of s.t. that is considered offensive.

Century: *(n.)* a time period of one hundred years.

Character: *(n.)* a person in a novel, play, or film.

Characteristic: *(n.)* special quality, *(syn.)* trait.

Characterization: *(n.)* a description of the character of s.o.

Chemical: *(adj.)* relating to chemistry.

Chess: *(n.)* a board game for two players, each starting with 16 pieces (chessmen) that are moved across a board divided into squares (chessboard) in an attempt to capture the other player's pieces.

Chord: *(n.)* three of more musical notes played together.

Chubby: *(adj.)* fat, *(syn.)* plump.

Civil War: *(n.)* in the USA, the war between the North and South from 1861 to 1865.

Clarity: *(n.)* clearness.

Classical: *(adj.)* related to the literature, art, architecture, etc. of ancient Greece and Rome.

Clever: *(adj.)* intelligent and quick at understanding.

Closed-minded: *(adj.)* unaccepting of the beliefs, ideas, and opinions of others.

Coincidence: *(n.)* the chance happening of two or more events at the same time.

Collapse: *(v.)* fall down or break up.

Collision: *(n.)* a crashing together.

Colloquialism: *(n.)* an informal expression.

Commerce: *(n.)* the buying and selling of goods and services within a country and with other countries.

Common: *(adj.)* ordinary, having no special quality.

Communication: *(n.)* the act of passing on information, feelings, etc.

Communicatively: *(adv.)* effectively giving and receiving information.

Compete: *(v.)* participate in a contest.

Competition: *(n.)* 1. the act of trying to win or achieve more than an opponent or opponents. 2. the people, as a group, whom one is trying to do better than, esp. in business.

Complex: *(adj.)* having many parts or details that make s.t. hard to understand or deal with, *(syn.)* complicated.

Composer: *(n.)* person who writes music.

Composition: *(n.)* how something is put together.

Con: *(n.)* reason(s) against s.t.

Concentration: *(n.)* close attention.

Concept: *(n.)* general idea.

Condemn: *(v.)* strongly express disapproval of s.o. or s.t.

Condition: *(n.)* external factor.

Conduct: *(v.)* direct.

Confidence: *(n.)* a belief in one's abilities.

Confident: *(adj.)* with strong belief in one's abilities.

Conflict: *(n.)* an argument, disagreement.

Confront: *(v.)* deal directly with s.t. difficult or dangerous.

Connection: *(n.)* relationship (between people, actions, ideas).

Conscious: *(adj.)* known.

Consciousness: *(n.)* awareness.

Conservative: 1. *(adj.)* slow to change, cautious. 2. *(n.)* one having a political view of keeping traditional and often proven ways of doing things.

Constructively: *(adv.)* helpfully, usefully.

Contemporary: *(adj.)* of today, *(syn.)* modern.

Context: *(n.)* the setting and circumstances surrounding a statement or an event that help determine its meaning.

Contrast: *(n.)* a sharp difference in shade, form, or meaning.

Contribute: *(v.)* participate positively in s.t.

Controversial: *(adj.)* causing disagreement or dispute.

Controversy: *(n.)* public disagreement, usu. involving strong opinions and an important subject.

Conveyor: *(n.)* s.o. who makes information known to others, messenger.

Cool: *(adj. infrml.)* excellent, admirable.

Cope: *(v.)* face difficulties and try to overcome them.

Core: *(n.)* the most important, basic part of s.t.

Corporate: *(adj.)* related to a business, esp. one that is incorporated.

Corporation: *(n.)* a business with a legal status (incorporated).

Correspond: *(v.)* match.

Corroborate: *(v.)* indicate that s.t. another person said is true.

Counterpart: *(n.)* person or thing that is like another person or thing.

Counterproductive: *(adj.)* not useful, damaging.

Courageous: *(adj.)* brave.

Courteous: *(adj.)* having good manners, polite.

Crack open: *(phrasal v.)* break apart with force.

Craft: *(n.)* a boat, airplane, or space vehicle.

Crazy: *(adj.)* making no sense, foolish, insane.

Criteria: *(n.)* rules used to judge s.t., standards of measurement.

Critic: *(n.)* a person who reviews and gives opinions about art, music, film, etc.

Critical thinking: *(n.)* reasoning with careful evaluation and judgment.

Criticize: *(v.)* point out faults in s.o. or s.t.

Crucial: *(adj.)* extremely important, *(syns.)* critical, decisive.

Cue: *(n.)* a sign or signal, esp. one used to start an action.

Culinary: *(adj.)* related to the kitchen and cooking.

Cultivate: *(v.)* study and develop a fine understanding, such as of art, music, or books.

Cultured: *(adj.)* having knowledge of art, music, books, etc.

Curb: *(n.)* the edge of a sidewalk that borders on the street, *(syn.)* a curbstone.

Curriculum: *(n.)* the courses offered at an educational institution (school, college, etc.).

Cylinder: *(n.)* a shape or object with a flat, circular top and bottom and straight sides.

D

Damage: *(v.)* hurt, injure.

Deal with: *(phrasal v. insep.)* interact with s.o. or s.t., esp. in business.

Dean: *(n.)* academic administrator, frequently the head of a college.

Death row: *(n.)* a place in prison where prisoners who have received the death penalty are kept.

Decade: *(n.)* a period of ten years.

Decision maker: *(n.)* a person within a group or organization who has the power to decide.

Decline: 1. *(n.)* a weakening, *(syn.)* deterioration. 2. *(v.)* refuse, usu. politely.

Decorative: *(adj.)* quality of making s.t. look attractive, ornamental.

Deemphasize: *(v.)* place little or no importance on, *(syn.)* not stress.

Defense: *(n.)* 1. a means of protecting from danger. 2. the legal protection in a court of law of a person accused of a crime.

Defense mechanism: *(n.)* a response, either instinctive or learned, to protect oneself from real or imagined danger.

Delta: *(n.)* a flat, low-lying area of land shaped like a triangle made by a river entering a sea.

Democrat: *(n.)* a member of one of two major political parties in the USA.

Demographics: *(n.pl.)* information and statistics about groups of people used esp. in politics and marketing.

Depend: *(v.)* rely on, trust in.

Descend: *(v.)* go down.

Deserve: *(v.)* earn, be worthy of, *(syn.)* warrant.

Desirability: *(n.)* quality of being worthwhile or valuable.

Destructive: *(adj.)* causing great damage, *(syn.)* devastating.

Determination: *(n.)* strong will.

Determine: *(v.)* conclude, decide, find out, *(syn.)* ascertain.

Development: *(n.)* growth, progress.

Devise: *(v.)* create, develop.

Devoid: *(adj.)* empty, lacking.

Devouring: *(adj.)* eating up quickly.

Diagram: *(v.)* draw with markings to show how s.t. is put together or works.

Dilemma: *(n.)* a difficult choice between two (usu. undesirable) alternatives, *(syn.)* quandary.

Disappointment: *(n.)* sadness over the loss of s.t. expected or hoped for.

Disguised: *(adj.)* hidden, covered up.

Disposable: *(adj.)* capable of being thrown away after use.

Distinction: *(n.)* difference.

Diversity: *(n.)* differences among people in race, ethnic group, religion, etc.

Documentary: *(n.)* a film or television program based on facts and/or historical records.

Doggone: *(exclam. of)* annoyance or surprise.

Double: *(v.)* make two times as much.

Downhearted: *(adj.)* feeling sad, *(syn.)* discouraged.

Drama: *(n.)* a play, esp. a serious one, for acting on a stage.

Dwell: *(v.)* live, *(syn.)* reside.

Dynamic: *(adj.)* producing change and activity.

E

Earthly: *(adj.)* related to everyday concerns on Earth, not heavenly.

Economic: *(adj.)* related to material wealth and its management.

Edible: *(adj.)* able to be eaten, eatable.

Editing: *(n.)* deleting, improving, or correcting s.t.

Editor: *(n.)* one who corrects, clarifies, and shapes written and recorded works.

Editor in chief: *(n.)* person in charge of those who correct, clarify, and shape written and recorded works.

Editorial writer: *(n.)* a person who writes opinions in a magazine or newspaper.

Effective: *(adj.)* having the result that one wants.

Element: *(n.)* part, aspect.

Elizabethan drama: *(n.)* plays written during the reign of Elizabeth I of England, or related to that time in history.

Emancipation Proclamation: *(n.)* the announcement that freed African Americans from slavery in the USA in 1863.

Emerge: *(v.)* appear.

Emigrate: *(v.)* leave one's country to live in another.

Emotional: *(adj.)* having strong feelings.

Emphasize: *(v.)* place importance on, *(syn.)* stress.

Enrollment: *(n.)* the number of students registered or taking part in a class or school.

Entertaining: *(adj.)* amusing or delighting.

Entity: *(n.)* a thing, s.t. that exists.

Entrant: *(n.)* one who enters into s.t.

Entrepreneurism: *(n.)* starting a business with an idea, making it grow, and taking the risk of failure.

Entry level: *(n.)* in the lowest category of a type of job.

Environment: *(n.)* a set of social conditions that affect people, *(syn.)* atmosphere.

Ephemeral: *(adj.)* lasting only a short time.

Epoch: *(n.)* a period in geologic time or in history with a special character.

Escape: *(n.)* a temporary break from cares or worries.

Ethical: *(adj.)* related to moral or correct behavior.

Ethnic: *(adj.)* related to group characteristics, such as race, country of origin, religion, or culture.

Evaluate: *(v.)* study and make a judgment about.

Evolve: *(v.)* develop, change.

Exaggerate: *(v.)* say s.t. is better, worse, more important, etc. than it really is, *(syn.)* overstate.

Excerpt: *(n.)* a selection quoted from a large written or spoken work.

Expand: *(v.)* grow larger.

Expect: *(v.)* want and believe that s.t. will happen.

Expel: *(v.)* send away for a reason, *(syn.)* dismiss.

Explore: *(v.)* investigate or study an issue.

Explosion: *(n.)* a sudden large increase.

Exposure: *(n.)* subjection to an influence.

Expressive: *(adj.)* showing obvious emotion.

Exquisite: *(adj.)* perfectly beautiful, outstanding.

F

Face: *(v.)* meet with courage, confront.

Fantasy: *(n.)* a product of the imagination, *(syns.)* daydream, illusion.

Fascinating: *(adj.)* very interesting, *(syns.)* absorbing, engrossing.

Fauna: *(n.)* the animals in a specific place or time period.

Feature: *(n.)* 1. important part or characteristic. 2. the mouth, chin, nose, eyes, etc. of the human face.

Fiction: *(n.)* a type of literature based upon the author's imagination as opposed to fact.

Field holler: *(n.)* a chant sung by people while working on the land.

Field: *(n.)* an area of activity, interest, or study.

Figure out: *(phrasal v.)* solve, understand.

Fine art: *(n.)* painting, drawing, music, dance, literature, drama, and architecture.

Fiscal: *(adj.)* related to taxation and spending of government money.

Flexible: *(adj.)* capable of changing and adapting to new circumstances.

Flora: *(n.)* the plants in a specific place or time period.

Food styling: *(n.)* the presenting of food in an artful manner.

Forbidden: *(adj.)* not permitted, *(syns.)* prohibited, banned.

D–F

Frame (of mind): *(n.)* one's mental attitude at a specific time.

Free jazz: *(n.)* highly improvised jazz with little formal structure and tempo and with irregular timing.

Freedom of expression: *(n.)* one's right to communicate ideas and views freely, without threat of government interference.

Freedom of speech: *(n.)* the right to speak or write what one wishes without government interference.

Freelance: *(v.)* work as an independent, self-employed person usu. for a variety of companies.

Frustrated: *(adj.)* irritated, disappointed, angered; the feeling that results when one is prevented from doing s.t. one wants to do.

Frustration: *(n.)* the feeling (of irritation, disappointment, anger) that results when one is prevented from doing s.t. one wants to do.

Funk (in a funk): *(n.)* feeling sad and low, *(syn.)* depressed.

Futurism: *(n.)* an early twentieth-century art movement that emphasized the sounds and movements of the modern age.

G

Gain: *(v.)* obtain, acquire.

Gangsta rap: *(n.)* a type of music in which the artist speaks, accompanied by a strong rhythm, about the reality of crime and violence in urban America.

Gap: *(n.)* empty time or spaces.

Gathering: *(n.)* a meeting, social function.

Generation: *(n.)* average period of time for people to become adults, approximately twenty-five to thirty years.

Generous: *(adj.)* ready to give, giving.

Genius: *(n.)* a person with extraordinary intellectual ability.

Genre: *(n.)* a specific type of literature, art, or music grouped according to a style or subject.

Gifted: *(adj.)* having special natural ability.

Global: *(adj.)* relating to all the world, worldwide.

Global village: *(n.)* the entire world and its people as one community.

Globalization: *(n.)* the spread of s.t. worldwide.

Glorify: *(v.)* praise s.t., making it seem more honorable and positive than it actually is.

Go: *(n.)* a Japanese board game with small black and white pieces.

Gothic: *(adj.)* a style of European architecture in the twelfth to sixteenth centuries.

Gourmet: *(n.)* a person who knows a lot about and enjoys fine food and drink.

Graffiti: *(n.pl.)* (used with a sing. or pl. v.) writings and drawings on walls, often rude, funny, or political.

Grandiose: *(adj.)* magnificent, splendid.

Gratification: *(n.)* a sense of pleasure and satisfaction.

Grind to a halt: *(v.)* stop.

Grit: *(v.)* press one's teeth together hard, usu. during difficult moments.

Guy: *(n. infrml.)* a man.

H

Hamlet: *(n.)* a tragic play about a prince of Denmark, written by William Shakespeare.

Hang up: *(phrasal v.)* end a telephone conversation by putting down the phone.

Harmony: *(n.)* 1. several notes played at the same time to produce melodious chords. 2. peaceful cooperation, *(syn.)* accord.

Hearing: *(n.)* the sense of receiving sound through the ears.

Heritage: *(n.)* something passed on from one generation to the next, tradition.

Hispanic: *(n.)* person of Latin American or Spanish descent.

Homesickness: *(n.)* a feeling of sadness when s.o. is away or missing one's home.

Horn: *(n.)* a musical instrument, usu. made of metal, that creates sounds when air is blown into it.

Hostile: *(adj.)* hateful, angry.

House: *(v.)* shelter s.t. or s.o.

Human resources: *(n.pl.)* personnel, employees.

I

Identifying: *(n.)* recognizing the characteristics of s.o. or s.t.

Identity: *(n.)* one's sense of self.

Idiot: *(n.)* person of little intelligence.

Ignorant: *(adj.)* unknowing, uninformed.

Ignore: *(v.)* pay no attention to, overlook.

Imitator: *(n.)* s.o. who copies a way of doing things from another.

Impact: 1. *(n.)* effect, impression. 2. *(v.)* affect, influence.

Implement: *(v.)* start, put into action.

Impolite: *(adj.)* showing bad manners, rude.

Impractical: *(adj.)* not realistic, not sensible.

Impression: *(n.)* a feeling or idea about s.o. or s.t.

Improvise: *(v.)* perform in a creative or inventive manner rather than following a script or musical score.

In the face of: *(adv.)* in front of, when confronted with.

In spite of: *(adv.)* instead of what might be easy or logical.

In tandem: *(n.)* two together.

Independent: *(n.)* a United States voter who chooses not to be affiliated with the Democratic or Republican party.

Individualism: *(n.)* a belief that one should behave according to his or her own beliefs.

Individualistic: *(adj.)* related to thinking and behaving according to one's own beliefs.

Industrialized: *(adj.)* developed in commercial production and sales.

Industry: *(n.)* a specific type of manufacturing.

Infer: *(v.)* guess based on thinking about some information, *(syns.)* surmise, deduce.

Inference: *(n.)* an educated guess based on some information.

Inferior: *(adj.)* lower in quality.

Influence: *(n.)* the power to change or persuade.

Inner-city: *(adj.)* of a city's central area, esp. a poor area or slum.

Innovative: *(adj.)* creatively made or improved.

Interact: *(v.)* communicate with s.o. through conversation, looks, or action.

Internet: *(n.)* a huge international computer network of electronic mail and information services.

Internship: *(n.)* a job one does for little or no money in order to gain experience in a business or profession.

Interpersonal: *(adj.)* between people.

Interpret: *(v.)* decide on the meaning of s.t. that is not clear or understood.

Interpretation: *(n.)* an explanation, decision about what s.t. means.

Intolerant: *(adj.)* lacking kindness or understanding toward people who are different, *(syns.)* bigoted, prejudiced.

Intrapersonal: *(adj.)* within one's own mind.

Introspective: *(adj.)* quality of looking inside oneself and thinking carefully.

Intuitive: *(adj.)* related to feeling, not learned knowledge.

Inventive: *(adj.)* able to make things or solve problems in a smart, clever way, *(syns.)* creative, resourceful.

Invest: *(v.)* put (money) into a business idea or activity in the hope of making more money.

Investigate: *(v.)* look at something carefully, examine.

Investment: *(n.)* giving toward or putting money into s.t., especially in a way that involves commitment.

I.Q. test: *(n.)* examination that measures the ability to learn, understand, and

F–I

use information; an evaluation of smartness (intelligence quotient).

Issue: *(n.)* a topic or matter of concern.

J

Jazz: *(n.)* a form of American popular music that combines flexible rhythmic background with solo and ensemble improvisations.

Journey: *(n.)* a trip, esp. a long one.

Juicy: *(adj.fig.)* unusually interesting, *(syn.)* scandalous.

Justice: *(n.)* the law when it is applied or carried out in a fair way, fairness.

K

Kindergarten: *(n.)* class that four- and five-year-old children attend the year before entering the first grade of school.

Kinesthetic: *(adj.)* relating to body movement and position.

Kink: *(n.)* problem, defect.

L

Ladder: *(n.)* two bars joined to each other by steps, used for climbing.

Lazy: *(adj.)* disliking and avoiding work.

Lead: *(adj.)* most important, as with the first story on the front page of a newspaper.

Leaden: *(adj.)* made of lead, unusually heavy.

Leadership: *(n.)* direction and control of others.

Legitimate: *(adj.)* reasonable, justified.

Liability: *(n.)* disadvantage, drawback.

Liberal: *(n.)* (in politics) one who proposes changes; progressive.

Lifelong: *(adj.)* lasting through one's lifetime.

Limitless: *(adj.)* infinite, without end.

Linguistic: *(adj.)* relating to the study of languages.

Link: *(v.)* connect things or concepts together.

Literacy: *(n.)* the ability to read and write.

Loan: *(n.)* a sum of money borrowed at a rate of interest.

Logical: *(adj.)* 1. showing good sense, reasonable. 2. using a system of reasoning.

Longing: *(n.)* a strong desire or emotional need, *(syn.)* yearning.

Loud: *(adj.)* having an intense voice, noisy.

Loyalty: *(n.)* faithfulness, devotion.

M

Marker: *(n.)* a sign.

Market: *(n.)* the combination of makers, sellers, and buyers of a product or service on a local, national, or international level.

Marketing: *(n.)* promoting and trying to sell goods and services.

Materialistic: *(adj.)* having the idea that wealth is an important goal in life.

Maxim: *(n.)* a saying about a principle of behavior or living.

Maximize: *(v.)* get or demand the most from s.t.

Mechanism: *(n.)* a way or means of doing s.t.

Media: *(n.pl.)* the combination of television, radio, news magazines, and large-circulation newspapers.

Medieval: *(adj.)* related to the Middle Ages.

Mentor: *(n.)* a teacher and friend.

Merit: *(n.)* proven ability, achievement.

Microcosm: *(n.)* a small, complete version of s.t. larger, a sample.

Microwave oven: *(n.)* a cooking appliance that uses short-frequency electromagnetic waves.

Minimize: *(v.)* reduce or limit s.t., lessen.

Minority: *(n.)* a number or group that is less than half of the total.

M.I.s: *(n.)* (multiple intelligences) a theory that describes several different types of smartness.

Misleading: *(adj.)* bringing one to the wrong idea, action, or direction, *(syn.)* deceiving.

Mismanage: *(v.)* organize poorly.

Moderate: *(n.)* one who is in the middle.

Modernization: *(n.)* change adhering to contemporary standards.

Mood: *(n.)* an emotional state or feeling, such as happiness or sadness.

Moral: *(adj.)* relating to what is right or wrong.

Motivate: *(v.)* give or provide a reason to do s.t.

Motivation: *(n.)* a reason to do s.t.

Motive: *(n.)* a reason, purpose for doing s.t.

Multiculturalism: *(n.)* relating to several different cultures.

Multiple: *(adj.)* many, numerous.

Mysterious: *(adj.)* having no known cause, such as s.t. supernatural or secret.

Myth: *(n.)* story from ancient cultures about history, gods, and heroes.

N

Naturalist: *(n.)* a person who studies plants and animals.

Neat: *(adj.)* precise and orderly.

Negative: *(adj.)* doubtful about s.t., critical.

Neutral: *(adj.)* not on either side in a disagreement, debate, war, etc., *(syn.)* impartial.

Newsstand: *(n.)* a small store or place that sells newspapers and magazines.

Noble: *(adj.)* having strength of character, high ideals, and honorable intentions.

Nod: *(v.)* move the head up and down to express agreement or approval.

Notion: *(n.)* an idea or belief, esp. one that is unclear or unreasonable.

Nutritionist: *(n.)* a trained person who specializes in the study of healthy eating practices.

O

Obstacle: *(n.)* s.t. that gets in the way and stops action or progress.

Obvious: *(adj.)* easy to see or understand, clear.

Omen: *(n.)* a sign of s.t. that is going to happen in the future.

Open-minded: *(adj.)* willing to listen to or consider the opinions and ideas of others.

Open: *(adj.)* willing to listen to new ideas, opinions, etc.

Opera: *(n.)* a theater art in which a story is set to music.

Opponent: *(n.)* person who take the opposite side in a fight, game, contest, etc.

Originate: *(v.)* (cause to) begin, come from.

Outcast: *(n.)* a person who is rejected by society.

Overcome: *(v.)* successfully fight against.

Overture: *(n.)* an introductory or opening piece of music.

P

Packaging: *(n.)* the material, design, and style of containers for goods to be sold.

Pajamas: *(n.pl.)* loose shirt and pants made for sleeping.

Paradigm: *(n.)* a model or concept used as a standard by which people evaluate, understand, and often act.

Paraphrase: *(v.)* explain the meaning of s.t. that has been said or written by using different words or phrases.

Parking lot: *(n.)* an area used for parking cars, often watched by an attendant.

Partial to: *(adj.)* fond of, having a special liking for.

Passion: *(n.)* strong emotion or devotion.

Path: *(n.)* route, road.

Patient: *(adj.)* willing to wait for s.t. to occur.

Peaceful: *(adj.)* calm, quiet, without troubles.

Pediatric: *(adj.)* concerning the care of children.

Penetrate: *(v.)* break or enter into.

Perceive: (v.) become aware of s.t. through the senses (sight, hearing, touch, etc.) or by thinking.

Performer: (n.) person who performs for an audience, such as a singer, dancer, actor, or musician.

Persevere: (v.) continue working toward a goal despite difficulties or obstacles.

Perspective: (n.) 1. a way of seeing things, point of view, opinion, (syns.) an angle, slant. 2. the set of beliefs, interests, attitudes, etc. that contributes to one's judgment on issues and events.

Pertain: (v.) relate to s.t.

Pervasive: (adj.) widespread, common.

Petition: (v.) formally request a court to take an action or change a law.

Phenomenal: (adj.) unusual, remarkable.

Plagiarism: (n.) a work or idea of someone else taken and used or presented as one's own.

Play down: (phrasal v.) treat s.t. as unimportant, minimize.

Political: (adj.) relating to affairs of the state and government.

Politician: (n.) person who runs for elected office, such as president, governor, or mayor.

Pop art: (n.) a mid-twentieth-century art movement focusing on everyday objects and images.

Portray: (v.) describe s.o. or s.t. in a particular way.

Possessiveness: (n.) quality of having a strong desire to control things or people.

Powerful: (adj.) strong, having great force.

Practical: (adj.) capable of acting in a sensible, efficient manner to obtain useful results.

Pre-selection: (n.) a choice that is made before the final choice, limiting the possibilities.

Predict: (v.) indicate what will happen in the future, (syn.) foretell.

Prehistoric: (adj.) of or relating to a time before history was recorded through writing.

Prejudice: (n.) an unfair opinion for or against s.o. or s.t. that is not based on reason.

Press: (n.) newspapers, magazines, and television news organizations.

Prestige: (n.) qualities, such as excellent reputation, wealth, and power, that bring admiration or honor.

Prevent: (v.) stop from happening.

Primary or primary election: (n.) in the USA, an election by a political party to choose its candidate to run in a general election.

Primitive: (adj.) simple, rough, from an early stage of development.

Print: (n.) written form.

Pro: (n.) a reason for or in favor of s.t.

Produce: 1. (v.) create, invent s.t. from the mind (writing, composing, painting, etc.). 2. (n.) food products, esp. vegetables.

Profit: (n.) money remaining after business expenses are deducted.

Progress: (n.) advancement, movement toward a goal.

Progressive: (adj.) related to making changes or reforming old ways, (syn.) alternative.

Proliferation: (n.) a rapid increase in number, a multiplication.

Propaganda: (n.) information made official and public, esp. by a government, to persuade people of s.t.

Proposal: (n.) s.t. that is suggested as a possible plan.

Prosecution lawyer: (n.) the legal representative of the state who tries to convict criminals.

Psychiatrist: (n.) a medical doctor who treats mental diseases.

Psychic: (adj.) related to or influenced by the human mind.

Psychoanalysis: (n.) a method of psychiatric therapy developed by Sigmund Freud in order to explore and explain unconscious fears, conflicts, and thoughts.

Psychotherapist: (n.) a person trained in psychology and the treatment of mental disorders, but who is not a medical doctor.

Psychotherapy: (n.) treatment for emotional and other troubles that involves talking to a trained psychotherapist.

Psychopath: (n.) a person with a mental illness that makes him or her dangerous to others.

Punishing: (adj.) disciplining, quality of making one pay for doing s.t. wrong.

Purity: (n.) a characteristic of s.t. that is without badness or sin.

Purse: (n.) a woman's handbag.

Pursuit: (n.) an activity that one dedicates time to.

Putter: (v.) move forward slowly and ineffectively.

Q

Quadruple: (v.) make four times as large.

R

Race: (n.) any of the groupings of human beings categorized by physical type.

Radical: (n.) one with very strong nontraditional beliefs, esp. one who wants change in politics or religion.

Rage: (n.) strong, uncontrolled anger.

Rank: (n.) one's position in society or within an organization.

Ranking: (n.) a place in an ordered system, a position of value, honor, or success.

Rare: (adj.) not often encountered, (syn.) infrequent.

Rational: (adj.) showing logical thought, (syns.) reasonable, sensible.

Reactionary: (n.) one who doesn't want changes, esp. in government or business.

Reasonable: (adj.) referring to a logical or sensible approach or attitude.

Reasoned: (adj.) thought out logically and rationally.

Receiver: (n.) a device that takes in signals, as for a radio or telephone.

Recover: (v.) get s.t. back, get control again, (syn.) retrieve.

Recurring: (adj.) happening again and again.

Rediscover: (v.) find s.t. again.

Reflective: (adj.) thoughtful in a deep, serious, contemplative way.

Refuse: (v.) decline, not accept.

Regardless: (adv.) disregarding, no matter.

Region: (n.) a geographical area.

Registered: (adj.) officially enrolled, such as a legal voter.

Reheat: (v.) heat s.t. again.

Reject: (v.) refuse, not accept.

Reliance: (n.) dependence, a condition of needing s.t. or s.o. for support or help.

Remnant: (n.) leftover, thing that remains.

Renaissance: (n.) the fourteenth through the seventeenth centuries in Europe, when classical art and ideas became popular again.

Repository: (n.) a place where things are kept.

Representation: (n.) act of creating a realistic image in a picture or sculpture.

Repress: (v.) keep s.t. secret and out of reach.

Republican: (n.) a member of one of two major political parties in the USA.

Research: (n.) the intense study of a particular subject.

Researcher: (n.) s.o. who conducts a study on a specific subject, (syn.) investigator.

Resentment: (n.) a feeling of anger about s.t., unhappiness, (syn.) bitterness.

Reserved: (adj.) cool in one's behavior, not showing feelings, (syn.) restrained.

Resources: (n.) Possessions or qualities of a country, organization, or person.

Respect: (n.) approval and honor for s.o.'s or s.t.'s good qualities.

Retire: (v.) leave the workforce and stop working.

P–R

Revealing: *(adj.)* showing s.t. that was previously hidden.

Reviewer: *(n.)* a person who writes about the good and bad points of s.t.

Revolutionary: *(adj.)* wanting or causing a complete change, as in government, economy, or a field of study.

Rhythm: *(n.)* a regular beat, especially in music or movement.

Rhythm and blues (R & B): *(n.pl.)* (used with a sing. v.) a type of modern American music with a strong beat influenced by blues and jazz.

Rhythmic: *(adj.)* having a regular beat, as in music.

Rigid: *(adj.)* stiff, unbending.

Risk: *(n.)* a chance or danger of losing s.t. important for the possibility of a larger gain.

Rivalry: *(n.)* an ongoing competition between opponents.

Rough: *(adj.)* difficult, not totally safe.

Rub off on: *(phrasal v. insep.)* act in a similar way, *(syns.)* affect, influence.

Run: *(v.)* direct and make decisions, *(syns.)* manage, supervise.

S

Sane: *(adj.)* mentally healthy.

Scholarship: *(n.)* a loan or grant that pays for study.

Scrabble: *(n.)* a board game in which the players compete at creating words with letter blocks.

Seat: *(n.)* the base, the location.

Secular: *(adj.)* not religious.

Security: *(n.)* protection from danger or loss.

Self: *(n.)* the individual, the essential identity of a person.

Self-determination: *(n.)* a person's will or intention to decide his or her own fate.

Self-development: *(n.)* the process of growth and progress within oneself.

Self-doubt: *(n.)* a feeling of not being confident about one's abilities.

Self-employed: *(adj.)* related to working in a business owned by oneself.

Self-esteem: *(n.)* a feeling of liking oneself, a sense of self-worth.

Self-image: *(n.)* how one perceives oneself.

Sensationalistic: *(adj.)* exciting in a negative way, arousing curiosity with exaggerated information.

Sensitive: *(adj.)* able to sense or feel strongly or finely.

Sequence: *(n.)* a continuing and connected series of acts (events, steps, etc.).

Setting: *(n.)* surroundings or environment.

Shotgun: *(n.)* a long gun (not a handgun) used mostly for hunting.

Sight: *(n.)* the physical sense of seeing.

Significance: *(n.)* meaning.

Skill: *(n.)* the ability to do a particular task.

Skimming: *(n.)* reading or looking through s.t. quickly.

Skit: *(n.)* a short, often funny scene that is acted out.

Slip of the tongue: *(n.)* s.t. said involuntarily that reveals unconscious thoughts.

Smell: *(n.)* the sense for which the nose is used.

Snare: *(v.)* net, catch.

Soar: *(v.)* fly high through the air with no difficulty.

Sociable: *(adj.)* friendly, liking to be with other people.

Social: *(adj.)* of or about people and society.

Social ladder: *(n.)* expression used to describe social classes of people from lower to higher.

Socializing: *(n.)* being with other people in a friendly group for talking, dining.

Solution: *(n.)* an answer to a problem, a way of solving it.

Solve: *(v.)* find an answer or solution for s.t.

Sophisticated: *(adj.)* 1. complex, refined. 2. with high-class tastes and understanding, *(syn.)* worldly.

Soul: *(n.)* popular American music created by African Americans that combines gospel music and rhythm and blues.

Spar: *(n.)* a pole on a boat or ship—e.g., mast.

Spatial: *(adj.)* relating to space or area.

Species: *(n.)* a biological classification of a group of living things.

Spirit: *(n.)* the nonphysical part of a person, made up of thoughts, emotions, etc., *(syn.)* soul.

Spiritual: *(adj.)* of or about the nonphysical part of a person, made up of thoughts, emotions, etc.

Split: *(v.)* divide s.t. by cutting or breaking.

Spread: *(v.)* cover a surface by pushing s.t. toward the edges of the surface.

Stamina: *(n.)* the ability to be active for long periods of time.

Standard: *(n.)* s.t. common, accepted.

Start-up: *(adj.)* beginning.

Stereotyping: *(n.)* using a too-simple and often mistaken idea to describe a particular group.

Stoop: *(n.)* the stairs or small porch in front of a house or building.

Storehouse: *(n.)* place where supplies or things are kept.

Straightforward: *(adj.)* clear, direct, without complications.

Stress: *(n.)* the degree of force put on a part of a spoken word.

Strong willed: *(adj.)* firm and forceful in one's ideas or actions, *(syn.)* willful.

Stuff: *(n.)* a general word for unnamed or unknown things.

Styling: *(n.)* making or creating s.t. in a special, artful way.

Subjective: *(adj.)* related to personal feeling and opinion rather than facts.

Sup: *(v.)* (old usage) eat the evening meal.

Superficial: *(adj.)* lacking in seriousness, limited in understanding.

Superstition: *(n.)* the belief in magical or supernatural beings and events.

Support: *(v.)* be in favor of.

Suprematism: a geometric, abstract, revolutionary school of art in early twentieth-century Russia.

Sure fire: *(adj.infrml.)* sure to work as expected, *(syns.)* certain, definite.

Surface: *(v.)* appear.

Surrealism: *(n.)* an early- to mid-twentieth century art movement focusing on the images of dreams and the unconscious mind.

Survive: *(v.)* continue to live or exist, esp. for a long time or under hard conditions; endure.

Switch: *(v.)* change or exchange.

Symbol: *(n.)* sign, mark, picture, or other object or event taken or understood to be the representation of s.t. else, esp. s.t. important or meaningful.

Symmetrical: *(adj.)* balanced and in proportion, with two parts that are mirror images of each other.

T

Take charge: *(v.)* assume control of s.t.

Talent: *(n.)* having the ability to do s.t. easily.

Talkative: *(adj.)* liking to talk.

Tap: *(n.)* hit lightly as with the fingers.

Taste: *(n.)* the sense of flavor that comes from experiencing foods and liquids on the tongue.

Technically: *(adv.)* in a practical sense.

Technique: *(n.)* method of doing s.t.

Telephone booth: *(n.)* an enclosure containing a public telephone.

Tempo: *(n.)* the rate of speed or rhythm of s.t.

Temporary: *(adj.)* not lasting, passing, impermanent.

Tend: *(v.)* 1. lean, incline toward in attitude, preference, action, etc. 2. watch over, care for.

Tendency: *(n.)* an inclination or leaning in attitude or behavior.

Tenement: *(n.)* a crowded, low-quality house or apartment building.

Term: *(n.)* a group of words or an expression.

R–T

Thankful: *(adj.)* appreciative, *(syn.)* grateful.

Theatrical: *(adj.)* related to the theater.

Theme: *(n.)* a central idea or main pattern.

Thrilling: *(adj.)* intensely exciting.

Throbbing: *(adj.)* beating strongly, usu. from pain, *(syn.)* pulsating.

Tolerance: *(n.)* acceptance, esp. of beliefs and behavior different from the dominant culture.

Touch: *(n.)* the feeling of s.t. against one's own skin.

Traditional: *(adj.)* related to the passing of customs and beliefs from one generation to another.

Tragedy: *(n.)* drama in which s.o. suffers because of a personal flaw and hostile outside forces or events.

Trait: *(n.)* a characteristic, *(syn.)* attribute.

Transform: *(v.)* change from one shape or appearance to another.

Transition: *(n.)* a change from one condition to another.

Trap: *(v.)* catch and confine or hold s.o. or s.t. against their will.

Tribe: *(n.)* a social unit made up of people, groups, and/or families who share the same culture, leader, and ancestry.

Trick: *(v.)* deceive, mislead.

Tricky: *(adj.)* needing special care or technique in doing s.t. difficult.

Trio: *(n.)* a group of three, esp. singers or musicians.

Triple: *(v.)* make three times as large.

Trumpet: *(n.)* brass wind musical instrument with high-pitched sound.

U

U.S. Bureau of Labor Statistics: *(n.)* a United States agency that gathers numerical information to characterize a sample of the population of workers in the country.

Ultimately: *(adv.)* in the end.

Unattainable: *(adj.)* not achievable, not reachable.

Unattractive: *(adj.)* uninteresting, unappealing.

Unconscious: *(adj.)* an uncontrolled part of the mind that affects our thoughts and behavior and stores memories, desires, and fears we are unaware of.

Uneasiness: *(n.)* nervousness, worry.

Unedited: *(adj.)* not corrected, left in original form.

Unintended: *(adj.)* not planned, not meant to be.

Universal: *(adj.)* found or practiced everywhere.

Universe: *(n.)* the stars, planets, other heavenly bodies, and space taken together.

Unsophisticated: *(adj.)* unworldly, simple.

Untrustworthy: *(adj.)* dishonest and unreliable.

Urban: *(adj.)* related to the city.

Urbanize: *(v.)* make citylike in nature.

V

Validate: *(v.)* confirm.

Value: 1. *(n.)* worth. 2. *(v.)* appreciate, think s.t. is important.

Valued: *(adj.)* appreciated.

Vast: *(adj.)* wide in area, *(syn.)* immense.

Venture: *(v.)* act with some risk of harm or loss of money.

Verbal: *(adj.)* referring to either spoken or written language.

Victim: *(n.)* s.o. or s.t. that suffers from an accident, crime, illness, or bad luck.

Visible: *(adj.)* able to be seen.

Vision: *(n.)* foresight, ability to imagine the future.

Vocal color: *(n.)* characteristics of the voice having interesting variations.

Vocation: *(n.)* one's livelihood, work.

Vow: *(v.)* swear, solemnly promise.

Vulnerable: *(adj.)* likely to be hurt or made to feel bad.

W

Wander: *(v.)* go from place to place without a fixed plan or goal.

Weapon: *(n.)* a tool used to harm or kill.

Weird: *(adj.)* strange, *(syns.)* odd, bizarre.

Wheelchair: *(n.)* a chair with wheels, used by a person who cannot walk.

Whining: *(n.)* a long, soft, high cry.

Wilderness: *(n.)* land in its natural state, esp. a large area unspoiled by humans.

Wisdom: *(n.)* knowledge, understanding learned from experience.

Withstand: *(v.)* last in spite of.

Workforce: *(n.)* all workers employed nationally, regionally, or in an individual business.

Workplace: *(n.)* the setting or place where people do their jobs.

Worldwide: *(adj.adv.)* all over the world.

Worn: *(adj.)* threadbare, ragged.

Worth: *(adj.)* good enough for, deserving.

Wound: *(v.)* cut, puncture, or otherwise hurt by striking s.o.'s body.

Y

Yale: *(n.)* a prestigious university located in New Haven, Connecticut.

T–Y

TAPESCRIPTS

Chapter 1
What Will I Do When They Find Out I'm Me?

Listening 1

Walter Anderson

During the last two decades I've had the rare and the wonderful opportunity to meet some of the most noble and achieved people on earth. I've met the heads of nations, people who've created great art, great literature. I've met people who've run corporations and done it successfully. I've met some of the best teachers America has, some of the greatest scientists. With every famous and celebrated person that I've met, the most famous of actors and actresses, I've asked each one of them a question: "When it's dark and you're alone, do you ever say to yourself: 'What will I do when they find out I'm me?'"

I've never failed to get a nod with the question. Every one of them said yes. What was it that I and they were afraid others would discover? That I am inferior . . . that I am vulnerable . . . that I deserve to be rejected. You see, I thought for years that I was the only human being who, when it was dark and I was alone, worried that others would find out that I was not quite good enough . . . that I could be hurt . . . that maybe I didn't belong. I know now that every sane human being worries that others will find out that they're inferior . . . they're vulnerable . . . they deserve to be rejected. Every one of us, when it's dark and we're alone, says, "What will I do when they find out I'm me?"

Over the course of my life I have learned seven rules that have served me well. If you will, seven rules to live by. And the first and most important is to know

who is responsible. I am responsible. When we begin with those three words, we can build a new life, even a new world.

The second is to believe in something big. Believe in something big, your life is worth a noble motive.

Three, practice tolerance. You'll like yourself a lot more, and so will others.

Fourth. Be brave and remember that courage is acting with fear, not without it. It's the difference, if you will, between Rocky and Rambo. Rocky's courageous, because Rocky continues on even though he's afraid. Rambo, on the other hand, has no fear. He's a psychopath. That's not courage.

Fifth, love someone because you should know joy. When we're children, the need to be loved is phenomenal. When we're adult, the need to love is greater.

Six. Be ambitious. No single effort will solve all of your problems, achieve all of your dreams, or even be enough. And that's OK. To want to be more than we are is real, and normal, and healthy.

Finally, number seven. Smile, because no one else can do that for you.

Listening 2

Walter Anderson

I was raised in a tenement, and one night my mother asked me to go across the street to the telephone booth (we had no telephone in our apartment) and call my brother. Now I don't remember what the telephone call was about, but I'll remember that as long as I live because when I hung the receiver back up my hand had blood on it, and I reached up and touched my face . . . my face had blood on it. Whoever had used the telephone before me had been either hurt or wounded, which was not unusual in the neighborhood I grew up. And I opened the bifold doors and I looked to my left, I looked to my right, and I ran across the street, and I ran up the steps to the tenement, went into our apartment. I washed the blood off my face and hands before my mother could see it.

A little later I went back down stairs and I sat on the stoop . . . now it's never quiet, really, in New York, but it was relatively quiet . . . the sounds of the city around, and I was alone. And I started to think about this mysterious person whose blood I had worn, and I became angry, I became enraged, and I vowed "I'm getting out of here," and I meant it.

It was in that moment that I first began to accept responsibility for my own life.

Listening 3

Johanna: The one I practice and live by is be ambitious. No single effort will solve all your problems, achieve all your dreams, or even be enough, and that's OK. To want to be more than we are is real, and normal, and healthy. I don't like the word *ambitious* because in my language it's not like a positive word. I like to say something like, "I have goals and I like to achieve them. And always have goals in your mind."

And the one that I would like to practice is practice tolerance. You'll like yourself a lot more, and so will others. I think I'm not very patient, and sometimes I think I expect more from people than they can really give me.

Rista Luna

For me the one I practice is say I am responsible. I think that it's not just being responsible because you take care or you achieve what you have to do but it's also because you are responsible for being happy, for being sad even if you . . . if I feel bad it's because I don't allow myself to feel good. So I think I can do something. I always can do something for feeling better myself.

And the one I like but I cannot practice very well is practice tolerance, because I think sometimes you know that everybody is not perfect but you always want things done the correct way and you can lose your patience. I can lose my patience. I can lose my patience, because I always try to do things the best I can and I get like mad when somebody doesn't do the same thing.

Metta

Believe in something big. Your life is worth a noble motive. This is something that I've definitely come to believe in because as we grow up we are put into a large society where sometimes we think we are just a small microcosm in this large, large society and we don't think we have a noble purpose of why we are on this earth. But if you really begin to think about it we've all been put here for some reason, and once you find your reason and you decide it's a noble reason it really makes you see why you are even on this earth and what your life is for and it gives you a very strong purpose for getting up every day and for doing the best you can to basically help make this world a better place.

Be brave; remember courage is acting with fear, not without it. If the challenge is worth it, you're supposed to be nervous. This is something that I'm definitely working on now in my life. Most of my life people haven't known that I have been afraid because I'm a good actress. So my outside looks brave, but inside I'm shaking with fear. But I've come to realize that this fear can be used to make you stronger in this goal that you're attempting. And if you use the fear constructively . . . letting yourself [say] "Yes I am afraid, what am I afraid of? Let's look at it. And let me take it with me into attacking this thing that I'm trying to accomplish here." And you'll see in the end that, yes, your fear was there but that's OK, but in the end you'll probably be successful.

Video

Walter Anderson

Let's begin the program with Walter Anderson, whose boyhood home was a tenement in Mt. Vernon, New York. As a young man he found self-respect serving our country in Vietnam. There in the wreckage of war he found an old typewriter and composed a poem he called "Just What Is Vietnam?" That poem and his love of reading eventually led Walter to his position as editor of *Parade*, the most widely read Sunday magazine in the world.

"My father was a violent alcoholic, and I was often safer on the street corner than I was in my own bed. My father would beat me for a variety of things. It infuriated and enraged him if he saw me reading because my father was not literate. And it was painful for him to see me read. My mother, though and nevertheless, encouraged me to read. Years after my father's death, I asked my mother, 'Ma, why did you do that? Why did you encourage me to read when you knew Daddy would beat me?' And she said, 'I knew if you would learn to read and you would read, somehow you'd find your way out. Every child needs a place.' And I lived in a violent home in a violent neighborhood, but there was this library. I could open a book. I could read it. I could be anyone. I could be anywhere. I could do anything. I could imagine myself out of the slum."

Walter parlayed his love of writing into a job at a New York newspaper, the first step up the ladder on his way to editor of *Parade* magazine. A leader in advocating the power of literacy, Walter has never forgotten the magic of books and how the gift of reading helped him to succeed.

[Anderson reads.] "Brother Bear was just crazy about space grizzlies." [Reading continues. Anderson narrates over the reading.] "Each of us needs to feel we have power, that we have control of our lives. Literacy empowers. Reading frees us. Reading was my ticket, not only from poverty, but from abuse. Someday I'm going to have to look back over my life, and the big things, being editor of *Parade,* writing books, appearing on television, aren't really going to be memorable. What's going to matter is whether or not I affected a life. Whether or not I helped a child grow."

Ladies and gentlemen, Ruth Peale, wife of the late Norman Vincent Peale, presents the Horatio Alger Award to Walter Anderson.

Anderson: "On this night, it has never been more clear to me that human beings can transform themselves, that each of us can do more, that a boy who grew up with a volatile childhood could someday stand on a stage like this with the Horatio Alger Award in one hand and one of the century's great Americans in the other. Thank you for the opportunity."

Dorothy Brown

There's an old folk expression that says, "On the edge of a ravine, that's where you'll find the most beautiful flowers." That vision reflects the dramatic success of Dr. Dorothy Brown, whose dream, even as an orphan child, was to become a surgeon.

"I was told, 'Well, you add it up and it just cannot be done. You're a girl, you're black, you're poor, and it just can't be done.' I didn't pay any attention to that. I just kept right on, dreaming my dreams. I was going to be a doctor. I was going to have on a white gown and a white hat, I said, and a white something on my face, and I was going to be a cutting doctor. When I was thirteen, my biological mother came and took me out of the orphanage. She told me that 'You have enough education now. You have to do like the other colored girls do in Troy.' And I went into domestic work."

But after work Dorothy kept at her dream, studying in secret in a closet by the light of a sixty-watt bulb. Abandoned by her mother again, she was taken in by an elderly couple, the Redmonds.

"I was sixteen years old when that family accepted me, and they were poor people. And they both told me that they loved me. And they said, 'The only thing we want you to do is stay in school and behave yourself.' That wasn't hard. Then I lived with them, and they were the only real parents that I ever knew."

In 1959 Dorothy accepted the position of chief of surgery at Riverdale Hospital in Nashville. She was the first African American woman to serve in Tennessee's General Assembly. Dorothy still makes house calls and continues her association with the orphanage that raised her.

"I went back to the orphanage where I had been as a child, and I talked to the children, and I told them that you never feel sorry for yourself because you had to be placed in an orphanage, that you were just as good as anybody else, and you could be just as big and just as famous, but you had to have a dream and then you had to stick with that dream and really make it come true. I understand that I've been traveling on God's highway 'cause for no other reason do things mesh like they meshed for me."

Ladies and gentlemen, Wallace Rathsmassan, retired chairman of Beatrice Foods, presents the Horatio Alger Award to Dr. Dorothy Brown.

Brown: "Where else but in America could such an incredible dream as mine have ever come true? Thank you."

Ben Carson

The Horatio Alger Awards now honors one of the world's leading pediatric neurosurgeons. He's recognized internationally, especially for a delicate twenty-two-hour operation that separated Siamese twins joined at the head, just two of the many children around the world who owe their lives to this remarkable man.

"I was by far the class dummy. No one ever had to worry about getting the lowest mark on a test as long as I was around. I was the kid who was always making funny noises when the teacher turned her back. Whenever there was a joke about a dummy, they used to just substitute my name to make it realistic for everybody."

Growing up in the Detroit projects, Ben seemed destined to live a life of violence and poverty until his mother turned his life around. "And when my mother saw my report card, she was horrified."

Carson's mother: "I went home and told he and his brother that they had to turn the TV off and start going to the library and getting books and make a book report and submit it to me."

Carson: "I began to be able to explore the world through the books, and I began to read about people who used their minds to make not only their own lives better but the lives of people around them, and within the space of a year and a half, I went from the bottom of the class to the top of the class."

Ben's pride of accomplishment spurred him on first through medical school, then to the top of his field in pediatric neurosurgery, where his devotion and talent continues to save precious lives.

Former patient: "My favorite hero in the world is Ben Carson 'cause he saved my life."

Carson: "It doesn't matter if you came from a broken home, from a racial minority, from dire poverty, from the worst grades imaginable. If we develop our God-given talents and have faith in God, there is nothing in this world that they can't accomplish."

And now Horatio Alger member Johnny Cash presents the Horatio Alger Award to Dr. Benjamin Carson, Sr.

Carson: "I want to thank God, and I want to thank America for still being the kind of place that a person who's born on the wrong side of the tracks can live in and accomplish anything they want, even brain surgery. Thank you."

Chapter 2
Legacy of the Blues

Listening 1

(Intro- Robert Johnson singing one of his songs) **still current?**

Steve Tarshis

OK. We're here to talk about the blues. What is the blues? The blues is a number of things. It's both a genre, in other words a style of music, but it's also the language, a certain type of musical language that was different from the European heritage of Bach, Beethoven, and Brahms, etc. that formed the basis for American music as a whole.

It probably originated around the year 1900 in a relatively small area of the country called the Mississippi Delta. Now, the Mississippi Delta was a place where many Blacks had emigrated to work in after the Civil War was over. And it was a wilderness area that they helped to clear and then to plant.

The blues itself, as I said, developed around 1900, and that's a significant year because it was about one generation after slavery was over. So, in essence, it was one of the first, maybe the first, musical cultural expressions by Black people in America as a freed entity.

Now, technically, the elements of blues consisted of the old work songs and field hollers that were sung in order to make the work go by more quickly. But blues began probably the moment when these songs and field hollers were put to music, put to a harmonic background. In other words, chords, usually on the guitar, were played. Another way of looking at this was the songs . . . the work songs and field hollers that probably had their origins in African music met the harmonies that were introduced by the Europeans to Black people in America. And when these two elements were combined, that's where blues first came into being.

Now the piece that we were just listening to was by Robert Johnson, who was considered by many to be one of the finest of the Delta blues performers and the one who sort of sent the music on its way into an urbanized period. American musicians later took the blues and elements of the blues and used it to create all the popular music forms, including rock 'n' roll, rhythm and blues, and jazz. That's why blues is considered to be so important and is such a powerful music to listen to.

Listening 2

Q: The style of jazz that you do is known to have a bluesy slant. Why do you think it has this blues slant to it?

Junior Mance: Good question. Well, I grew up in a blues environment; I mean my musical growing up was in a blues environment. I'm sure you've heard the term Chicago blues, which sometimes can be very misleading . . . but when I was growing up, Chicago really was a blues environment . . . Bluestown. All the famous blues singers were all based in Chicago
. . . people like Muddy Waters, Memphis Slim, and even Dinah Washington, who I worked with later, was from Chicago. And I guess it just rubbed off.

My mother liked the blues. My mother would always buy blues records, and my father too. And my father liked all music, though. But my mother was very partial to the blues, and she would buy either blues records or boogie woogie records, which was the first style of piano playing that I learned.

Q: In all these years of playing jazz and the blues . . . just as a performer, what was your greatest blues experience? Was it with a particular performer . . . was it a place?

JM: Well probably Dinah, I would say, Dinah Washington. In fact, that was one of the best experiences in my career anyway . . . playing with her. Well, you know, she was known as queen of the blues. But she did more than just blues, ya know, but her singing always had a blues tinge to it. You know, everything. She could sing the prettiest ballad and just put so much feeling into it, but it was always that bluesy feeling. So, I think, this is how she got the title of being the Queen of the Blues.

Q: What was the blues to her? Could you define her type of blues?

JM: Dinah—in fact, I've heard people ask Dinah this same question—Dinah seems to say there's all kinds of blues. Like, a lot of people think you have to be sad to like the blues. That's not true. There's a happy blues . . . a sad blues, you know, and Dinah would cover it all. Like, if she, say, if she was in a relationship where she had a good man . . . you

know what I mean, in her terms . . . oh, she would sing songs about that and just give you a good feeling when the song was over, you know. And then on the other hand, if she was downhearted, if, well, say, take that same man, if he left her or something, if the relationship was over, she could really put you in a deep funk, you know, like you know, and you could really feel it. You know so . . . it's hard, I don't think any one mood makes the blues; the blues can be all moods.

Q: Well, is this a new development that the blues would be happy? It seems like its origins would be sad.

JM: No, no, no. It goes all the way back to when the blues originated, to Bessie Smith and to all those people. Bessie Smith and all of them. They sang . . . a lot of the blues that Bessie sings . . . I mean a lot of the blues that Dinah sings came from some of the things that Bessie did. Yeah. It's always been that way. There are some singers, some performers, who get more into this depressive type of thing. You know, like they used to say, Billie Holiday, whenever she sang the blues it was always depressing, you know.

Q: Was it? Do you think?

JM: I think so when she sang blues. I'm not talking about when she sang other things too. You know like her most famous one was a thing called "Billie's Blues." I think she says "My man don't love me . . . treats me awful mean. He's the meanest man I've ever seen," you know. She was into that more, but she wasn't what you would call a blues singer. She just sang the blues sometimes. But even the male blues singers like T-Bone Walker, or I'm going way back in time now you know or Muddy Waters, they would sing both, you know, the happy blues and the miserable blues.

Q: Is there something you can say, a description about how you feel about being a blues/jazz performer? How do you feel about the music?

JM: I like it. I love it, yeah. And I don't get in any certain kind of mood to have to play the blues; I just like all blues, you know, yeah. Like Ray Charles say: "You can't lose with the blues."

Q: Can you describe . . . is there any difference, if we're talking about definitions of different types of music, is there a difference between jazz with the blues, jazz without the blues, is jazz different from the blues?

JM: Oh yes. Blues . . . well in the beginning, blues was very much the basis for jazz. You know the jazz idiom came out of the blues way back, we're talking about. . . . But since then . . . jazz goes through so many evolved . . . evolutions . . . it evolved so much, there are just many, many types of jazz now. You know you can't just pigeonhole . . . just take it and say "That's jazz" because it covers so much, you know this is what keeps it interesting. That's probably why I like jazz . . . because I listen to everything in jazz. I'm still more partial to the bluesy type of jazz, you know. But you know there's . . . it's like you take a person who doesn't know anything about jazz, you know, and you ask him, "What is jazz?" Depending on who they hear first it can be very . . . it can be a bad experience, or it can be a good experience, you know. Say someone who has never heard jazz, you take him to a Count Basie concert or turn him on to a Count Basie record or something, they're more than likely going to like that, you know, because they can snap their fingers to it, they can pat their feet to it, but then you can get a little more, I don't know the word I'm looking for, I guess intellectual, for want of a better term, and say play something by Cecil Taylor, what we call avant-garde jazz, that person who's completely oblivious to jazz may not like that, you know, because it's entirely different, but it's still under the heading of jazz. Or they could go the other way. This could be a person who maybe has listened to classical music all their lives, people like Mahler or Hindemith or Stravinsky or something, and they hear something like that and they may like it and they may not like the Count Basie thing or the Ray Charles thing or whatever.

Q: Could you tell me what you think about how the blues has affected other forms of music, like rock 'n' roll, and things like that, American music in general?

JM: I think it's a basis just like it was for jazz for rock and roll also, because a lot of the more famous rock and roll players they admit that they got a lot of the stuff they do from jazz, like the Rolling Stones; when they first got very, very popular they had B. B. King as their opening act. And they admit that they got a lot of stuff from B. B. King and people like that. The Beatles also, the same way.

Bonus Listening

Boogie Woogie

(music)

The reason I made that one so long is because I did two different versions of boogie woogie . . . there's boogie woogie (**Music**) with one bass, then there's this other bass, which is probably more common (**Music**). That's what they call a "walking boogie woogie bass." It's strange; now that was the first thing I learned how to play when I was a kid musically, but it's hard for me to play boogie woogie now. I don't know; I guess it's that two-hand coordination . . . because now the way that jazz goes . . . like modern jazz . . . piano players don't use their left hand as much; they depend more on the bass player and the drummer for keeping the bottom. But back then the bass players played differently also, so there were more "two-fisted" piano players then.

Bebop

(music)

Bebop was more or less music that was, I think, was born at Metten's Playhouse, which used to be a famous jazz club about 118th St. Just off 7th Ave. That's where Charlie Parker, who was probably the main innovator of bebop, and Dizzy, Charlie and Dizzy both, I think it was a joint project, but Dizzy used to give more credit to Charlie Parker than anything else. Well, Charlie Parker did come up with this new style that just opened everybody's eyes. I said, "Oh, wow, what is that?" But at Metten's Playhouse and this is, oh, I guess back in the early forties, maybe, or late thirties, Dizzy Gillespie, Charlie Parker, Thelonius Monk, Kenny Clark—well, even Coleman Hawkins—they were a little older than he was, but even he was in on the movement too for want of a better term. But that's more or less their music. It's a little more sophisticated, I think. It's different from boogie woogie; boogie woogie is all blues. You know, bebop is all sorts of songs, not just blues. I just played (**Music**) that was one of Charlie Parker's compositions; that's the melody.

Free Jazz

(**Music**)

I don't know much about free jazz. I never got into it. I tried to listen to some of it. Some of it I like. It's just maybe not my cup of tea, but some of those people work hard at doing it, so I'm not going to knock it. It's free.

Listening 3

Come Rain or Come Shine
J. Mercer and H. Arlen

I'm gonna love you
Like nobody's loved you
Come rain or come shine
High as a mountain
Deep as a river
Come rain or come shine
I guess when I met you
It was just one of those things
But don't ever bet me
Cuz I'm gonna be true
If you let me

You're gonna love me
Like nobody's loved me
Come rain or come shine
Happy together, unhappy together
Now won't it be fine
Days may be cloudy or sunny
We're in or we're out of the money
But I'm with you always
I'm with you
Come rain or come shine

Mannish Boy
M. Waters

Oh yeah, oh yeah
Everything, everything
Everything's gonna be alright this morning
Oh yeah, wow, yeah
Now when I was young boy
At the age of five
My mother said I was gonna be
The greatest man alive
But now I'm a man
Way past twenty-one

I would believe me baby
I have lots of fun
I'm a man

I spell M - A- H - I - N
That rubber thin man
No B, O child, Y
That means mannish boy
I'm a man
I'm full grown man
I'm a man
I'm a natural born lover's man
I'm a man
I'm a rolling stone
I'm a man
I'm a hoochie coochie man
Setting on the outside
Just me and my mate
You know I'm made to move honey
Come up two hours late
Wasn't that a man

I spell M - A- H - I - N
That rubber thin man
No B, O child, Y
That means mannish boy . . . Man
I'm full grown man . . . Man
I'm a natural born lover's man . . . Man
I'm a rolling stone
Man child
I'm a hoochie coochie man
The lines I shoots
I will never miss
When I make love to a woman
She can't resist
I think I go down
To old castle's dude
I'm gonna bring back my second cousin
That little Johnny cockaroo
All you little girls
Settin out that line
I can make love to you woman
In five letters time
Ain't that a man

I spell M - A- H - I - N
That rubber thin, I'm grown
No B, O child, Y
That means mannish boy . . . Man
I'm full grown man . . . Man
I'm a natural born lover's man . . . Man

I'm a rolling stone
I'm a Man child
I'm a hoochie coochie man
Well, well, well
Hurry, hurry, hurry, hurry
Don't hurt me, don't hurt me child
Don't hurt me, don't hurt me, don't hurt me child
Well, well, well

Video

Carolina Underground

Hello. I am Carolina Slim. Man, yeah!

I was born in South Carolina. I come to New York City after the Korean War. I got married up here, and I stayed. My wife used to come to Carolina, and I met her that way. And I come to New York and started staying. Every day called for 'nother, another day called for another, and after a while I found myself in New York for 35-40 years. But I'm still from South Carolina.

I like playing in the subway station because it's never a minute of deadtime; it's never a minute of loneliness. Everything is just fresh all the time. I just love playing out in the public. Free. Free to the people.

I grew up from a musical family. Brother, sister, cousin, friend—everybody I knew played music. Organs, pie plate, tin pans, bucket, ledge, anything. I'm a drummer. I play bass. A good musician plays everything. They classified me as electric acoustic Piedmont blues. You know, you do it, they'll put you in a class; don't you worry 'bout that. I play the guitar. It's electric, but I play it in an acoustic guitar style. And the blues is from the Piedmont region, 'round North Carolina and upper part of South Carolina. That's the Piedmont region.

I was told a few times that blues was usually a true story. That convenient. A lot of people, when they say blues, they think of hard times. I guess some of that is included. But there are happy blues and there are sad blues. But I play mostly more of the simple everyday street man type of blues. I play behind the old man Johnny Lee Hooker who did "Mae Belle." I guess I could been recorded myself, but everybody just didn't make records. Everybody didn't wanta make records. Everybody didn't go through what it took back in those days to make 'em, and like that.

I'm never fast; I always got a minute to spend with somebody. If somebody asks me something, I've got time and children, oh boy, if it's a small child come up to me and try to ask me a question, I'm gonna take time out until I can understand what the child wants.

Deep down, if you did anything towards the public, you will have a remembrance. A lot of the blues that I played when I was a boy fourteen years old, I play 'em right today. They don't get old, or they don't get out of style. They gets better.

Chapter 3
Food: Business & Pleasure

Listening 1

Gary Goldberg

I'm going to talk with you today about a love affair, and this is America's love affair with fine food, which I call the art of cuisine, and America really is in love with fine food. I can give you so many examples of that. For example, there's a proliferation of great restaurants of every type in this country, not only in New York, which I think is perhaps the greatest restaurant city in the world other than Paris, but in Los Angeles, San Francisco, in the Napa Valley, Seattle, Chicago, Boston . . . fine food and fine restaurants everywhere.

There are also dozens of food and wine magazines and dozens of cookbooks that come out every year . . . *Gourmet*, *Bon Appetit*, etc. Some of them have been around for many years, some of them are brand new, but they just keep coming. We also have a proliferation of gourmet shops in this country (fancy food shops, they're sometimes called), and they sell fresh produce, they sell prepared foods, packaged foods, you can buy a whole wonderful dinner already prepared for you, take it home and just reheat it. They sell gourmet coffees, teas, desserts, everything. There's also an explosion of cooking schools, both for professionals and nonprofessionals.

As a director of a cooking school in New York City, the New School Culinary Arts Program, I of course have insight into this area, and I can tell you it is amazing. We have literally tripled our enrollment in the last six years, and we have over 5000 students a year. And it's not just true here; it's true in cooking schools all across America.

You might ask why people study culinary arts. And there are many reasons. Of course, the first is as a career, because it really is a wonderful career area. There are many jobs available. For example, in the year 2005 the U.S. Bureau of Labor Statistics says there will be 12 1/2 million jobs available in this area . . . 46% growth in positions for chefs, 44% for managers, etc. It's amazing!

Now, also one of the advantages of being in this field is enormous flexibility. You can travel from city to city and get a job, which you can't do in a lot of areas, so it affords you travel; it affords you independence and a certain amount of security. Chefs also have become stars. They appear on television, they write books, they do yacht trips. I mean they're really . . . many of them become famous and have achieved fame and fortune, and of course that's a goal many people strive for. There are also many other choices of careers in this area. Not just chefs and caterers and bakers, but you can be a food stylist, you can be a food editor, you can be a nutritionist, and then there are fields you can go into. We give one-day courses for people who are changing careers—for example, How to Create Your Own Specialty Food Product—and we have a young man named Joe LaMotta who's the son of Jake LaMotta, the famous boxer that Martin Scorsese made a film about, *Raging Bull*. He's come out with a new tomato sauce called LaMotta's Tomato Sauce. Then we have another young man, Joseph Banano, Jr., who is a New York City firefighter and also a fitness trainer, and he took a course on how to get a cookbook published and came out with a best-selling cookbook called the *Healthy Firehouse Cookbook*. So you really can change your career and do it successfully in this area.

People who change careers to become food professionals do it, I think, primarily, though, because they love it. For example, I'm a career-change person. I changed careers when I was in my late twenties. I always loved food. I decided to make my avocation my vocation, do something I really love. And I think I'm very fortunate because I love coming to work every day.

Now, there are a number of students who take courses, many of them at the New School, as an avocation or as a hobby. They want to learn to cook at home for themselves, for enjoyment, for entertaining. And for them, I think, the primary motive is cooking as fun. It really is fun. It's something that gives you immediate pleasure. It involves all the senses. It allows you to socialize with people, to interact, to cook for entertaining.

Also, there's something enormously creative about cooking. And I think that's why cooking is often considered an art—the culinary arts—because you're creating something that's beautiful, artful, imaginative, hopefully delicious, and in spite of all that it's ephemeral, it doesn't last very long; we make it, we eat it, and it's gone. But this is one creative process that has immediate gratification, and not many things in life do.

Also, it's perhaps less expensive to eat at home, so if you learn to learn to make good food at home, you can save money, you can cook what you like, you can cook healthy and nourishing foods, and also we've discovered a whole generation of young professionals who never learned to cook because both their parents were working so there was no one cooking at home. Now they've discovered that they want to cook for themselves; they've discovered how exciting and delicious this is to cook for themselves and for friends.

One of the most famous American cookbooks of all time is called *The Joy of Cooking*, and I really think that's what Americans are doing. They're rediscovering the joy of cooking and of eating. One of my great friends who was a very large and very jolly French lady came to America to be a chef and caterer; I think she said it best: "People who love food are happy people."

Listening 2

Marjorie Vai: I'm speaking with Emel Basdoğan (EB: oh, pretty well pronounced.). Thank you, who is co-owner and editor-in-chief of the largest selling food magazine in Turkey; in fact, it's the largest selling magazine in Turkey. Emel, how did you get started with this project? Where did you get the idea to start a food magazine in Turkey?

Emel Basdoğan: Well, food was always a passion for me, but it was a coincidence in a sense. I had a friend who was a magazine editor in a different area. We felt that there would be a boom of interest for food. So we thought we would make a food magazine. We also knew of the other examples of food magazines in the world. It seemed the time was right for Turkey to have one.

MV: So how did you actually start the magazine?

EB: Our interest in food was something romantic, but business is *not* romantic, we knew that. We planned very well. First we looked for financial support from food companies. But, understandably, none of them wanted to share our risk. We asked them instead if they could assure us that they would buy a certain volume of advertisements. This was a minimum guarantee for us, and so this was important financial help.

MV: So in the end it was very easy to get the start-up money?

EB: No, actually, it wasn't. Two young ladies coming and saying that they have nice ideas. You know, this wasn't very exciting. But because I had experience in food commercials, I was known and had connections in the food industry, and my partner had experience in publishing . . . this was proof that we could do it! But even they were surprised at how successful it was! In the end it was very good for the whole food industry to have a food magazine because it raised product awareness.

MV: Once you had the magazine, how did you market it?

EB: We had a very limited budget, so we couldn't do any advertising. We planned that we would sell the magazine in supermarkets as well as newsstands.

MV: Wasn't this something innovative for Turkey, selling magazines in supermarkets?

EB: Here and in Europe this is very common, but in Turkey, supermarkets are only for bread and butters, that kind of thing. They resisted it. It took six months to persuade them that magazines, especially a food magazine, wasn't out of place in a supermarket. In the end they agreed . . . just because I insisted . . . but now they are very happy because they are making a lot of money too.

MV: So, what's the attraction of food? In the U.S. also, I believe, three of the top ten selling magazines are food magazines. Why is food such an involving topic? It's not just survival, is it?

EB: No, it's not just eating.

MV: What is it, then?

EB: I think food helps you to come out of the walls of your small world. You can enter a new world,

new cultures, knowing new materials and learning new tastes . . . it opens windows. Also, it affects all the sense—touch, sight, smell, taste, and hearing—when someone compliments you on your cooking, you know. And I think, because it affects all the senses it is wonderful for self-education. You must learn to coordinate all the senses. With food, it's not work; it's pleasure and self-development at the same time.

Listening 3, Part 1

Marjorie Vai: So how did you get into the food business? What's your history in work?

Irene Khin Wong: Well, I was in investment banking field, and a good friend of mine who's in the travel field got me into food and travel area, and he inspires me to do a restaurant. There wasn't any Burmese restaurant per se at that time. And I can really share what is Burmese food and what is Burma like. So that made me wanted to open up a restaurant, a Burmese restaurant.

MV: But now you've become, since then, since you had the restaurant you've become a real expert on Southeast Asia, you've traveled all around Southeast Asia learning first-hand about the different cuisines, and . . . how did you make that transition from just Burmese to that?

IKW: During my restaurant years I found out that there are other Asian cuisines, and other Asian countries that is just as fascinating as my country, so I want to explore more on that area rather than just restaurants per se.

MV: So how do you feel about your work?

IKW: I like it very much now because I deal and I work with other food lovers and I share a lot of information with them as well as they share a lot of their background and their experience with me. So every day, every moment is different, and I can never tell what it's gonna to be like the next day.

MV: What do you think it is about food that's so appealing? Dealing with food?

IKW: Well, food is really universal, it's interacting with people, people's personality, and food really brings out the personality and characteristic of a person. And I always tell people that when you do a restaurant, it's not . . . you don't think of the dollar sign first, you have to think of opening out your living room (MV: Oh, that's nice.) and business will have to come later on.

MV: Oh, that's a great way to look at it. Good. OK.

IKW: Thank you.

Listening 3, Part 2

Marjorie Vai: How did you get into the food business? Where did you start professionally?

John Massachio: Where did I start? I always tended bar part-time since I got married. Even before I got married . . . which is a good thirty years ago. And very early I wanted to get into the restaurant business, but I didn't do too much about it but tend bar. And finally in the late seventies I decided that I would get serious about going into the restaurant business, I went to culinary school, I gave up my job tending bar to become a waiter to learn the service end of a restaurant business, and that's how it all began. I mean, I was always interested in food, I always loved to eat, I loved to go out to restaurants, my family were great . . . my mother was a great cook . . . and I was a little chubby kid who loved to eat. And my mother said when I was lost she could always find me in the kitchen . . . no matter whose house I was at.

MV: What was the first restaurant you opened?

JM: I had a little place on Mulberry Street, just south of what is now considered Little Italy, but at one time it was a part of Little Italy. And we had twenty-six seats. And it was good; it was my first restaurant, I did all the cooking, and I got my experience there.

MV: What was it called?

JM: It was called the Mulberry Bush.

MV: And now at La Dolce Vita. When did you start La Dolce Vita?

JM: I started on Spring Street. It'll be ten years August sixth.

MV: And how do you feel now about being in the restaurant business?

JM: I mean, I love the business and I love entertaining people and feeding people and I love the cooking aspect of it, but presently I'm bogged down with paperwork, and I can't do what I really like to do.

MV: And what you like to do is . . .

JM: Cook, and entertain, and make people happy.

Chapter 4
Us and Them: Creating the Other

Listening 1

John Mayher

One of the things that's fascinating about the way the human mind works is the importance of categorizing that is part of our whole way of thinking about the world, and coming to know it. Starting as very little children, we begin to categorize things into good and bad, hot and cold, sweet and sour, or edible, inedible. And we do that with people too. And our families help us do that with people. They teach us who's in our family and who's not. Who's in our tribe, so to speak, and who's not. Who's in our neighborhood and who's not, who are strangers and who are friends. And part of that is a whole process of creating groups that we think of as ours and groups that we think of as somehow the other.

Now this was probably a very helpful thing to do when we were young . . . as a species . . . 50 . . . 60,000 years ago, when it was really important to be able to tell who was in our tribe and who wasn't. But now it's become counterproductive because many times this characterization of other people becomes stereotypical and we give negative traits to those other people based on our categorization of them because simply we don't know them very well. They are other than we and we don't understand them, they do things differently, they eat differently, they look different, and so they somehow are frightening to us. And so we want to keep them away, keep them separate, and we give them negative traits. We think that they are lazy, we think they're avaricious, we think that they're untrustworthy. All of these kinds of things get associated as stereotypes with particular *Other* groups.

And so where we are is in a dilemma, because on the one hand there's nothing we can do about the way our brain categorizes; we will always categorize. We have to. It's the way our minds work. But what we can do is we learn to think about differences, differences among people as well as differences among clothing or food or what have you, as good rather than necessarily as scary and bad, so that we can think about people belonging to different groups and learn to value them, to say Ah! They aren't like my family, they aren't like my tribe, but that's an interesting tribe, and I'd like to know about them. We can learn to value the differences without putting our tribe higher than their tribe, or their tribe higher than our tribe. Unfortunately, we don't do that very easily. We really like when we make a category to also give it a value . . . to say this category, my tribe, is more valuable than that category, your tribe.

So, I think, in the world we need to find ways to teach each other tolerance for differences in a kind of active way, in which we want to learn how to recognize that the country we live in and the world we live in is populated by human beings who have enormous amounts of stuff in common. We're much more alike than we are different, and yet we do have different color hair and different color eyes and different color skins. But do these things really make a difference? Well, they do make some difference, and it's important to recognize that they do. But do they mean that we should be hostile to people . . . we should kill people? I don't think so . . . and yet we have historically killed people because they had different religion, because they had different skin color, because they belonged to a different country or because they spoke a different language. And none of those things are going to create the possibility of a community in which we can all live together. If we keep fighting, we're not going to live together, so if we're going to be good citizens of the world, we need to learn how to live with each other.

Listening 2

Linda: Oh, ya know, Michael, I really wanted to talk with you about something today. I'm so annoyed and frustrated, and I guess 'cause you're a man, I'll bring it up with you.

Michael: Uh oh, a man thing.

Linda: A man thing . . . and a woman thing, as always. You know, I've got this friend, a guy, and I've known him for so long, and he's obviously going through a bad situation now and feeling a lot of pain, and I can't get him to talk to me. I mean, is this a guy thing? If this were a woman, there would be no problem talking.

Michael: Well, what do you want him to talk about?

Linda: I want him to tell me how he feels; I think he's hurting. And I think he's keeping it inside, and it isn't good.

Michael: Well . . . I suppose you could look at it as being a guy thing, but I . . . it's the way that men and women talk about things that's different. I mean, generally, if a man was going to talk about something, he wants to talk about it because he has a problem and he wants to get a solution to it. Whereas if you talk to a woman, they just want to talk about how they feel about things and sort of work through it that way. It's a longer, slower, deeper, more revealing, all that kind of thing, conversation. And guys just want to talk about . . . this is my problem, so what do you think the solution is, or how should I fix it?

Linda: Well, that's all very nice and practical, but how do you get from that point of having a problem and jump all the way to solving it if you don't have that middle part of talking about how you feel? How do you know what your options are, what solutions are possible? I don't get it.

Michael: Well, it's not that you're jumping across things; it's just that . . . like if people have a . . . I think men and women both have a spectrum of things; there's the emotional part of them, and there's the problem-solving part of them, or something like that, and I think women tend to go more toward revealing their feelings and talking about that kind of thing. It's not . . . and men just say, "Well, it doesn't really matter how you feel about it because obviously you're really upset about it, so why don't we just not talk about that, because it's obvious and let's just get on to the solution." You know . . .

Linda: You know, it's interesting you said problem solving because I just saw a video recently about how, as early as pre-school, little girls and little boys problem solve differently.

Michael: Ah ha!

Linda: Yeah, it's true.

Michael: OK.

Linda: They show these little kids, they were maybe three or four, in a classroom, and the boys somehow got into a conflict over a truck. And guess how they dealt with it?

Michael: How? (laughs)

Linda: They threw the truck on the floor and started hitting each other.

Michael: Uh huh.

Linda: Typical, right? Typical male stuff. Now the girls . . .

Michael: Very direct.

Linda: Very direct.

Michael: Very direct.

Linda: That's what you're saying, though, isn't it? Aren't you saying that? OK. At the end I guess they solved the problem, but it was a little bit on the violent side.

Michael: Um hm.

Linda: Now, the girls in the same classroom were videotaped having also a conflict over who was going to play the mommy when they were playing house. And it got to be a problem 'cause all the girls wanted to be Mommy. What do you think happened?

Michael: Um . . .

Linda: You think they threw the doll?

Michael: No, I don't think they threw the doll, and they probably didn't pull hair.

Linda: No, they didn't.

Michael: What did they do?

Linda: Basically, they started to cry first; everybody was crying.

Michael: OK.

Linda: And then there was some whining, but they solved the problem by talking about it. And it was amazing, even though they were little . . . they would say, well, you know you were Mommy yesterday, you can be the mommy tomorrow, I'm going to do it today. And in their rather unsophisticated way, they talked about it. And when they were angry, they said they were angry. And at the end one of the girls was chosen to play the mommy, and they solved the problem. Now, why can't you do that?

Michael: Well, that's exactly what I was talking about.

Linda: No, it's not!

Michael: Yes, it is! They talked . . . the girls talked their way through, and about how they feel, and

you did it and trying to problem solve and all that kind of thing, and it takes some time and they reach their solution . . . the boys just went *bam!* You know . . . they just solved the problem right away without talking about it.

Linda: I think this must be genetic; I really do.

Michael: Well, actually . . . oh, caveman, right? Going back to the caveman.

Linda: Well, I didn't say that, but I just think there must be different mechanisms for dealing with problems (M: Right.) . . . that men have and women have, you know? And I feel bad that you don't do it our way. (laughs)

Michael: Oh, oh well, you know . . . thank you for your sympathy and your understanding. (laughs)

Linda: Anytime, Michael.

Listening 3

Neal: I'm a Democrat, and my view of the Republican and Democratic parties, at least in part, is this. In this country individualism is very important. And individualism means among other things that people on the basis of their hard work, their intelligence, and their determination can get ahead. They can be successful and they can climb the social ladder, or they can fall down the social ladder on the basis of their merits, on the basis of what they do.

Republicans want to basically remove government and lower the impact of government so that some people can succeed wildly and some people can fail amazingly badly. Whereas Democrats want to put some limits on that. Democrats do not want to make everybody alike, but they want to put some limits on how high those who succeed can go, and how low those who fail, or never succeed, can fall.

And I think that is good public policy. I think the Democrats have got it right. Because if the gap between those who have and those who have not becomes too great, there's enormous resentments built up at the bottom and enormous . . . at the top, enormous disdain for those at the bottom. And that is not a good and healthy social condition for any country.

Thomas: Basically, I think that a Democrat, or a Democratic administration, is trying to gain supporters by taking care of their needs. Or they are establishing a method of distributing wealth to various groups so that they can vote for them. Whereas the Republicans, I think, are more entitled, more considerate of the individual's needs, the individual taking care of themselves, and having less government and more responsibility for themselves.

Basically, I support the Republican party because I feel that the government does more to me than what I can do for myself. I think if they had less government I would be able to be more successful and to be able to create greater wealth and take care of my needs and my immediate family.

Stephen: To my way of understanding, the two major political parties in this country are the Democrats, the more liberal party, and the Republicans, which represent a more conservative point of view. Both of these are generally along scales that have to do with political and social and fiscal issues. Democrats tend to be more interested in finding ways that the government can expend the resources of the country in support of individual people. And the Republicans tend to find ways to expend the resources through organizations, traditionally businesses or other large groups of people. They both have legitimate reasons for why they think one way might be better than the other way. The Democrats always tend to be seen as the party that represents the working person. And the Republicans tend to be seen as the party which represents invested capital. And so to me those sort of define the two different ways that the parties can be seen. And it's not . . . although it sounds fairly clear-cut, it gets a little bit complicated because ours is a country which is based on an economic system which is capital focused, so the contributions of the individual are measured in terms of capital as well, so it's not as clear a distinction as it might otherwise sound to be. So now I am neither one of those. I am registered as an Independent. I have always been registered as an Independent because at the time that I first had to face the decision as to which way to go, I couldn't really decide which was the . . . neither one of the parties really defined, in its entirety, the way I felt about anything. Independents have . . . one of the nice things about being an Independent is that you don't get a lot of propaganda from any one of the parties; rather, you're really left alone to make up your own mind about things because your name isn't on any mailing list. One of the major negatives to it, however, is

that you don't get to participate in the pre-selection process, our primary process, which is the process through which candidates are selected before they stand for national election. So Independents can't vote in primaries because primaries are party events, and I'm not a member of any party.

But . . . and sometimes that's very frustrating, but I feel that the trade-off is that I feel I can make a much more objective decision between the parties and I can split my vote without feeling like I'm being disloyal to any group, so I can go into the voting booth and vote for a Democrat for one office and a Republican for another office and feel that I'm being true to myself without betraying a loyalty to some external party.

Video

I Wish I Had a Map

IT: I had some problem with the fact that some people didn't know really where Italy was. They were asking me . . . saying, "Yeah. I know, that's in Europe," and looking like, "Isn't it?"

GK: Well, I say, "You know it's Mediterranean. You know the Mediterranean Sea." And they say, "Yes." And I say, "Well, do you know Turkey?" "Yeah." "Well, it's between Italy and Turkey. Just in the . . . right in the middle."

IN: "Where is India? Is it somewhere near Africa? Is it somewhere in the Middle East? Are you from the Middle East?"

AF: Well, it wasn't the knowledge about Kenya specifically. It was more about knowledge of Africa as a whole. And because I found that there wasn't first of all, the knowledge about specific countries. You know, there was this view of Africa as, you know, one big country. Like one black hole. And outside of that there wasn't any knowledge.

SP: Some people think that Spain is in South America or in Mexico.

KO: They know where is Japanese . . . Japan, but they don't know where is Korea.

AF: When I was applying to colleges to come here, I had some schools, write, you know, Kenya, South Africa.

GK: I just, you know, smile . . . but I keep my thoughts to myself.

AF: Sometimes I just ignore people because I just don't have time, you know, to deal with that level of profound ignorance, and yet again sometimes I also refer people to the library.

GK: If they don't know where Greece is, that means that they don't want to know where Greece is.

AF: I wish I had a map.

IT: They ask me about the 3 M . . . that is, macaroni, mafia, and mandolino which can . . . or you can substitute mandolino with mama anyway. Which kind of pasta you have. They ask me for recipe . . . if I know how to cook this and that . . . if I can cook for them sometime.

AF: It's, you know, populated by, you know, savages swinging from trees.

IN: Do you eat meat? Followed by . . . do you worship cows?

AF: Someone asked me if, you know, we eat lions at home.

IN: Do you go to school on elephants?

AF: Are there cars in Kenya?

IN: Planes, trains, automobiles . . . we have them all.

AF: Were you living in a tree before you came here?

IN: Do you speak English?

AF: If it's a news program, what does the African woman in the scene look like? She is surrounded by flies, has at least one baby hanging off of her and she's exposed, you know, her body is exposed, either her breasts or whatever it is . . . or, you know, like a mule of the world, you know, toiling in the sun.

SP: They think that we are all very Catholic, and we go by the book, you know, no sex before getting married and no abortion, and all the children you want, go to Mass every Sunday.

IT: They expect you to wish to become a mother, to get married, something that's, you know, maybe not in my dreams, like taking care of the house.

SP: They think that women are submissive. They do what their husband wants them to do and they stay at home taking care of the children.

IT: I really hate cooking. And, you know, I'm not the kind of woman that, you know, can be classified as a would-be housewife or, you know, a would-be mother. I just hate children.

AF: The stereotype of Africans is that Africans are, you know, hypersexual, you know, base, immoral.

ITM: Basically, the stereotype of Italian men is to be

romantic and . . . I don't know how to say it, basically romantic and seductive with women.

SA: There is a myth about Latin lovers.

IT: It's true they think of me as an Italian madonna, you know, as the symbol of fertility.

AF: You're some kind of exotic fruit somehow because you're from somewhere else.

IT: I think that it's really embarrassing!

Chapter 5
Art, Society, and the Artist

Listening 1
Charles Olton

As an art historian I am interested in why art occurs in human communities. I study fine art, but what I say could apply to other forms of art. Art always occurs in contexts . . . social, historical, political, economic conditions are part of the context of art. Art, in other words, reflects those conditions. It either protests against them or celebrates them in one way or another.

Art also reflects its own traditions. There are connections and influences that artists cast upon one another.

When I look at a painting, I always look for the contemporary influences . . . the social and political and economic influences that helped shape the painter's ideas. And I also look for what the painting builds on or rejects in its own artistic tradition.

We call these influences the context of art or the conditions that give art its character. Let me give you an example: Renaissance art. The contemporary condition of Renaissance art was the end of the Medieval period, the decline of Medieval political organizations, the decline of Christian church power, the rise of the nation state, the increase of capitalism and wealth, and the discovery of the New World.

The artistic context of the Renaissance was a rejection of mystical themes, a rejection of Gothic forms, and a return to the Classicism of ancient Greece and Rome, which artists believed was more rational, had a greater clarity of form, and which focused on more universal concepts of beauty.

We can also think of context when we consider other kinds of art forms. Let's think of another art form of a much different kind . . . modern graffiti, which we might think of as modern cave painting. In the ancient times, prehistoric man painted their experiences, their fears, their angers, their ideas on the walls of caves. Today, modern graffiti painters put them on the walls of cities. And in so doing they express the economic conditions in which they live, urban poverty, anger, protest. They are political and social outcasts often, and they express their ideas in this way.

Graffiti art also reflects an artistic rejection of the traditional materials of art, of paint and paper. Instead, graffiti artists use spray paint, and they paint on the urban environment itself.

What we said about graffiti or about Renaissance art could also be said about many other artistic, visual expressions . . . illustration, for example, political cartooning, its subjects and its visual forms reflect a context, just like Renaissance painting, just like graffiti. Or design, modern design which reflects modern interests, needs, designs, desires, fears, and tastes. Modern design too has a context, both artistic and social.

In conclusion, whenever we look at a piece of visual art, we need to think about its context, because the context will help us understand its meaning.

Listening 2

Marjorie Vai: In Dean Olton's talk, he discusses the fact that art always exists in a context. And he talks specifically about two contexts, the social context, which includes social, political, etc. factors, and the artistic tradition; that's a different context. We're now looking at two pieces of art here, and I was wondering if we could discuss them, or if you could discuss them in those terms. The first is an African stool, and maybe you can tell us a little bit more about that. What was the social context of that stool?

Brian Brooks: This stool was used by the chief to assert his power and his rank and his status as a chief. The artist uses the image of a woman as the conveyor of the powers of nature, and the chair itself is an image of this woman holding up the king.

MV: OK, and what about the artistic traditions within which this piece appeared?

BB: The artists of this culture were required to use one single block of wood without cutting any pieces apart from each other. The whole form had to be made from one single piece. And the artist did several things that are within his tradition. The artist exaggerates the size of the head so that the idea that the spirit dwells within the head, as the most important part of the body, is understood. And also the artist plays down the role of the fingers and the toes and the feet as well. You also see that to get the idea of rank and status of this woman as a conveyor of nature, as a way to communicate nature, that the headdress is one that is traditionally known as a headdress of somebody who has high status and rank, and also the marks on her body is also a sign of rank, much the way you would see a sergeant have stripes on his arm to signify rank.

MV: Is there anything that you think this artist might have done that is innovative and a little different? Is there anything special about this piece?

BB: Yes. If you can imagine this being a cylinder like a tree originally, and you look from the top down, you would see spiral rings that come from the outside and move to the . . . get smaller as you get closer to the center of the stool, the part that the king sits on. And also at the same time you can see rings on the woman's face, and those rings are perfectly lined up with the symmetrical, the balanced left and right of the eye, the nose, the lips in the center of the face. They're also rings that emerge from a trunk that came out of the tree, and the artist's choice to use a branch in this particular place on this particular tree makes it very, very significant and also a very strong piece and a connection to both the tree but also as the stool itself.

MV: Oh, that's very interesting. OK, the second piece we're looking at is a Jacques Villon, called *La Philosophe*, and it's a twentieth-century piece of art. Could we first, again, discuss the social context that that came in?

BB: Yes, artists at this time, especially within this particular style that is known as Cubism, were responding to the tradition of painting the human figure, but in this case the artist was also aware of how photography, but also moving images of film, were now probably considered more objective and better able to represent nature as the way it is seen. So artists that were working in the Cubist tradition were very, very aware of this; also they were, by some thinking, that they anticipated Einstein's theory of relativity and the fact that time can be experienced in different ways depending on a person's experiences.

MV: And that shows up in the way things are broken up on the surface?

BB: Yes, and what's happening here is that since the nineteenth century the artist's still working with traditional forms like the figure but approaching the form in entirely different, radical way. You see that the details that we assume we would see on a figure, such as fingers, anatomy details of the nose, the mouth, the feet, and other particulars, are deemphasized, and what is emphasized more so is the design of the picture. The use of triangles and shapes in some kind of harmony, musical harmony with each other as important to the picture as the figure itself.

MV: So, in other words, the African sculptor was more or less following the artistic traditions of his time, whereas this Cubist picture was sort of revolutionary compared to the . . .

BB: Yes, and I think that that's a good way of putting it; I think that these are both working within . . . one is working within a tradition that was expected that the artist would work in, that is, the Luba artist, needing to fulfill the requirements and follow this tradition, and in general Cubism was a rejection against earlier traditions.

MV: Great, thank you.

BB: Thank you.

Listening 3

One can analyze epoch after epoch—from the Stone Age to our own day—and see that there is no form of art which does not also play an essential political role.

Through art we express our concept of what nature is not.

Art is nothing but humanized science . . . Music is but a living application of mathematics.

Painting completes culture, helps human relations, and explores the mysteries of the universe.

In order to speak more concretely we may call (art) the grandchild of nature, and from these same things is born painting. So therefore we may justly speak of it as the grandchild of nature and as related to God himself.

Art does not reproduce the visible; it makes visible.

Art is either plagiarism or revolution!

Video*

remnants by Reiko Tahara

Telephone conversation

Hello, Mabu?

Oh, hi, Sister?

Yeah. How are you?

I'm fine.

How's Tokyo? As usual?

Yeah, yeah, nothing changes . . .

* *Telephone conversation (in English, cross fades from Japanese conversation)*

Oh, hi, sister?

Yeah. How's your life?

Umm . . . OK.

How's Tokyo? As usual?

Yeah, yeah, nothing changes.

How's Mom and Dad?

They're doing fine.

So . . . how's your school?

School?

Yeah.

Nmm . . . bad.

(Laughter) Bad? What do you mean, "bad"? Are you doing OK at school?

No, I think I've failed. (laughter)

I know. That's what Mom told me. But why do you skip the classes so often?

I don't know. I don't like economics. So boring.

Well, what are you gonna do? You spent two years to get into this college, didn't you?

Yeah, but . . . what can I do? That's the only school that I got into.

* *TV commentator (male voice)*

In Japan, "change" is the word on everybody's lips. Japanese salary-men and women are fed up with the status quo. They wanna change the system that has made Japan the world's number-two economic superpower.

*Italicized parts are in Japanese.

* Woman's voice

Tradition and modernization. Others and myself. Is there anything real? Or is everything imaginary?

People are dancing in each era, in each style. In my imagination? In their imagination? Or someone else's intention?

She is walking down the street in New York City. A strange glance exchanged. And we pass by. Why can't I smile at her? Why do I need to smile at her? It's not necessary. Am I judging the other? Or scared of seeing my reflection on the other?

Running. I am running. I guess, I'm afraid of accepting all the symbolic meanings of images that I create. So I start listening to my family.

* Woman's voice

Japan is heaven now, grandma says.

*Grandma's voice: "If you recall the days during the war, Japan is now like heaven."

Why? Are we all dreaming? Or are we all dead? No, no, she says. You don't know the difficult time. We should appreciate the people who rebuilt Japan. I know she really likes sitting in the backseat of her grandchildren's cars while they drive.

* Telephone conversation

So, why don't you change your school?

You mean, why don't I lose a couple of more years for those stupid exams?

Well, you're still young.

Not really.

You told me you wanted to be a teacher. I think you can do it if you really try hard.

You say that because you're woman, and you're not here.

*Woman's voice

A fun time at the summer festival. Japanese tradition in my sister's memory.

* Sister's voice: "It's so crowded at a summer festival and everybody's happy . . . it would be so fun to have those things."

Tradition seems so far away. Tradition and modernization, both are fantasies. We buy and make products to satisfy our fantasies. Efforts to look stronger and more sophisticated becomes another tradition.

My sister wore both traditional and Western wedding dresses when she got married. She looked very beautiful in the Western wedding dress.

TV commentator (male voice)

The Japanese have assembled their vision of America, product by product, and made it their own.

Woman's voice

Japan is now like America, Grandma says. Why not? America was the role model of postwar Japan, wasn't it? She never expected that Japan would really become like America.

*Grandma's voice: "I never thought Japan would really become like America."

The archetypal image of future Japan via the image of America, or the West was just a mirror reflection. It never comes out. It is never reached.

Don't worry about tradition, Grandma says. History is moving, but we don't change anyway. Saying so, she smiles.

Family conversation—Woman: *"Is Japanese tradition. . . . "* Little boy: *"What is 'tradition'?"* Woman: *"'Tradition' is . . . something like . . . I'll tell you later!"* (laughter of Grandma and little boy)

* Telephone conversation

I think you can do it if you really try hard.

You say that because you are a woman, and you're not here. I'm the first son. I know I'm supposed to graduate from college, work for a decent company, get married, and have kids.

Yeah, but . . . do you think you can do it?

I don't know . . . I just need a little time to think. Everything goes so fast here. I feel so out of place.

* Brother's voice: "I've got to do it, anyway, but . . . this sense of time, time, time seems discouraging me to go on."

* TV commentator (female voice, crossfades from B's voice)

In four years, they will be graduated from college and, you know, you will be the backbone of Japanese society. You will be her salaried workers, your white-collar workers, sitting in your offices nine to five. . . .

* Brother's voice (crossfades from commentator's voice): "It's time that is important in Japan. Starting work at nine and finishing at five, extra work till

eight . . . I don't fit in those things . . . I don't, can't . . . I can't fit, I guess."

* *Woman's voice*

Shu, my sister's first son. He is making a yard. What's this tallest building, Shu? He says it's his father's company. How about that gray building? He says it's his father's company, too. The same answer to the third building.

We find a small red brick in his yard. Is it also your father's company? No, it is Shu's house. His very very tiny house.

A briefcase outside his yard. It's my dad's bag! Don't you know? Shu says with a triumphant look.

* Family talk—Mom: *"What's the tallest building, Shu?"* Shu: *"This one? This is my papa's company."* Shu: *"Look, look! I made this all!"* Shu: *"This one is Papa's company. A very very tall papa's company!"* Grandma: *"Which is your house, Shu?"* Shu: *"Shu's house is a much much smaller one. This is my house!"* (laughter) Shu: *"This is Papa's bag."*

Family talk in airport—Announcement: *"Final announcement for the passengers of Canadian Airline flight number . . . "* Dad: *"Isn't that your flight?"* Woman: *"This is it! This is my flight. Via Toronto . . . "* Sister: *"She said that was the final notice."* Woman: *"OK, OK. I will be going now."*

* *Woman's voice* (crossfades from family talk)

The impression that Shu has of his father cruelly resembles the one that I had of my father until the day he retired. How many bags do they need to carry while people talk about "changes"?

I ask my father to talk to me in front of the camera. He says, "Of course not. Give me your question sheet. I'll type up the answers and send it back to you."

*Family talk at airport—Woman: *"Will you promise you'll write the answers and send them back to me?"* Father: *"Hurry up. You'd better go now."*

TV commentator (male voice)

There are two attitudes in Japan now, the old—shikata-ga-nai; what can you do?"—and the new—we'll manage. Hell, we're not gonna take it anymore." If the Japanese people get mad enough, that could be real change, and improve U.S.–Japan relation . . .

Woman's voice

I wonder how my mom can always be so optimistic and nonchalant. Maybe because she is religious. Maybe it's an inherited character from Grandma. Or it's the good tradition of the Japanese mama. Tradition is something unspoken being passed on in each family. Look at your sister. She is holding her baby just in the same way as I was holding all of you.

If we are spiritually independent, nothing would bother us, my mother says. But how about Japan's cultural independence? Not from America, or the West. But from Japan's corporate world, which they have totally trusted. How much they have admired security. And how much we are bored with it. My sister's message for her kids is, again, to be independent.

Woman's voice

It is spring. I'm trying to finish this film. A few days ago, my father called me and said Shu entered a very good private kindergarten. He walks proudly under the cherry blossom tree.

* Family talk—Woman: *"What will you become when you are bigger, Shu?"* Shu: *"Of course a doctor!"* Grandma: *"Ohohohoho."* (laughter)

A good kindergarten. A good elementary school. A good junior high. Shu has already started climbing the steps of the Japanese competitive world to bring security to his family.

*Family talk—Woman: *"So who do you think are controlling our lives now?"* Shu: *"Control..!"* Woman: *"Leave 'control' alone, Shu."* (laughter) Grandma: *"It is, after all, congressmen's job to decide those matters."*

Still running through the haunting images of others. My family . . . they weren't others. I thought I knew them. I thought they knew me. In a sense, it was true. Now, my family members are the others locked into video images existing in my own imagination. What they speak in the images do not stop me, nor my brother, from running. But their words have unspoken power to make us speak to others.

*Family talk—Brother: *"It's so sour, seriously!"* (laughter) Brother: *"These are the oranges we took from our yard."* Mom: *"I'm making orange jelly for Reiko so that she can bring it back with her to America."* Sister: *"Reiko, Reiko, Mabu said he* *wouldn't take it anymore. Mabu, why don't you eat more!"* (laughter)

There are things which do not need to be spoken. And there are things which do need to be spoken. Generation to generation. People to people. Voices to be heard. Generation to generation. People to people . . . to be heard.

I never imagined what those dancing people were thinking about. I was scared. But also, I knew I always wanted to dance with them.

Chapter 6
Smarts!

Listening 1

Mara Krechevsky

Traditionally, people have thought of intelligence as being a single entity, something that you can measure with a test like an I.Q. test. And usually people think of intelligence as involving primarily linguistic and logical/mathematical kinds of abilities. Scores on these tests have been very important in school, for instance, in selecting students for special programs like gifted and talented programs.

In 1983 Howard Gardner came up with a different notion of what an intelligence is. He devised a theory called the theory of multiple intelligences. And this theory says that an intelligence should not be defined by how people perform on individualized pencil and paper tests . . . which, usually, as I said, tap linguistic and mathematical capabilities. But, rather, we should think of intelligence as representing the ability to create a product or to solve a problem that is meaningful to all of us, in cultures all over the world. So he wanted to look at what are the meaningful kinds of products, and roles and tasks that people perform and then what is involved in leading up to these projects, products, roles, and so forth.

He had a set of eight criteria that he used to determine whether or not an ability counted as an intelligence. For instance, he looked at whether he could identify these abilities in the brain; he looked at special populations such as savants, autistic individuals, and highly gifted individuals. He looked at whether he could identify core capacities or key abilities for each intelligence like rhythm and pitch

in music. And he looked at what was valued in different cultures. And then, based on these kinds of criteria, he came up with a list of seven, and currently there are eight, intelligences. These intelligences are linguistic and logical/mathematical, the two that many of us usually think of as involving intelligence. People who can communicate easily through language or individuals who can use or appreciate abstract relations, in the case of logical/mathematical. But then he also identified five and now six other intelligences, including musical intelligence, which allows people to create, communicate, and understand meanings made out of sound, spatial intelligence, which makes it possible for us to perceive visual or spatial information and then perhaps transform this information. Bodily–kinesthetic intelligence, which refers to using your whole body or parts of your body, like your hands or your mouth, to create products or solve problems. And then finally two personal intelligences: intrapersonal intelligence, which refers to a very good understanding of yourself and how to use an understanding of yourself, what are your strengths and weaknesses, to be effective in the world. And interpersonal, which refers to the ability to understand other people and to interact effectively with them.

Most recently, he's also identified what he calls a naturalist intelligence, which is someone who is very sensitive to the natural and physical world around them—flora and fauna and so on. A gardener or a farmer or a botanist are examples of individuals with naturalist intelligence.

Listening 2

MV: Well, you know in this unit we're talking about multiple intelligences, the seven intelligences as opposed to the traditional two intelligences. And although I might have some questions about this, what I think is really, really interesting about this is that . . . it can make teachers aware that people have different learning styles. And that if they have different learning styles and they address those different learning styles and sort of adapt their teaching, that it might help with the learning process. But I was wondering if we could look at it today and go through these seven intelligences and see if there's some way, if a student looks at themselves and looks at these descriptions and decides that they have, you know, they're strong in one area and they're strong in another area, how they can change their behavior as learners and perhaps help themselves with that. So why don't we go through them one at a time? And, of course, the first is linguistic intelligence.

Victoria Kimbrough: Yeah, that one seems like anyone that has the linguistic intelligence is just going to naturally be able to learn languages. And almost all of the things that apply to them would apply to being a good language learner.

MV: Actually, this was another thing that was very comforting about this; I remember in the old days, if you thought you weren't good at linguistic things and language, that you couldn't be a good language learner, and I think now this is helping us to be aware that we can even if we're not so strong.

VK: Right, I think we'll find a lot of ways that other people that don't necessarily have a concentration of linguistic intelligence can still be good language learners and use their intelligence type to be good language learners.

MV: Now the second one is logical/mathematical, and this might be the trickiest. But I kind of think that since logical/mathematical may involve patterns and that, that people who are good at this might find some comfort or might find some security in looking at the patterns in languages and being comfortable with them so that they feel that they have some kind of base.

VK: Right, and seeing how different patterns relate to each other using the . . . because almost every book will have some sort of grammatical diagram in it somewhere. And people who have the logical/mathematical intelligence might want to pay more attention to those grammatical diagrams, or paradigms, as they're called. Or even if the book doesn't have them, the person with the mathematical intelligence might want to take what they've learned in class and put it into a diagram (**MV:** Yeah, that's a good idea.) of some kind so that they can see the patterns more clearly in the diagram.

MV: Yeah, they should get some satisfaction out of that because they have a sense of patterns and things.

VK: And even fill in blanks in patterns that weren't necessarily brought up in class. That would be like a puzzle.

MV: Or even finding books that are organized that way outside of the classroom, books.

VK: Yeah, exactly, looking . . . if the classroom book is organized more communicatively and with not so much grammar in it, they might find a book that emphasizes patterns.

MV: Now, spatial intelligence, I guess that's the one I associate with visual intelligence and art although it is other things, but I tend to think of it as visual. Obviously, pictures would help this kind of person. (**VK:** Right.) And what other kinds of visual stimulus do you think?

VK: Well, I think this . . . people with this kind of intelligence would do real well to concentrate on watching television and connecting words to what's going on, on television. Looking at images and then even making images in their mind when they're trying to learn vocabulary words, they might want to imagine something that would help them remember that word and (**MV:** Oh, that's a good idea.) images that way.

MV: Connecting it with images. And things like magazines and comics, using them as resources, and maybe to extend your idea of vocabulary, when they see a picture, connect it with a word in a magazine, they might put a list together and put them on cards, and keep them.

OK, the next one is musical intelligence, and this one is another one that I think is a little tricky and stretching it a little; I have a hard time getting beyond the sense that people with musical intelligence can pick up the rhythm and the sounds of the language, which is very, very helpful. But what other things do you think might come up with musical intelligence?

VK: Well, I think that people who have that kind of intelligence would feel particularly comfortable working with songs and learning the language through songs, putting a rhythm and a beat to the words that they're learning.

MV: Yeah . . . that's very interesting, 'cause the philosophy, in a sense, in this book is to do something else and language is sort of a by-product (**VK:** Oh . . . yeah.), and the songs are like that. If you really love getting into the music, and you sort of automatically memorize the words and then later realize you know all that language, that might be a great approach for somebody like that.

VK: And there are lots of songs that tell stories, and so the stories . . . not only do you remember them better and remember the vocabulary better, but it forms a natural context for the language, because you've got the story along with the music . . . that helps.

MV: And also a lot of songs have a lot of colloquialisms in them and idioms. OK, the next one is bodily intelligence, physical intelligence, physical skills, liking to do things with your body, or just liking to do things, really, people who like to fix and put things together—what are some ideas that you might come up with, with that?

VK: Well, I think that anything that you would be able to do as you're learning would be a help.

MV: Games, physical games.

VK: And connecting gestures (MV:Yeah, that's a good one.) to what . . . because language is so full of these gestures, and body language is so important when you're learning a language, that people with this kind of intelligence might be particularly drawn to always putting together the language that they're learning with the expression, with the movement, with the way the body moves, and they might really enjoy learning the way people interact physically with each other in that culture.

MV: OK, the next is interpersonal intelligence. Which has to do with the way that you relate to other people. This is people that are very good at relating well to other people, and this is sort of an easy one for language I think. (VK: Right.) I guess this is where, when we tell people take risks and go out, if you live in an English-speaking country, and get out there and talk to people and ask them questions, and find yourself in social situations, this is a good one for that.

VK: Even if you don't live in a country, you can call an English-speaking embassy and ask for information or call, get the phone numbers of your classmates and just call them up if you're a person who likes to work with other people, just be sure you'll enjoy actually talking to other people.

MV: So that's pretty straightforward. Now intrapersonal is, my understanding of it is that it's someone who is reflective. And I remember, way back when I was learning French, that I would sort of think of the way that I use language and practice putting sentences in my head and then analyze it

and remember was this the way to do it, and have sort of imaginary little conversations in my head, and I wonder if that isn't an expression of that kind of skill?

VK: Oh, yes, and that's an interesting way to do it. I know that sometimes I will plan when I'm trying to speak another language, I always plan what I'm going to say in my head before I say it, so I think that's an extension of that. And keeping a journal would be another thing that someone that is more introspective might enjoy doing.

Listening 3

Karen: After reviewing the different intelligences I find myself to be linguistic, physical, musical, and a combination of interpersonal and intrapersonal. In my work as assistant to the deans at the New School for Social Research for eight and a half years, I have brought to the job many different skills, and I feel that the interpersonal and the intrapersonal are the very important skills in that kind of job where you deal with everybody . . . and you deal with people in the administration and you deal with people on the street and you deal with students who are . . . put their lives in your hands for four years. I am problem solving, constantly, every day. It's very stressful. But I'm a good advisor, and I'm able to listen to people's problems and get them solved quickly.

And also on the side there I was finishing my bachelor of arts degree at the New School. And on Saturdays and Sundays I would be singing, professionally singing. I sang at the Apollo, I sing at weddings and funerals (which is the downside), but still work, and I enjoy that a lot because I believe that you can touch people that you don't even know by sound.

I feel that my outgoing personality and my need to get information across to people who I feel are not getting it is what has allowed me to go forth and carve out what I hope to be a career in media . . . in the media. And I would love to be an assistant producer for public television. And I believe that my ability to work and solve problems and to see what is important in people and bring it to the forefront is a very big asset for public TV and something that the world needs. And I also believe that in public television you can bring forth various kinds of music. And I believe that jazz, which is where my roots are, is something that portrays what's in your heart, which is why I love the music. And I feel that is really important . . . and what people need to see and you don't see that on regular commercial television, and I really think that that would be an asset to the world, not just my small society.

George: In reviewing the seven categories I was actually quite pleased to find that what I doing in my professional life, as well as (to a certain extent) my personal life, was corroborated or validated by the. . . by my complete agreement of three of the descriptions. I'm a public relations professional; I'm director of communications at a university. And I found that I related very much with most of the issues on the interpersonal intelligence description in terms of being comfortable, in terms of being a good advisor to people, in terms of having several people you could consider a good friend. I think I do and I should professionally and personally have exemplary interpersonal skills and enjoy that part of myself, so I guess that's why I'm pretty satisfied with what I do for a living. The other two areas that I related to most strongly were the linguistic area—I write a lot, I read a lot, I speak a lot to groups. And then the visual and spatial intelligence. A good part of what I do in my professional life is working with artists and art directors and designers; in my personal life I go to museums.

Robert: After reviewing the descriptions of the different categories, I should say that in my life I already do so many different things and have had to develop skills that involve so many different areas that fit into many of those descriptions that I wouldn't say that one was completely me. Although my strongest ones were, I would say, intrapersonal, visual, and then interpersonal intelligence . . . with mathematics following close behind. In my life, having my own business, running a photography department at a university, and also being a creative artist requires everything from administrative duties, which are very logical . . . then I also have a strong need to be alone, to think, to work things out, to basically isolate, where I would even say intrapersonal is my strongest because almost all of those descriptions fit. And then also obviously being creative—the visual impacts everything and impacts all of the others. In the administrative work that I do, I mean typically everything ends up being visual no matter if I'm trying to make it that or not. So I

mean I just feel like I have three different areas physically in life. So I guess that I would say that some of the descriptions are quite accurate, but it depends which area of my life I'm moving in at the moment.

Chapter 7

Crime as Entertainment

Listening 1

Robert Polito

Detective fiction, as you know, begins with the short stories of Edgar Allen Poe in the middle of the nineteenth century. But you could say that crime fiction starts much earlier—in fact, you could probably say that American literature begins with the crime novel, Charles Brockton Brown's *Wieland*, published in 1798, in which a character hears voices telling him to kill his family.

Politicians and editorial writers like to condemn contemporary literature and film for its reliance on violence and shock. But their attitude, it seems to me, amounts to a kind of historical amnesia. One of the things they forget, for instance, is that Shakespeare's Globe theater burned down when a cannonball that was fired off during one of the scenes in Henry VII landed on the roof and set it ablaze. So shock value was obviously a great part of the appeal of Elizabethan drama.

Murder has been the subject of so much great literature, from the earliest Greek tragedies which are, in fact, about almost nothing else, through Shakespeare's *Hamlet* and *Macbeth*, and on into the present. And I think the appeal really is ultimately quite serious. Murder is still one of those events in which the universe appears to crack open and every crucial ethical, moral issue jumps out at you, impossible to ignore.

Perhaps violence can seem more acceptable when it is safely confined to the classics, and more distant from us in space and time. Modern media, such as television crime shows, video games, and gangsta rap in music, can make violence seem something absolutely pervasive and new. But, of course, violence was as real a force for the original audiences of the classics as it remains for us today.

Listening 2

David: I saw *Natural Born Killers* the other day, and I thought it was really cool.

Robyn: You did? Oh I just, I couldn't go see *Natural Born Killers*.

David: Really?

Robyn: Yeah, I just think the whole idea of it is so terrible. (D: Yeah.) It's just it's violent, and. . . .

David: It's weird, but I think it's, like, a good kind of escapism type of thing, you know, I mean. . . .

Robyn: Well, how can you feel like you're escaping when you're seeing people being killed? I mean . . . I, really, I respect Oliver Stone as a director, but I think it's sort of irresponsible to sensationalize crime like that.

David: Right. Yeah, well, I agree, I certainly understand, but it's like . . . I don't know, because it's a movie and because it's in the context of a movie, I think it's very easy, at least for me, to just kind of view it . . . not as like . . . I mean certainly I wouldn't say, you know, I think someone should go out and just kill people, I mean in real life I would be obviously totally against that. But as, like, a movie, you know, just like you can see things or read a book or think about things that you would never really do. But, just sometimes, like, living that experience can kind of have a cathartic effect of just like cleansing out that violence that's inside of you, or something, that you might see in the movie, or something, and you kind of connect with it, and you live it, and you feel it and then when the movie's over it's over and then you can kind of go back and be just a normal person again. If that makes sense.

Robyn: But don't you think that all of that violence is damaging to us? We're exposed to it so much. Oliver Stone (D: Right) makes a film about two teenagers who, you know, are really cool because they're killing people (D: Right) and on TV you see violence all of the time; all of these magazine shows are always doing crime stories. And I just think it's everywhere. We need more beauty in our lives. (D: No, I totally, I agree.) I think it has a bad effect on us.

David: But by the same token if you create only, like, beautiful movies or something like that, that's denying a very real part of reality and the human character which is, I mean there is . . . Everyone does have a dark part of themselves. You know that not everything in life is beautiful, and only, to like, present that is going to create an additional false sense of reality.

Robyn: Well, there just, there needs to be a balance.

David: Yeah, I mean I'm totally behind supporting positive values and stuff in films. Especially for kids, you know, that are still in that process of kind of forming their own identity. But for adults, I mean, I don't know, I guess at my heart I'm basically a very libertarian type of person. I mean I believe in the First Amendment. I believe that people should have the ability (R: but . . .) to see or do or think whatever they want as long as it's not negatively impacting society.

Robyn: Well, that's just the point. I believe that liberty is important but it's also a responsibility. (D: Oh, of course, I totally believe that.) I don't believe that there should be a law against making these films, but at the same time I think that our freedom means that we have the responsibility to try to do something positive in our world.

Listening 3

John Douglas

One of the things I've discovered in my ten years of selling murder mystery books . . . both through discussing the subject with writers, going to conferences and in my own reading and observations that very near the heart of the whole phenomenon is a longing for understanding about the roots of injustice and even the cause of death and people long to have that . . . the roots of those things exposed and eradicated . . . or taken away. So whether . . . let's put it this way, people are so troubled by injustice in their daily walk, and by the incomprehensibility of violence, that whether they want release from that uncertainty and fear by reading a story where the roots of the violence and injustice are isolated and ripped out of the social fabric or whether, on a cruder level, they simply wish to blow away all those things in a satisfying burst of violence, why either of those releases can be available through various types of crime fiction.

Laura Morgan

I show all sorts of films to students, and in a dark room they express their feelings very freely, and often when on the screen someone is being hurt . . . beaten up . . . tortured . . . killed . . . the students laugh, and in the darkness no one can see them and I feel they are expressing themselves quite freely. And what they're expressing is quite frightening because they're showing that they enjoy . . . watching someone else being hurt. It may be because it's not them if they're the victors, maybe because, well, they can get up and walk out of the theater and vicariously experience danger and death and then survive, but it's quite frightening to me and it reminds me of an old saying that the difference between tragedy and comedy is point of view: if something bad happens to someone else, it's a comedy; if it happens to you, it's a tragedy. And, of course, film audiences are spectators always.

Video

Narrator: Peter Montgomery is on Death Row, convicted of murder in the first degree for the killing of Carlos Ramos, a parking lot attendant, on the night of February 14th. Montgomery's defense lawyers are trying to stay the execution, claiming the crime was committed while Montgomery was sleepwalking and therefore not in his right mind.

Peter Miller, Defense Lawyer: My client was not in his right mind. He should be sent to a psychiatrist, not to the electric chair. The jury found evidence to condemn my client, who is now only a week away from death.

Geoffrey Scott, Psychiatrist: I can tell you that somnambulists are capable of committing this crime, but I cannot say whether or not Mr. Montgomery was sleepwalking at the time of the crime.

Narrator: The following is a section of the dramatized video made by the New York Police Department while reconstructing the crime.

Police assume Montgomery got up from bed pretending to be sleepwalking at approximately 2:54 a.m. He walked to the kitchen, picked up the murder weapon, and went out to find his victim, Carlos Ramos.

Many witnesses testified to having seen Montgomery walking the streets in his pajamas as he was heading towards the parking lot. A security camera in the parking lot at 243 Grand Avenue captured the images when Montgomery entered the parking lot and first spoke to Carlos Ramos.

Minutes later, Montgomery leaves the parking lot in a silver car.

That same car, a silver Mazda with plate numbers 723 XLM, was reported stolen from the parking lot and was found by police the morning of February 15th in front of Montgomery's apartment building. Ramos's body was found severely slashed and unrecognizable.

Montgomery: I didn't know what I was doing when I killed Carlos Ramos.

Mrs. Montgomery: My son always did strange things when he was sleepwalking.

Mrs. Ramos: Carlos was such a good son. He always brought money home to take care of his little sisters. He had such a promising future.

Margaret Harris, Prosecuting Lawyer: Peter Montgomery passed by the parking lot in his pajamas various nights before. He was planning the whole thing to get away with the murder of Carlos Ramos, and he must be punished for it. The jury has done the right thing.

Sandra Reinhart, Psychiatrist: Even if Mr. Montgomery was sleepwalking before the murder, he would have woken up with the violent actions.

Montgomery: I never learned how to drive a stickshift car. I'm very frightened of them, and there are a lot of witnesses that could have told you I never would have driven one in my right mind.

Reinhart: Sleepwalkers are not in control of their actions. They obtain abilities they don't normally have because they are not conscious of their fears.

Scott: Sleepwalkers look like they are awake, but they're not. The dream takes over, and there is a whole different set of rules. I'm sure all of us can recall a dream where we were acting very differently than we would in "real life."

Harris: Montgomery must be a very smart man because, I must admit, it's hard to believe that a person with no prior record planned such a perfect crime.

Miller: It is absolutely impossible for someone to acquire capacities like driving and beating someone up as well as violent behavior unless he was not aware of what was happening. He had no motive. He didn't even know the victim, and there is not one reasonable explanation.

Mrs. Montgomery: Peter would not kill a fly. He was a . . . he's such a good boy. I can't understand this at all.

Montgomery: In the name of God, I promise I had no intention of killing anyone, much less someone I didn't even know.

Anthony Koppeloff, Detective: The other set of keys to the car was never found, which means someone else has that set of keys. And when I went and spoke with Montgomery's doorman, he confirmed to me that people came in prior to Montgomery leaving, which means Montgomery could have been brought to the parking lot by somebody else.

Harris: Montgomery has seen the video and the evidence, and neither he nor his lawyers can prove that he didn't do it.

Miller: No one could establish when Carlos Ramos was actually murdered. I strongly suspect he was killed after Montgomery left the parking lot.

Scott: Somnambulists are generally passive people who will delightfully receive and obey orders. It's very possible that a third person led Montgomery in and out of the parking lot, and that he was just doing what he was told.

Witness: I was walking by the parking lot, and I thought it was kind of strange to see someone driving in his pajamas. Seconds later two guys go into the parking lot, and I didn't think anything of it.

Narrator: Two other men did walk into the parking lot, as was shown by the parking lot security camera, but they were regarded as regular clients.

Mrs. Ramos: Carlos had such a strange feeling that something bad would happen to him that day. He owed some money to some bad people.

Montgomery: The day after the murder I found a lot of drawers open, and I couldn't find any money. I figured I had done some things in my sleep, but it could have been someone else was in my apartment. A lot of people know I sleepwalk.

Psychic Reader: I see Carlos. He wants to tell you something.

Mrs. Ramos: What is it?

Psychic Reader: He wants to tell you that he's close by. That he's near a river.

Mrs. Ramos: Purgatory.

Psychic Reader: Oh no, he's not dead. He's alive, but he's just hiding.

Miller: The body of the victim was so cut up that it is hard to believe the kitchen knife did the job. No

one was able to recognize the victim since the dental slides could not be matched. It could perfectly be someone else.

Harris: If that is not Carlos Ramos, then where is he?

Mrs. Ramos: My son could be alive. He could be hiding someplace to be safe.

Koppeloff: There's another person missing. His name is Stephen Gomez, and he has the same physical characteristics as Carlos Ramos.

Narrator: Both the prosecutor and the jury agree in saying that no credibility can be given to the psychic reader Mrs. Ramos visited. They believe Carlos Ramos is still dead.

Miller: This could cause unrepairable harm to my client, made believe that he is a murderer. We will have to sue.

Montgomery: I repeat, I am innocent and I should be given another chance . . . what a terrible nightmare.

Narrator: As Peter Montgomery still awaits execution, people all over the world are having their say. The defense is trying to arouse support from public opinion.

Second Narrator: If you think Peter Montgomery is innocent and should be acquitted, please dial 1-800-STY-LIVE.

Narrator: And so is the prosecution.

Second Narrator: If you think Peter Montgomery should be executed, please dial 1-800-YUR-DEAD.

Chapter 8
Work in the 21st Century

Listening 1

Vivian Eyre: In 1987 the Department of Labor asked the Hudson Institute to conduct a study on how the changing demographics in the country would affect the workplace in the 21st century. This study, which is known to us now as "Workforce 2000," showed three important issues to business: one is that the face of the American workplace will be changing, that 33% of the workforce will be minorities, with major growth in Asian and Hispanic communities. The second thing it showed is that there will be a globalization of business, and what that means is that business is going to need to expand to foreign markets . . . and third, that technology will be a part of every worker's job, regardless of the job, regardless of the level within the company.

Today, business is trying to understand these changes and to cope with them, and so are employees. We've held in the past a traditional view about employers, that somehow employers will take care of us, they'll know our career path, and once we get in that career path we'll succeed. But there's a new thinking coming today where people are starting to think about their own careers, and they're starting to call themselves "Me Inc." In other words, think about my skills as if I were a corporation. This means that I have to regularly evaluate: "What are my strengths? What are my liabilities?" and to be able to build on my strengths and minimize my liabilities.

What we learned from the Hudson Report is that by the year 2000, every new entrant into the workplace can expect to have ten jobs by the time he or she retires. These future jobs are going to require more skills. Skills in technology, in reading, in math, and in critical thinking. So people who are going to be successful are going to need to be lifelong learners. So think about it—for the first time in our history, age will no longer determine the beginning or the end of a person's education.

Listening 2

Vivian Eyre: After twenty-five years in human resources, people often ask me if I have any tips for how the average person can be successful. And some of those ideas are first of all, to really continue your education; a high school degree is no longer going to be enough for even the most entry level positions. Second, find a teacher who can really teach you business skills. Business skills such as computer skills, business finance, and communication and interpersonal skills. Those skills will be so important as you try and advance up the corporate ladder. Third, to take charge of your career by asking yourself, "Will this new position teach me anything new?" Third, or fourth rather, is to learn about the company's culture. Just as we come from different cultures, so every company has a different culture and a different tradition. And these

traditions impact on who gets ahead. If you can find a mentor who's been successful in your company, they can teach you about how the company is doing things and who are the people who are the most effective. They'll also help you find opportunities to be more visible in front of decision makers. Remember that the workplace is not your family, and that means that you're always being evaluated. That there's an expression in business today, which is "What's the value added?" In other words, what has this person contributed over and above their job description? So it's important to remember to speak up about your ideas. Since business today moves so quickly and is ever changing, it's so important to come to work with an open mind and with flexibility so that there's a willingness to try something new. And finally, and perhaps in my mind most importantly, to cultivate courage within, to persevere in the face of obstacles, whether those obstacles mean having the stamina to pursue an extensive job search or to have the strength to overcome or to withstand others' biases or prejudices.

In summary, business today demands lifelong learning, and we can begin this right now by asking ourselves, "How can I grow? How can I be better than yesterday?"

Listening 3

Mary Esther: My name is Mary Esther Malloy. I coordinate a certificate program in teaching adult literacy at the New School. I'm also in graduate school studying anthropology. And I'm a dancer, and I feel very fortunate to have had very satisfying work since leaving college—teaching and studying and dancing. And now that I'm arriving at thirty, I'm trying to figure out what I really want to be doing in the future, and I'm realizing more and more how critical it is to me that I'm involved in the arts in some way. That I can bring my involvement in the arts, in theater and dance, into my work. So I'm casting about. It's not easy. It involves risks. And I'm searching for what I should be doing.

Marcello: My name is Marcello, I'm Italian and I came to the United States five years ago, 1991. When I came over here, I was still keeping a very Italian idea of work, which is very rigid; it's something that you start and you keep forever and never changes. Since then I had to learn to abandon this idea quickly. I have been involved in a number of activities, a number of jobs. I started as a waiter because it seemed to be, it seemed to be like everybody else was doing . . . and I managed to work myself . . . my way up to become a manager in the same restaurant, which is what I'm still doing right now. I'm also been always interested in journalism, and so I . . . worked as a freelance for Italian newspapers for a while, but I also learned to keep changing and keep evolving, so right now I'm starting a company where I am using my activity as a freelance to coordinate other freelancers. So what I can say is that it's something that you have to change constantly. You have to learn to rediscover yourself all the time, and you have to be prepared in getting involved in things that you had no idea you could do.

David: Right now I'm an English teacher at two different schools, and I also have a technology business, a technology based business which basically creates English materials on the computer to be distributed over the Internet. This is kind of in tandem with one of my early childhood hobbies and fascinations, which was with computers, which has always been a big part of my life. In the future I plan to continue to expand my business, which helps schools and companies implement technology into their workforce, both from a perspective of training them to use it and also training them to create new things to be able to distribute over the Internet, and to . . . obviously to continue my education, possibly get a Ph.D. and continue teaching.

Chapter 9
The Dreaming Self

Listening 1

Patricia Simko

We're going to talk a little bit today about dreams. Dreams are important in our psychic life, and they've always been important in the history of human consciousness. As early as ancient Egypt, people spent time and energy investigating their dreams. And dreams are also universal; everybody dreams, and not only does everybody dream, but everybody dreams a lot.

Dreams contain direct messages from our unconscious minds. And that is the value of a dream. It was in fact through dreams that Freud originally even came up with the idea of the unconscious. However, it's difficult to really gain access to the unconscious mind. It's hidden and there are few ways that we can know what's going on in our unconscious. One way is by slips of the tongue or by unintended behaviors, like losing your keys.

But dreams are a direct and unedited communication from the unconscious which is also the source of all creation and the source of our whole identity. The unconscious mind is also the storehouse for limitless interactions and the repository of information that we've had forever. In a way you could say that your unconscious mind runs you. The unconscious tells us who we are . . . who we want to be . . . how we interact . . . how we think . . . what we create . . . how we relate . . . and what our defenses are. It is our dreams that inform us about the content of this repository. And our dreams that paint a picture of what's going on in this dark place.

In a way our dreams are a gift to us, for they offer us information about what runs us. We can always decline this gift because you can be sure that if it is declined the same message will come back again and again until we pay attention to it.

Dreams never lie. They never fool us. However, they do not speak directly. They will tell us what we want to know if we know how to figure them out. Our dreams are painfully honest, but they are also highly disguised. We need to know the tools to work with our dreams in order to get to the truth.

Our dreams bypass our conscious brains. In so doing they also bypass all the tricks of our conscious brains, like our defense mechanisms, our editor, all concepts of social desirability, and the unique gift we have for fooling ourselves. Our dreams never fool us; they will tell us what we think . . . what we really believe . . . what we wish for . . . what we hope for . . . what we dread the most, and in so doing, they give us a picture of our struggles . . . of our inner life. As that inner life comes to correspond with our outer life, we can join forces with our unconscious in moving forward in our lives. And our dreams can also help us take this next step in resolving problems.

Listening 2

Jane's Dream

I am in my car stopped at a curbside. I want to pull out, but another car stops next to me, blocking my movement. There are two of my co-workers in this car. After a time they pull away, and I can move my car again. Now I am driving along the road, but my car won't go. It starts to putter, and finally it stops totally.

In analyzing Jane's dream we start with the first step which is to tell the story in terms of the theme. Jane says: "I'm stuck; I can't move forward because my co-workers are blocking me. But even when they disappear I still cannot make progress."

In step two, Jane speaks about the day's events. "On the day of this dream I had been at work. I wasn't able to attend an important conference that I had been looking forward to because two other employees needed help. My boss told me to stay at my desk and help them. I was angry."

In step three the characters are described: two co-workers and Jane.

Step four describes the feelings of the dream. Jane says: "I felt anxious when my progress was blocked. And I was frustrated when I couldn't get my car to go forward."

In step five the symbols of the dream are examined. First, Jane looks at the people. She says: "They are my co-workers, two women. I've had feelings of being blocked at work because of co-workers. They remind me of my sisters. Growing up I had two sisters; they were older than I, and they would often tease me and make me do the chores that they didn't want to do. I never felt I could get away from them and get out on my own."

Next Jane speaks about the objects in the dream. "My car, I move around in my car. It is the vehicle that takes me places. I think my car represents progress . . . my energy, or my forward motion in life or in a job."

Then Jane speaks about the meaning of this dream to her inner self. She speaks as the car; she says, "I am Jane's car, I want to move ahead but I can't, this other car won't let me out. I feel blocked. The other car is bigger than I; I can't fight it. I feel weak and inadequate. And all I can do is wait. When the other car finally moves, I see that I can't really get going. I can barely move. I'm grinding to a halt. I just can't do it."

Jane's dream tells the story of her feeling blocked and frustrated in her progress or her journey. This dream captures the heart of Jane's uneasiness with competition and with rivalry. In her present life she feels blocked by competitive co-workers who don't care about her situation. In her early life it was her sisters who kept her from making progress on her own. Perhaps it is this early dynamic that has made Jane vulnerable to similar situations and feelings of collapse in the face of competition.

Frustration and anxiety are stirred up when present day life situations like Jane's interaction at work trigger unresolved early problems around Jane's rivalry with her sisters.

Listening 3

Bill's dreams

There are certain symbols that keep reoccurring in some of my nightly dreams.

One. I've been cast into a theatrical production, either a musical or an opera. And everyone assures me that I know my lines, and I know my part, and I know my music although I don't sing at all. And I'm very nervous and very fearful that I'll make a fool out of myself and everyone concerned. But they reassure me that once the curtain rises it'll all come to me. There is the blare of trumpets as the overture sounds. And then the cue is given and the curtain rises, and I'm about to sing; I look out and the entire theater is empty and devoid of people. There is no orchestra, and the entire theater is in darkness.

Another recurring dream I have is that I'm being pursued by something or someone and they're getting closer and closer behind me. I run, but for some reason I can't run as fast as they or my feet are leadened. And just when they're about to catch me, to snare me, I spread my arms and I soar in escape from them, high above the earth.

The third dream is when I sail my boat. It's a beautiful sailboat and I'm sailing across the ocean . . . maybe to Europe or to Polynesia, and there is always a storm that comes up and the clouds get gray. And it is fearful, but I steer my craft into the wind of the storm, and as the storm rages the sails are broken and they fall on the ship. They fall into the water and begin to turn my craft off course. But, when the storm clears, I make a temporary sail out of the broken mast and spars, and I sail to a beautiful island where there is always exquisite fruit.

Robyn's Dream

I was in my grandmother's house. My mother and my grandmother were there. We were upstairs, and I could see the kitchen, my grandmother's bedroom, the hallway, the closet door in the bathroom, and the front door. I could see a blanket, my grandmother's wheelchair although she was not in it, and all of the furniture in the rooms. My grandmother was looking for something, saying to me that she knew where it was. I went to my mother and said: "Mom, Nana is looking for her things, and we moved them." I then went out the front door into the front yard of my grandmother's house. There is a wooded area in the front of the house, and I walked toward it. One of my relatives, I can't remember who, told me to go ahead. As I walked into the woods, I could see a big fire. Around the fire were several of my relatives from both my mother's and my father's side of the family. Everybody was talking. It seemed like a social gathering, and I felt that they had been waiting for me to arrive.

Teacher's Notes

Chapter 1
What Will I Do When They Find Out I'm Me?

Page 2

Listening 1

A. Before You Listen

1. Discuss the definitions of *fear* and *anxiety* with the class. You might want to write these words on the board and elicit ideas from the students before introducing the definitions for discussion. Do the same with the word *confident*.

   Elicit responses to the question "What makes people feel anxious and lose confidence?" This may be a good opportunity to explore students' anxieties about the ESL classroom. Now have students fill in the chart individually. Tell students to imagine how they would feel in the situations if they have not experienced them.

2. Students should answer questions a–d in small groups. There are no correct answers. You may choose to discuss the results as a class. You may want to make the third question more concrete by asking students if they can think of one person they know who is confident. How can they tell? You can ask students to list three characteristics.

Culture Note

Have students read the Culture Note. Ask them to compare this information to their own culture.

B. Who Will You Be Listening To?

Introduce the lecturer's biography.

Page 3

C. Listening for a General Topic

Have students read the Listening Note. Emphasize to them that in order to listen well they need to relax. They should not listen for every word and detail. Now is a good time to get students used to this strategy, for it will serve them throughout the book.

Students should read the general topic possibilities on their own before listening to the recording. Students should listen to the uninterrupted lecture once before choosing the general topic.

Answer: 2

Page 4

D. Listening for Specific Information/Notetaking

Have students read the Listening/Notetaking Note on their own. Emphasize that they should not let an unknown word interrupt their listening or break their concentration.

Have students listen once and take notes. They should then compare their notes with a partner.

Answers:

1. I am responsible.
2. Believe in something big; your life is worth a noble motive.
3. Practice tolerance.
4. Be brave and remember that courage is acting with fear not without it.
5. Love someone because you should know joy.
6. Be ambitious.
7. Smile because no one else can do that for you.

E. Listening for Details

Have students complete the exercise items before listening. Students should check their answers with a partner.

1. Answers:

a. heads of nations

b. people who've created great art, great literature

c. people who've run corporations

d. some of the best teachers America has

e. some of the greatest scientists

f. the most famous of actors and actresses

2. Answers:

vulnerable; don't belong; able to be hurt; deserve to be rejected; not quite good enough

3. Answers:

Rocky; Rambo; Rocky

Page 5

F. Vocabulary and Dictation

Students should work together with a partner. Go over the instructions with the students. Tell them that they should not ask you to repeat anything. Read the sentences at a normal pace. Assure students that they will be able to check their answers. You may want to make a copy of the sentences available to students later.

Dictation:

1. During the last two decades I've had the rare and the wonderful opportunity to meet some of the most noble and achieved people on earth.

2. I've never failed to get a nod with the question. Every one of them said yes.

3. I know now that every sane human being worries that others will find out that they're inferior . . . they're vulnerable . . . they deserve to be rejected.

4. Believe in something big; your life is worth a noble motive.

5. Practice tolerance. You'll like yourself a lot more, and so will others.

6. Love someone because you should know joy. When we're children, the need to be loved is phenomenal. When we're adult, the need to love is greater.

7. Be ambitious. To want to be more than we are is real, and normal, and healthy.

1. Answers:

1. d
2. g
3. f
4. i
5. b
6. a
7. c
8. h
9. e

G. Expanding Meaning

Answers:

1. tolerance
2. rejected
3. decades
4. phenomenal
5. noble
6. sane
7. ambitious
8. nodded
9. vulnerable

Vocabulary Note

Draw the students' attention to the Vocabulary Note. You may wish to discuss it with them and give further examples on the board if necessary:

formal/informal   active/inactive

capable/incapable   complete/incomplete

Page 6

Listening 2

A. Before You Listen

Ask students the following questions to introduce storytelling. This may start a class discussion, but it should be brief.

- How is storytelling used to communicate with people?
- Why is it an effective way of communicating with people?
- How is storytelling used in your culture?

1. Now have students read the introduction to the story and the questions that they should focus

on. Encourage them not to stop reading if they come across a word that they do not know. They should concentrate on understanding the meaning of the story.

2. Students should discuss questions a and b in groups. Let them know that later in the chapter they will have the opportunity to tell a story of their own from beginning to end.

Page 7

B. Who Will You Be Listening To?
Students may read the information about Walter Anderson's story on their own, or you may choose to read it to them.

C. Understanding the Rhythm of English
You should go through each of the language patterns with your students. Emphasize the importance of rhythm in English. Ask students to compare this with their own languages. How is it the same/different? You might want to write the first sentence on the board and illustrate each pattern for your students in order to be sure that they understand. If students still feel unsure, write out the second sentence and let them mark the patterns together with you. Students should go on and complete the exercise in pairs. You may wish to circulate and check their progress.

Pronunciation Note

Emphasize the points being made in this note. For stress, give the classic examples of how the meaning can change with a change in stress; for example, *I scream, ice cream.*

Page 8

Answers for 1–3, page 7

I was raised in a tenement /and one night my mother asked me to go across the street to the telephone booth /(we had no telephone in our apartment)/ and call my brother. Now I don't remember what the telephone call was about /but I'll remember that as long as I live /because when I hung the receiver back up /my hand had blood on it,/and I reached up and touched my face/ . . . my face had blood on it./ Whoever had used the telephone before me/ had been either hurt or wounded,/ which was not unusual in the neighborhood I grew up. / And I opened the bifold doors/ and I looked to my left,/ I looked to my

right,/ and I ran across the street,/ and I ran up the steps to the tenement, /went into our apartment./ I washed the blood /off my face and hands/ before my mother could see it./

A little later /I went back down stairs /and I sat on the stoop . . . /now it's never quiet, really, in New York,/ but it was relatively quiet . . . /the sounds of the city around, /and I was alone. / And I started to think /about this mysterious person /whose blood I had worn, /and I became angry, /I became enraged,/ and I vowed, /"I'm getting out of here," /and I meant it./

It was in that moment /that I first began to accept responsibility /for my own life./

4. **Answer:** Walter Anderson sometimes speaks quickly and sometimes speaks slowly. He raises and lowers his voice. He speaks quickly and then slowly to create excitement and suspense when he talks about action. Example: "I looked to my left, I looked to my right, and I ran across the street."

   Walter Anderson lowers his voice to stress the seriousness of what he is saying. He then raises it again. Example: "I became angry, I became enraged, and I vowed 'I'm getting out of here,' and I meant it. It was in that moment. . . ."

5. Allow students to practice reading the story in pairs. You may want to try one phrase with them aloud to get them started.

D. Telling a Story
Students should work in small groups and be given some time to think about what they want to say before telling their stories.

Page 9

Culture Note

Have students read the Culture Note. This is a good opportunity for students to compare the information to their own culture.

E. Expanding Knowledge—Other Resources
1. Ask students:

- If you aren't confident, can you learn to be?

Discuss their answers before reading the course description and going on to the other questions.

2. Discuss these questions and the book illustrations. You may want to bring in other

examples of self-help materials or course descriptions for students to discuss. You can ask students if there are areas of self-improvement that they are interested in. A follow-up assignment may be for students to research and find a book, video, or course that would address their specific self-improvement needs.

Page 10

Listening 3

A. Who Will You Be Listening To?

Have students read the reminder of the seven rules and the Listening Tip before listening.

B. Before You Listen

Students should work in groups and go over the introduction to the listening exercise and the questions that the speakers were asked.

C. Listening for Specific Information/Notetaking

1. Students should listen once and fill in all that they can. They can then compare their answers before listening a second time.

2. Answers:

a. Be tolerant

b. Be tolerant

c. Ambitious

D. Personal Reflection

There are no correct answers. Remind students that they have limited time to discuss each speaker.

Page 11

Video

A. What Will You Be Watching?

Students can read the introduction to the Horatio Alger Awards on their own. You may want to discuss the meaning of the awards briefly as a class.

Listening Note

Have students read this before starting the video.

B. Notetaking

Students should work in pairs. Allow them to read the instructions and questions on the chart before starting the video.

Answers:

- What problems did they face growing up?

They were all poor.

Walter Anderson was abused by his alcoholic father.

Dorothy Brown lived in an orphanage. She was abandoned twice by her biological mother.

Ben Carson was poor, from a broken home, and everybody thought he was stupid.

- How did they overcome their problems?

Walter Anderson overcame his problems by reading and imagining a life outside of the ghetto. He took responsibility for his life.

Dorothy Brown overcame her problems by sticking to her dream and studying.

Ben Carson overcame his problem by studying at the library and doing well in school. He gained confidence in himself.

- Did they get help?

Walter Anderson was helped by his mother, who encouraged him to read despite the fact that his father would beat him for reading. She knew that this would help him find a way out.

Dorothy Brown was helped by the Redmond family, who took her in when she was sixteen. They told her that they loved her and were the only real family that she ever knew.

Ben Carson was helped by his mother. She made him go to the library, write book reports, and turn them in to her. This helped him to learn, do better in school, and gain confidence. The amazing thing was that his mother was illiterate; she could not actually read the book reports.

- What do they do now?

Walter Anderson became a journalist. Today he is editor of *Parade* magazine.

Dorothy Brown became the chief of surgery at Riverdale Hospital and the first African American woman to serve in Tennessee's General Assembly. She still practices medicine today and makes house calls.

Ben Carson is a pediatric neurosurgeon. He is well-known in his field for accomplishing a delicate 22-hour operation that separated Siamese twins joined at the head.

- How do they give back to society?

Walter Anderson is an advocate for literacy. He

works with children.

Dorothy Brown still helps people by practicing medicine and making house calls. She also goes back to the orphanage where she grew up to talk to the children there and encourage them.

Ben Carson saves the lives of children and has become a hero to the many children he has helped.

C. Analysis and Synthesis

Students will probably find that almost all of the points are illustrated in these stories. Be *responsible*, *brave*, *and ambitious*, and *believe in something big* are points that all three award recipients illustrate. Some students may feel that *love someone* is illustrated by the people who helped Walter Anderson, Dorothy Brown, and Ben Carson. *Practice tolerance* and *smile* are the two points that are not clearly illustrated in these stories. However, we see all three award recipients smile, and we can also assume that since they all had people who acted negatively toward them as children, they needed to be tolerant.

Chapter 2:
Legacy of the Blues

Page 12

Listening 1

A. Before You Listen

1. Elicit answers to the questions from students. You may have some students in your class who are particularly knowledgeable about music. Allow them to share their ideas with the class. Have the students list as many forms of American music as possible. Then compare answers as a class. Otherwise, you may choose to elicit forms of American music from the class as a whole and list them on the board. Some examples of types of American music are blues, rhythm and blues, rap, hip hop, acid rock, rockabilly, country western, jazz, bluegrass, pop, soul, and ragtime.

2. Students should work in groups and share the information they have about American music and the artists listed. They can list their favorite performers individually and then share their choices with their group.

Answers:

Madonna—rock 'n' roll

Louis Armstrong—jazz

Billy Joel—rock 'n' roll

Whitney Houston—pop

Page 13

3. Students should continue working in groups and answer questions a–c after reading the definitions.

Answers:

a. Many people think of the blues as sad music. It will be pointed out later in the chapter that blues songs can be sad; however, there are also happy blues songs.

b. The second definition, music, will be discussed in this unit.

c. Student answers may vary here. They may talk about feelings and traditions that have been passed on by the blues to Americans and to African Americans in particular. However, the legacy of the blues, as discussed in this chapter, is the music that was born from the blues. American music such as jazz and rock is rooted in the blues.

The time line should serve to give students a historical perspective of the time when blues music originated. They will hear in the lecture that follows that the blues originated around the year 1900, after the Civil War. Draw students' attention to the wars listed and to the Emancipation Proclamation, which freed the slaves in 1863. Ask students during which war slaves were freed. You might also point out that this happened less than 150 years ago. Students will likely understand that this is significant to the chapter because southern Black Americans developed the blues.

Page 14

B. Who Will You Be Listening To?

Have students read Stephen Tarshis's background information. Ask students to look at the map below and the picture and predict how they might be related to the lecture they will hear.

The Culture Note should be discussed with the class since students may have questions. If you are teaching in the United States, it is likely that

---

students have already heard the term *African American*. In America today, the terms *African American* and *Black* are used interchangeably by African Americans and other Americans. These are both considered to be correct terms; however, the usage of the term *African American* is growing because it is thought to be more inclusive, whereas the term *Black* refers to race only.

C. Listening for a General Topic

Have the students read the Listening Note. Remind them not to stop listening when they hear an unknown word. They will likely understand the lecture despite some unknown words. Students should choose one general topic of the three listed. You can have them check their answers with a partner.

Answer: 2

D. Specific Information/Notetaking

1. Students should work in pairs. Have students read the Summary Writing Note (p. 15). Remind them that they should not try to include details in their summaries. Questions a–e will help them focus on the important points to include in their summary. They should focus on listening for those points. Have students read the questions before listening and taking notes on a separate piece of paper. They can then work with their partners to write the summary.

Page 15

2. Student summaries will differ slightly. Do not expect their summaries to be exactly like the sample summary. However, they should be able to touch on all the main points.

Sample Summary:

The blues is a style, a genre of music that formed the basis for American music as a whole. It began around 1900, one generation after slavery. The elements of the blues are work songs from African music together with the harmonies of European music. One of the first Delta blues performers was Robert Johnson. He sent the music into an urbanized period. The legacy of the blues is popular forms of American music such as rock 'n' roll, rhythm and blues, and jazz.

E. Listening for Details

Students should work in pairs. They should read the statements before listening. You may want to

encourage them to make corrections before listening based on what they remember. Pairs can check answers with each other after the listening.

Answers:

1. Bach, Beethoven, and Brahms were *European* composers.
2. Blacks emigrated to the Mississippi Delta after the *Civil War*.
3. Blacks went to the Mississippi Delta mainly to *clear and plant*.
4. Robert Johnson was a *Delta blues* singer.
5. Jazz and rock *are* related to the blues.

F. Vocabulary and Dictation

1. Students should work in pairs. Have students read the Vocabulary Note. You may want to provide them with another example. Tell students that you should not be interrupted while you read the sentences. Reassure them that their answers will be corrected. Have the students read the vocabulary and the definitions before you begin. When you finish, have students check their answers with another pair of students.

Dictation:

1. [The blues] is a certain type of [musical] language that was different from the European <u>heritage</u> of Bach, Beethoven, and Brahms. . . .
2. [The blues] probably <u>originated</u> around the year 1900.
3. The Mississippi Delta was a place where many Blacks had <u>emigrated</u> to work in after the Civil War was over. And it was a <u>wilderness</u> area that they helped to clear and then to plant.
4. The blues . . . developed around 1900, and that's a significant year because it was about one <u>generation</u> after slavery was over. So, in essence, it was one of the first, maybe the first . . . musical cultural expressions by Black people in America as a freed <u>entity</u>.
5. These songs and field hollers were put to music, put to a harmonic background. In other words, <u>chords</u> . . . were played.
6. Robert Johnson . . . sent music on its way into an <u>urbanized</u> period.

Answers:

1. c

2. a

3. g

4. b

5. f

6. e

7. h

8. d

2. Again, students should work in pairs. Tell students that you will read some of the sentences in the same way you did before. They should try to write down each sentence and then compare their work with a partner. Partners should be able to fill in any gaps together. Circulate to make sure that students have the correct sentences when they finish comparing.

Page 16

Listening 2

A. Before You Listen

1. If the timing is right, you may want to ask students to do some research outside of class for this exercise. They can interview people to get explanations for the six types of music listed. Students can alternatively be assigned one of the six types of music and report their findings back to the class, sharing what they have learned. If this is to be done in class only, ideas can be elicited from the class as a whole, and the Glossary can be used for those terms not explained by class members. Encourage students to give specific examples of songs or performers to illustrate the terms. A variation would be to group or pair students together to work out the musical terms.

2. Students should work in groups. They should first read the names of the music samples. They may be familiar with some of them. Emphasize to students that this is a guessing game. They are not expected to know each form of music, but they should try to match the music with the term and performer based on the term meanings. Students should put the number of the sample (based on the order it is heard) next to their choice.

3. Students should write their own impressions of the samples in just a few words. There are no correct answers. Students can then compare

their answers and their comments. Once students have the correct answers, allow them to listen one more time so that they can listen for the correct matches and get a sense of the different types of music.

Page 17

B. Who Will You Be Listening To?

Have students read the background information on Junior Mance. Discuss the quotation with the students. You might ask them why they think Junior Mance feels it's hard to teach the blues.

C. Listening for Specific Information

1. Ask for volunteers to try to guess the meaning of the boldfaced terms.

2. Have students work in groups. Emphasize to students that they should focus on listening for the information asked in the questions. They do not need to understand every word. Allow students to go over the questions before playing the interview. Students should discuss their answers to the questions after listening.

Page 18

D. Interviewing

Students should work in pairs. Have students use the expressions on page 17 to answer the questions. For the last question, encourage students to share their feelings about music from their own culture and to describe or give examples of that music. You may want to give students a time limit.

E. Speaking Styles

Have students discuss their responses as a class.

Answers:

Steve Tarshis is more formal than Junior Mance. Steve Tarshis gives a lecture while Junior Mance talks about his experiences and reminisces. Steve Tarshis is more objective than Junior Mance. Junior Mance speaks about his feelings toward the blues while Steve Tarshis gives us a history of the blues.

F. Making Inferences

Students should work in pairs. Have the students read the quotations and discuss them before listening. Remind them that they are making inferences. They are applying what they know from the interview to the quotation. The difficulty of this task should provide a good opportunity for discussion among students. They may be able to complete some of the exercise before listening and then check their answers with a partner. You may go over responses with the class as a whole or circulate to check that students have responded appropriately.

Answers:

1. Yes. Junior Mance talks about Dinah Washington and how her music always reflected her own experiences.
2. No. Junior Mance says that there's a happy blues and a sad blues.
3. Yes. Junior Mance quotes Ray Charles saying exactly that. He loves the blues.

Page 19

4. Junior Mance says that the blues is a basis for jazz, but he does not seem to think that jazz is better than blues. He might not agree.

Bonus Listening

This listening is for students' enjoyment. They should not do anything but listen. Tell them that they will hear Junior Mance improvising and that in itself is interesting. They might not understand all of what he says, but they will understand the spirit of what he is doing here.

"West Africa and the Blues" is for students to read and discuss together in pairs or groups. Alternatively, you can discuss the information as a class. If there is somebody in your class with a music background, take advantage by allowing him/her to help the other students. Encourage students to think of examples.

Page 20

Listening 3

A. What Will You Be Listening To?

Students will listen to two full-length pieces of music. Although they will have a listening task to complete, they should really relax and enjoy the music.

B. Listening for Specific Information

1. Students should work in groups. They should first check for words they know, and share their knowledge with the group. They can then look up the words that they do not know in the Glossary. Listen for voices. If students seem to

be reading only and not speaking, circulate and remind them that they need to share what they know, guess, and discuss the words before consulting the Glossary.

2. Allow students to read the descriptions of each song. They should then listen and use the words above to describe what they hear. When the songs are over, have students compare their descriptions with members of their group. Descriptions may vary.

Sample Answers:

a. "Come Rain or Come Shine" by Dinah Washington is emotional, smooth, soft, mellow, and easy.
b. "Mannish Boy" by Muddy Waters is playful, loud, wild, repetitive, and vocally colorful.

C. Analysis and Synthesis

Students should continue to work in their groups and discuss the questions.

Answers:

1. Even though "Mannish Boy" is a simple song, it is interesting and exciting because there is a lot of feeling. It is vocally colorful.
2. Answers may vary, but students should be able to hear some connection between, for example, "Mannish Boy" and the style of the Rolling Stones.

Page 21

Video

A. What Will You Be Watching?

Before having students read the introduction to the video, you might ask them a lead-in question: How did the blues become popular in the very beginning? Students may remember Robert Johnson from the first listening and may be able to guess that blues singers traveled from place to place singing the blues for the public. Once you have elicited some ideas, have students read the introduction. Ask them what "the everyday street man type of blues" is, in their opinion. Have students read the Listening Tip. They should not be discouraged by the difficulty of the video; it's good for them to be exposed to an American accent that is likely to be unfamiliar to them.

B. Listening for Specific Information

Have students read the questions before listening. You may discuss answers as a class or have the students compare answers with a partner and circulate to see how students have done.

Answers:

1. Yes. He loves playing for the public. There's never a minute of dead time.

2. He became a musician because he comes from a musical family.

3. He says that there are happy blues songs and sad blues songs.

C. Comparison and Contrast

Answers will vary.

Chapter 3:
Food: Business & Pleasure

Page 22

Listening 1

Before reading the introduction to this chapter, ask some questions to the students to get them focused on work as it relates to the chapter.

- Is work always a pleasure?
- When is work pleasurable?
- Do most people do something they love for work?

Once students have answered these questions, have them read the introduction and ask them if they agree or disagree with the statements made.

A. Before You Listen

1. a. This activity is designed to show students how to work together to form a consensus. Students should look at the chart, and the class as a whole should agree on four or more items to be added to the list. This can be done by having students call out suggestions and asking for a show of hands to vote for each suggestion. An alternative to this exercise is to have students close their books before looking at the chart. You can then ask students to tell you the interests that they think many people have. Once you have listed some of their suggestions on the board, have students open their books and look at the chart. The board list may have

some of the same items as the book list. Those that are different can be added to the book list.

 b. Have students work on their own and rank the items on the list, using 1 for the most interesting and 10 for the least interesting.

 c. The class should now work together to agree on how the items should be ranked. The easiest way to do this is to call on students to offer their opinions for number 1, for example. Vote on the items that more than one student has placed as number 1. The majority will decide which item gets ranked number 1. Continue in this way to finish the class ranking.

  Students should read the Preparation Note. For the final project they will create a plan for their own business doing something they enjoy. Students should be encouraged to start keeping a journal of their thoughts throughout the unit. This will be helpful to them later on.

Page 23

2. Students should now be placed in small groups. Students can rank these motives for eating individually and then compare their responses with the other members of the group. They should discuss their reasons for making their choices. You should circulate to make sure that students understand each motive. Have other group members explain meanings when possible.

3. Students can individually list their three favorite places to eat and then discuss their answers with their groups.

4. Have the students read the Culture Note before beginning this activity. This should get them thinking about entrepreneurship and the food industry. Students should then create a single list of food professions together with their groups. When their list is completed, they can discuss the questions.

B. Who Will You Be Listening To?

Students should read the background information about Gary Goldberg on their own before beginning the listening exercises. Ask students if they know what is taught in a culinary arts school. The following are examples of courses that are taught in one culinary arts program:

How to Become a Party Planner

Commercial Bread Baking at Tom Cat Bakery

Great Holiday Pies: Sweet and Savory

Family Cooking: Parents and Kids Cook Pasta Together

Basic Techniques of Cooking: Four Day Workshop

Spotlight on Herbs

Introduction to the Wines of California

Page 24

C. Listening for a General Topic

Students should read general topic statements 1–3 before listening. When the listening is completed, they can check their answers with a partner. You may otherwise check answers with the class as a whole.

Answer: 2

D. Listening for Specific Information/Notetaking

Students should work in pairs. Have students read the introductory information before moving on to the tasks. After reading this information, students should look at the outline. After reading the instructions, and before listening, students should read the Listening/Notetaking Tips. Emphasize that students should (1) concentrate on recording the information that they need, (2) not stop if they hear a word they do not understand, but record it and move on, and (3) listen for the details and examples that the speaker gives. They are clues to figuring out the main idea. After emphasizing these points, allow students time to discuss with their partners for further clarification.

1. Students should work individually to take notes on the opening statement, the two main ideas, and the closing statement.

2. Students should now compare their notes from the listening. Once they have agreed on the information, they should fill in the outline in the book.

Answers:

Opening Statement: I'm going to talk with you about a love affair, and this is America's love affair with fine food. . . .

Main Idea: People study culinary arts for professional reasons, as a career.

Main Idea: People study culinary arts as an avocation or hobby.

Closing Statement: People who love food are happy people.

E. Listening for Details

Students should read the instructions and the details listed in the outline before listening. Remind them that they should be listening for specific information. Students should check the details that the speaker mentions in the listening. When they have finished, they can compare with their partner.

Answers:

Details: There are many restaurants of every type.

There are dozens of food magazines/cookbooks.

There are many gourmet shops.

There's an explosion of cooking schools.

Details: It's a wonderful career.

There are many jobs available.

People love it.

Details: They cook for themselves.

They cook to entertain.

Cooking is fun.

It involves all the senses.

It's creative.

It's ephemeral.

It has immediate gratification.

Page 25

F. Vocabulary and Dictation

1. Students should read the instructions. Tell students that they should not interrupt you or ask you to repeat anything. The vocabulary words listed are in the sentences that you will read. Tell students that they should try to understand the meanings of these words based on the sentences they hear. When the dictation is over, students should check their answers with their partner. You can circulate, or check with the class as a whole, to ensure that students have the correct answers.

Dictation:

1. America really is in love with fine food. I can give you so many examples of that. For example, there's a proliferation of great restaurants of every type in this country. . . .

2. We also have a proliferation of gourmet shops in this country (fancy food shops, they're

sometimes called), and they sell fresh produce, they sell prepared foods and packaged foods, you can buy a whole wonderful dinner already prepared for you, take it home and just reheat it.

3. I changed careers when I was in my late twenties. I always loved food. I decided to make my avocation my vocation and to do something I really love. And I think I'm very fortunate because I love coming to work every day. . . . There are a number of students who take courses, many of them at the New School, as an avocation or as a hobby. They want to learn to cook at home for themselves, for enjoyment, for entertaining. And for them, I think, the primary motive is cooking as fun.

4. . . . you're creating something that's beautiful, artful, imaginative, hopefully delicious, and in spite of all that it's ephemeral, it doesn't last very long; we make it, we eat it, and it's gone.

Answers:

1. f
2. d
3. e
4. b
5. a
6. g
7. c

2. Students should work with their partners to complete this exercise. They should fill in the correct vocabulary word based on the meanings they have learned. When they have finished, you can check answers with the class as a whole. An alternative is to have pairs check answers with other pairs as you circulate to ensure that all students have the correct answers.

   Have students read the Vocabulary Note before moving on. Give them time to check understanding with their partner.

Answers:

a. ephemeral
b. avocation/vocation
c. produce
d. motive
e. proliferation
f. gourmet

3. Read item 3 from the previous dictation. Again, read the passage twice, but do not repeat words in between readings. Students should write down as much as they can on their own. When they have finished, they can check their version of the dictation with a partner. You may then want to create small groups and have students fill in words they have missed by comparing with other group members. You can photocopy the passage you used and pass it out to each group so that students can check their work at the end of this exercise.

Page 26

Listening 2

A. Before You Listen

1. Students should work in small groups. Give students a limited amount of time to discuss the questions listed. Circulate and point out the issues—time, money, security, risk, and job satisfaction—as needed.

2. The group should read the instructions and the idea and planning options before beginning. Remind students that they must agree on the logical order of these steps to create their plan. Once students have decided on their plan order, they should read the information on problem solving that follows. Ask students to discuss problems that might come up during the various phases of such a plan.

B. Who Will You Be Listening To?

Students should read the information about Emel Basdoğan. You may want to ask the students to predict the kinds of problems Emel might have run into while starting her magazine. Ask if they know of a food magazine in their country. Who reads it? Once you have heard some ideas, move on.

Page 27

Listening Note

Remind students that they will need to adjust their listening to this particular speaker and of the importance of this listening skill. If you feel it appropriate for your particular class, this may be a good time to have students reflect on pronunciation difficulties particular to their native language, and those of their classmates. In a multilingual classroom, this topic may be useful in helping students to be more tolerant with their speaking partners in the future. When students understand that they are developing a valuable skill by listening to nonnative English speakers, their attitudes toward group and pair work may improve.

C. Listening for a Sequence of Events
Students should be placed in small groups. They should read the introduction and instructions on their own. Have students look at the outline before listening. They should also read the Listening Tip. Emphasize to students that the interviewer's questions will prepare them for what Emel will say, and will also tell them the order of events in Emel's story. Students can individually write notes in the spaces provided. They should then work as a group. They should compare information and agree on the correct answers.

Idea:

Interest: Passion for food

The product: Food magazine

Experience: Emel had experience in food commercials and connections in the food industry.

Ambition: To create a successful publication

Identifying the market: They thought that there would be a boom of interest in food in Turkey. Turkey did not have a food magazine.

Financial support: They looked for financial support, but nobody would take the risk. They got assurance that companies would buy a certain volume of advertising.

Packaging: A magazine

Marketing: They sold the magazine in supermarkets.

Page 28

D. Ordering a Sequence of Events
Students can read the instructions on their own. They will need to read Gary Goldberg's story individually. However, they should stay in their groups to discuss when necessary.

Page 29

E. Telling a Story
Students should now work in pairs using the language in 1 and 2. They should look at the chart they completed earlier and take turns retelling Emel's story. Students do not have to use every word listed. They should try to vary their stories

when possible by choosing alternative words to those their partner chose.

F. Telling Your Own Story
Students should now work in groups. They may need a little time to think of a story. When they are ready, they should take turns telling a business success story. The story can be about themselves, a friend, family member, or famous person.

Page 30

Listening 3
A. Who Will You Be Listening To?
Students should be placed in groups. They can read the introduction to Irene Khin Wong and John Massachio on their own. They can discuss the speakers' occupations and any words they have difficulty with for better understanding.

B. Listening for Specific Information
Have students read the questions before listening. They should also read the Culture Note on their own. Tell students that they should answer the questions as they listen. The questions themselves should help students focus on the information they need to listen for. When the listening is over, students should check their answers with members of their group. You can circulate to make sure students have the correct answers.

Answers:

Irene

a. She was in the investment banking field.

b. She opened a Burmese restaurant.

c. She changed because she wanted to explore other kinds of Asian cuisine.

John

a. He tended bar part time.

b. He went to culinary school and became a waiter to learn the service end of the restaurant business.

C. Analysis and Synthesis
1. Students should work in groups and answer the questions. They will not remember exactly what each speaker said, but they should remember some of the main ideas that these speakers expressed. Answers will vary depending on what students remember. They should discuss their answers and in so doing help each other remember.

Answers:

1. John's story is similar to Gary's. They both loved school and worked part time in restaurants, John tending bar and Gary as a waiter. They both learned about the service end of the restaurant business by waiting tables. They both wanted to open restaurants, so they went to school. John went to culinary school, and Gary studied food management. They both loved food before getting into the food business.

2. Irene loves sharing information with other food lovers. People share their experiences with her. Every day is different for her. She also feels that food involves interacting with people. She thinks of running a restaurant as opening your living room to people. Gary also loves entertaining people, feeding people, and cooking. They both see interaction with people as one of the great benefits of their profession.

3. **Gary:** Cooking is fun, gives immediate pleasure, allows you to socialize with people, allows you to be creative. Food can be beautiful, artful, delicious, and it's ephemeral. People who love food are happy people.

    Emel: Food helps you come out of your small world and enter a new world, new cultures. It affects all the senses and is therefore wonderful for self-education.

    Irene: Food is universal; it's interacting with people, people's personalities. Food brings out the personality and characteristics of a person.

    John: He loves food, to cook, entertain, and make people happy. Therefore, he thinks food makes people happy.

Page 31

Project

A. What Will You Be Doing?
Students should read the introduction to the project on their own.

B. Brainstorming
Students should work in groups. They should read the instructions and then begin their discussion. The goal of each student is to discuss his or her special interest with the group and get ideas from group members on an appropriate business to start, an appropriate product or service that is related to the

student's special interest. Advise students that they should help one another identify the business that is right for them. This will help them to continue the project.

C. Researching
1. Students are again working with their group. Each student again has a specific goal, to create interview questions for his or her specific area of interest. Students will used the questions listed as models but should make them more specific to their particular interest. Students will need to discuss their questions and ask their group for suggestions. Group members should help each other until all the students are confident that they have a good set of interview questions.

2. Students will work on their own. They need to identify an appropriate person to interview. The person they interview should have a job related to the area of interest that the student has chosen. It may not be possible for each person to find the perfect interviewee. Students should do the best that they can to find someone who is involved in the business they are interested in. Before students leave the classroom to interview, you may want to check with each student individually to be sure that they have identified an appropriate person, or to help them come up with ideas for people they might interview.

D. Planning
Students should work in groups. Again, the purpose of students working in groups is to share ideas, share suggestions, and help each other. Students should use their interviews and the organization of the question list to create a basic business plan. They should write their plan to be presented to the class. They should use the experiences of the person they interviewed to support their plan. As each student presents his or her plan to the class, you may want to ask the rest of the class to come up with questions or suggestions regarding the plan presented.

Chapter 4:
Us and Them: Creating the Other

Page 32

Students should read the introduction to the chapter on their own. When they have finished, ask them if they were able to picture the different groups mentioned in the text. Was there a specific image that came to mind? It is likely that some or all of the students will answer yes. Ask this how this ability to picture these groups in our minds relates to the subtitle of the chapter, "Creating the Other." Ask students to suggest what the chapter might be about. Listen to students' ideas, but do not answer the question for them. They will soon understand the subtitle.

Listening 1

A. Before You Listen

1. Students should work in pairs. Have students first discuss the vocabulary words with each other. They can help each other to define difficult words. They should use the Glossary only when both partners do not understand the meaning of a word.

2. Students should continue to work in pairs. Students should first use the words from the vocabulary list they feel are appropriate to describe Americans and the British. Ask students to add words of their own to these descriptions. Tell students that it is fine to be completely honest, even if some of the words used are negative. When students have finished, they should compare their work with their partner's. Ask students to notice similarities and differences in their descriptions. Do they have similar ideas about these two groups?

3. Students should now work in small groups. Each student should place a positive (+) or negative (−) value next to the words listed. When they have completed this task, they should compare results with their group. They will likely find that there are some differences in the values they have given the words. For example, while *talkative* may be considered a positive trait in some cultures or by some people, for others it is negative. As students discuss their answers, circulate and encourage

them to also discuss cultural perspective. If you are teaching in a multicultural classroom, this will be an interesting topic to explore. If you are not, you will probably find that students still have different answers based on their personal perspective. If you are in an English-speaking country such as the United States or Great Britain, you may wish to tell students which value people in your country tend to give to each of the descriptive words.

Page 33

4. Students should individually fill in the words that describe their particular group. It is important to emphasize to students that they may choose any group. They may feel more comfortable, for example, speaking about their profession than their religion. Also remind students that they should write words that "other" people would use to describe them. This will allow students to discuss how realistic people's perceptions of their group are. When they have finished, they should discuss their chart with the students in their group.

5. Students should discuss the questions. Remind them to give as many examples as possible of the influences that helped to develop their opinions. Students may need to speculate in order to answer the last question. Let them know that this is fine. Students should also help each other come up with ways that others may have developed ideas about their group.

6. Students should discuss these questions with their group. They will probably agree that it is difficult to accurately describe a group as a whole. Their differences of opinion when describing Americans and British will highlight this point. Students may need help with the idea of stereotyping. Circulate to make sure that students who understand the term explain it to other students. Students may also refer to the Glossary. It is important that students recognize that stereotyping is generally negative, while recognizing cultural diversity can be very positive. They should be allowed to struggle with the idea of how to differentiate between the two.

Page 34

B. Who Will You Be Listening To?

Students should read about John Mayher's background on their own before listening. You might want to ask students to predict what John Mayher means by "creating the other." Students should also read the Culture Note on their own. It may be a good idea to ask if someone in the class can define *multiculturalism*. If students are not sure of the meaning, encourage them to guess. The word parts *multi* and *culture* within the term should help students. They can also find the definition in the Glossary. If you wish to discuss this note with the class as a whole, you can ask students if multiculturalism is an important part of education in their country. If you are teaching in the students' country, ask them if, in their own experience, they have witnessed an emphasis on multiculturalism in education.

C. Listening for a General Topic

Students should work in pairs. Have students read the instructions on their own. They should then read the general topic statements below. They can ask each other for help if they have any difficulty with the meanings of the general topic statements. They may want to predict the answer before listening. Students should listen and choose the correct general topic statement. When the listening is over, students should compare their answers with their partner.

Answer: 2

D. Listening for Main Ideas

Students should work together in pairs. Instruct students to read the beginning of each statement on the left, and then try to find its matching half on the right. They should write the letter of the correct matching half in the space provided. Emphasize to students that their answers should, above all, make sense. They can determine if the answers make sense by thinking about the general topic. The completed statements should relate logically to the general topic. Once students have finished matching, play the listening. Students should check their answers during the listening. After the listening, partners can compare answers again.

Answers:

1. d

2. a

3. b

4 c

Page 35

E. Listening for Specific Information/Notetaking

Students should read the instructions for this exercise. Ask students to look at the example provided in statement 1. They may recall John Mayher's use of examples throughout the lecture. Have students read the Listening/Notetaking Strategy. Remind students of the importance of moving on when listening. They must write down as much of the necessary information as possible. However, they should not stop listening if they do not understand a word. There is always time later to look the word up in the Glossary.

Answers:

1. hot and cold, sweet and sour, edible and inedible.

2. tribe, neighborhood, friends

3. different, separate, negative

4. my tribe, interesting

5. hair, eyes

6. skin color, country, language

F. Vocabulary and Dictation

1. Students should work in pairs. They should read the instructions and the vocabulary words and definitions listed below. Have students work together to try to match any words and definitions they know.

2. You should then instruct them to listen to the sentences that you will read. They should not interrupt you or ask you to repeat anything. Reassure them that they will have the correct definitions for the vocabulary words by the end of this exercise. Tell students that the vocabulary words will be in the phrases you read. They should try to understand the meanings of these words within the phrases. When you have finished, students should work together in pairs to check their answers. You may wish to circulate to check answers, or to go over the answers with the class as a whole.

Vocabulary

1. One of the things that's fascinating about the way the human mind works is the importance of categorizing that is part of our whole way of thinking about the world. . . .

2. Now this was probably a very helpful thing to do when we were young . . . as a species . . . 50 . . . 60,000 years ago, when it was really important to be able to tell who was in our tribe and who wasn't. But now it's become counterproductive because many times this characterization of other people becomes stereotypical and we give negative traits to those other people based on our categorization of them because simply we don't know them very well.

3. And so where we are is in a dilemma, because on the one hand there's nothing we can do about the way our brain categorizes. . . .

4. But do they mean that we should be hostile to people . . . we should kill people . . . I don't think so.

Answers:

1. c
2. g
3. e
4. f
5. h
6. i
7. a
8. b
9. j
10. d

Page 36

Listening 2

A. Before You Listen

1. Students should be placed in small groups. Have students individually read the instructions and then proceed to list the most common types of categories and examples in the chart below. Point out the sample provided. Tell students that there are no right answers but that they should try to think of the most common types of categories. When students are done, they should compare their answers with their group. However, students should not change their answers.

2. Students should again read the instructions. Remind them that they should rate the categories according to what they think most stands out in other people's minds. This is not a rating of their personal opinion on the importance of each category. They should then discuss their responses with their group.

3. The two sayings at the top of the page refer to men and women. The *them* in the American saying refers to women. Students may or may not get this. They should try to answer the first question with their group: What group is it? Students should be encouraged to guess. If they do not guess correctly, that's fine. Tell them that the American saying refers to women. Students should then proceed to discuss with their group whether or not they included men and women in their chart, and how they would rate them. Students should look at the French saying at the top of the page. It means "Long live the difference" and refers to the differences between men and women. Encourage students to think of similar sayings and translate and discuss them with their group. Each group should then share these sayings with the class as a whole.

4. The class should split into two groups, men and women. If this is impossible in your class due to an extremely uneven distribution of men and women, then create two mixed groups and have students play gender roles as needed. One group should work on creating a list of women's traits and the other on creating a list of men's traits. The class should again be encouraged to be completely honest. When the groups have finished the lists, they should switch lists. Each group will then discuss the list they have received and answer the questions. When students have discussed each question, a class discussion should take place. Ask students to tell the results of this activity and how they felt about it. Were they surprised by the traits that were attributed to men and women? Why?

Page 37

A. Who Will You Be Listening To?

Students should read the background information on Michael Barrett and Linda Farhood-Karasava on their own before listening.

B. Listening for Opinions/Summarizing

1. Students should work with a partner. Have students read the instructions and questions 1 and 2 before listening. They should be instructed to take notes on a separate piece of paper. After the listening, students should compare notes with their partner. They should agree on answers to the two questions. They should summarize their notes into one sentence to answer the questions. You may wish to circulate to check students' answers since the actual sentences will differ from pair to pair. However, each pair should make the same points in answering the two questions.

Answers:

a. Men solve problems by getting directly to the solution.

b. Women talk about their feelings to try to understand their options and possible solutions before solving the problem.

2. Students should read the instructions on their own. They should then go on to complete the chart by indicating whether Michael and Linda would agree or disagree with the statements. Make sure that students read the Thinking Strategy. It warns them to read the statements very carefully. Students need to think about what the two speakers said during the listening. What position did they take?

3. After students have done this, they should check their responses with their partner. They are now ready to listen. Students should check their responses when they listen.

Answers:

	Michael	Linda
1.	X	✔
2.	✔	✔
3.	X	X
4.	X	X
5.	X	X
6.	✔	✔

Page 38

C. Speaking Styles/Perspectives

Students should work in groups. They should discuss where Michael and Linda belong in the areas of speaking style and perspective marked below. Students should be encouraged to give examples to support their choices. You may wish to go over each group's answers with the class and then, if answers differ, tell the class where the speakers belong for each line and why.

Answers:

- Michael is a bit more formal than Linda (M2, L3).

- Students may consider Michael more humorous than Linda since Linda's humor is somewhat sarcastic. They are both humorous and should fall somewhere in the middle (M2, L3).

- Both Michael and Linda are relatively open-minded. Linda asks for Michael's opinions, and Michael readily listens to Linda (M2, L2).

- Michael seems more objective than Linda. Linda is frustrated because she cannot understand her male friend. She relates to the topic more personally than Michael (M2, L4).

D. Comparing and Contrasting

1. Instruct students to look at the language below. They should discuss this language with their groups to help clarify meaning and/or recall it occurring in the dialogue between Michael and Linda.

2. Students should continue to work in groups. Each group should choose a topic of discussion, a or b. Once they have chosen their topic, they should try to compare and contrast using the language from the above exercise when possible. Students should keep in mind what has been said about tolerance between different groups. Remind them to try to be objective.

Page 39

3. **Through the Eyes of Children**
   Students should work in groups. They should look at the cartoon on the right and discuss their impressions. They should then go on to answer and discuss the questions.

Possible Answers:

Each child sees the other as another child, similar to and not different from himself. The adults, on the other hand, notice the difference in color immediately.

At some point between early childhood and adulthood, people learn to categorize based on differences. This sometimes includes attributing negative stereotypes to the other group. This seems to be something that we are educated to do, perhaps by our family, our society, and our peers.

As John Mayher suggested, we can learn to see the similarities between people. We can be active about educating people to appreciate differences in other human beings.

E. Bonus Listening

Students should first read the excerpt from *The Butter Battle Book*. Warn them of the nature of the excerpt. For example, *Yook* and *Zook* are fictitious words. The passage is intentionally absurd and therefore may not make perfect sense to the students from the start. They should listen to the excerpt being read. Students should be encouraged to enjoy Dr. Seuss's use of language. He is loved for the clever plays on words in his rhymes. When the listening is over, students should have a group discussion. They should try to relate Dr. Seuss's message to what has been covered in the chapter. You may prompt them by asking this: What would John Mayher's reaction to this excerpt be?

Page 40

Listening 3

A. Who Will You Be Listening To?

Students should work in groups. Before starting, you may wish to elicit from them the two major political parties in the United States. Then ask them what Independents are.

B. Before You Listen

The Culture Note should help students understand the basic political positions of the Democratic and Republican parties. Even if they are not familiar with the parties, they will have an idea of what it means to be to the left or to the right. The illustration has moderates from both parties in the middle, sharing the closest position to that of the

opposing party. In the center of the Democratic party are Liberals, and in the center of the Republican party are Conservatives. The extreme opposing positions are held by Radicals on the left and Reactionaries on the right. As stated above, Independents may go with either party and therefore do not hold a permanent place to the left or to the right.

C. Notetaking

Students should read the instructions before listening. They should take notes on the speakers' answers to the first question. When the listening is over, they should compare their notes with the other members of their group. When students have agreed on the speakers' responses, they should try to guess the political positions of all three speakers. Their guesses should be checked while listening to the speakers' answers to the second question.

Answers:

Neal is a Democrat.

Democrats

Democrats do not want to make everybody alike, but they want to put some limits on how high those who succeed can go, and how low those who fail, or never succeed, can fall.

Republicans

Republicans want to basically remove government and lower the impact of government so that some people can succeed wildly and some people can fail amazingly badly.

Thomas is a Republican.

Democrats

A Democratic administration is trying to gain supporters by taking care of their needs. Or they are establishing a method of distributing wealth to various groups so that they can vote for them.

Republicans

Republicans are more entitled, more considerate of the individual's needs, individuals taking care of themselves, and having less government and more responsibility for themselves.

Stephen is an Independent.

Democrats

Democrats are the more liberal party. They tend to be more interested in finding ways that the government can expend the resources of the country in support of individual people. They always tend to be seen as the party that represents the working person.

Republicans

Republicans represent a conservative point of view. They tend to find ways to expend the resources through organizations, traditionally businesses or other large groups of people. They tend to be seen as the party which represents invested capital.

D. Analysis

Students should read the questions and discuss them with their groups. Tell students that whether or not they were able to guess the political party of a speaker may be a good indication of how objective he was. If it was easy to guess, then that person probably made one party sound more positive than the other. Also, students can use the illustration in the Culture Note to understand how accurate each speaker was.

Possible Answers:

The speakers were all fairly objective. Thomas may have been the least objective since he said that Democrats distribute wealth to various groups so that they can get votes. This is quite negative. Neal also uses language such as *succeed wildly* and *fail amazingly badly*, which puts the Republicans in a negative light. Stephen's description of the two parties as liberal and conservative matches the information in the Culture Note. He may be considered the most objective speaker.

Page 41

Video

A. What Will You Be Watching?

Students should work in groups. They will hear foreign students complaining. It would be a good idea to tell students that the speakers in the video are speakers of English as a second language. They will have different accents, some of which will be unfamiliar to the students in your class. The importance of developing listening skills for understanding nonnative speakers of English was discussed in Chapter 3. Now is a good time to refresh students' memories about the importance of such skills.

B. Notetaking/Role-Playing

For the second part of the activity, students should be placed in four groups. Have students read step 1 before seeing the video for the second time.

1. Students should together choose one character from those listed. Once they have chosen one character, they should watch the video a second time. Each student should take notes on what the character says and seems to feel throughout the video.

2. When the video is over, students should compare notes. Students should try to agree on the information they have noted. If there is anyone in the class from the same country as the character the group has chosen, then the group should ask that classmate for more information about the topics discussed in the video.

3. Once the information on the character chosen is as complete as possible, the group should elect one person to represent that character. The people chosen from each group to represent the group's character should go to the front of the room. They should role-play a four-way conversation. Each student will represent the point of view of his or her character, bringing up feelings and comments from the video and any additional perceptions the student believes the character might have. You might instruct the students to act as though they are at a café discussing the difficulties they have encountered since arriving in the United States.

C. Map Reading

Students should work together in small groups. The speakers from the video and their countries are listed with numbers beside them. Students must put the number that corresponds to the country in the appropriate place on the map. Students will likely find this task difficult. They will know the location of some countries, but not others. When they have done the best they can in groups, ask them to reflect on their knowledge. Why do they know more about some countries than others? You may want to ask students for comments on this activity with the class as a whole. This will likely reveal that most students encountered the same problem and that there is a lot to be learned about the countries of the world.

Answers:

Consult an atlas, if needed.

Chapter 5:
Art, Society, and the Artist

Page 42

Listening 1

A. Before You Listen

1. First, discuss the questions listed at the top of the page with the students as a class. These questions should be used to introduce students to the topic of the chapter, art, and to get them thinking about some of the questions the chapter will address. Allow students to express their opinions regarding these questions and ask for examples when possible.

Students should work in small groups to discuss the questions in a and b. Again, students are being asked to give personal opinions, to discuss impressions and feelings toward art. There are no correct answers, but students should be encouraged to think about what they are seeing and how it makes them feel.

Page 43

2. Have students scan the vocabulary words below. Instruct them to use other group members as a resource for understanding new vocabulary. You may wish to circulate to help students with words that all group members are having difficulty with. Pay close attention to the words *spiritual, balanced,* and *harmonious.* Try to check that students understand these words.

Students should now use the words provided to describe the pictures on pages 42 and 43. They should discuss their word choices with one another and add words of their own whenever possible. Students should try to agree on the descriptions. A difference of opinion is acceptable if the students can logically support their word choices.

Sample Answers:

Girl Before a Mirror
complex, sophisticated, modern, strong

Poseidon
balanced, reasoned, harmonious, beautiful

Peruvian bottle
earthy, balanced, decorative, strong

David
strong, harmonious, refined, beautiful

The Actor Ichikawa
controlled, geometric, balanced

Never Again War
free, strong, romantic

Buddhist temple
mystical, peaceful, refined, harmonious

B. Who Will You Be Listening To?

Have students read about Charles Olton on their own.

C. Listening for a General Topic

Students should work in pairs. Have students read the instructions and the three general topic choices before listening. Students should listen once and choose the general topic. When the listening is over, students should check their answer with a partner.

Answer: 2

D. Listening for Main Ideas

Students should read the instructions and the main idea choices on their own. Direct their attention to the Listening Note. Students are advised to try to understand the entire listening before selecting the two main ideas. Since the speaker uses most of his time giving examples, the main ideas should be evident to students after understanding the examples cited. Students should listen and then choose the two main ideas that seem most logical.

Answers:

Art reflects its own traditions. This is one of its contexts.

Social, historical, political, and economic conditions are part of the context of art.

Historical Perspective

You should discuss the time line with the class as a whole. Have students study the time line and try to volunteer answers to the question. They should pay special attention to how periods relate to each other—e.g. the Middle Ages to the Renaissance—and the duration of the periods by comparing them to the twentieth century. This exercise serves to give students a general idea of the various periods mentioned when discussing art in this chapter. It might allow them to understand the historical contexts in which specific art occurred.

E. Listening for Details

Students should work in pairs, read the instructions, and first try to complete the exercise from memory. When they have done all that they can, they should listen again and complete the exercise, checking their answers as they listen. Students may not have used Olton's exact words, but words with the same meaning. Those answers should be considered correct. Circulate to check students' answers.

Page 45

Answers:

Middle Ages/Renaissance

The social, historical, political, and economic contexts:

- the end of the Medieval period
- the decline of Medieval political organizations
- the decline of Christian church power
- the rise of the nation state
- the increase of capitalism and wealth
- the discovery of the New World

The artistic contexts:

- a rejection of Gothic forms
- a return to the Classicism of ancient Greece and Rome, which artists believed was more rational, had a greater clarity of form, and which focused on more universal concepts of beauty

Prehistory/Today

The social, historical, political, and economic contexts:

- In the ancient times, prehistoric man painted their experiences, their fears, their angers, their ideas on the walls of caves.
- Today, modern graffiti artists express the economic conditions in which they live, urban poverty, anger, protest.
- They are political and social outcasts often, and they express their ideas in this way

The artistic contexts:

- Graffiti art reflects an artistic rejection of the traditional materials of art, of paint and paper.
- Instead, graffiti artists use spray paint, and they paint on the urban environment itself.

F. Vocabulary and Dictation

1. Students should work in pairs. Ask students to read the instructions, the vocabulary words, and the definitions before you begin. They may want to complete what they can before the dictation. Tell students that that they should not interrupt. Students should understand the meaning of the vocabulary from the sentence in which it appears. Have students complete the exercise as you dictate. When they have finished, students should compare their answers with their partner.

Dictation:

1. Art always occurs in contexts . . . social, historical, political, economic conditions are part of the context of art.
2. In the ancient times, prehistoric man painted their experiences, their fears, their angers, their ideas on the walls of caves.
3. Today, modern graffiti painters put them on the walls of cities.
4. And in so doing they express the economic conditions in which they live, urban poverty, anger, protest.
5. They are political and social outcasts often, and they express their ideas in this way.

Answers:

1. c   2. g
3. d   4. e
5. f   6. b
7. a

2. Tell students that you will read a passage from the lecture. They should not interrupt while you are dictating. They should write down as much as they can and then compare their work with their partner. If students still have gaps in their passage, combine pairs and have students again compare their work. They should be able to agree on the completed passage. When they have finished, show them the actual passage and have them correct their work.

Dictation:

When I look at a painting, I always look for the contemporary influences . . . the social and political and economic influences that helped shape the painter's ideas. And I also look for what the painting builds on or rejects in its own artistic tradition.

Page 46

Listening 2

A. Before You Listen

1. Students should work alone. Emphasize to them that they should write how the art makes them *feel*, which is not the same as describing likes and dislikes. They should describe emotions rather than opinions.

2. Students should work in small groups. They should show the other members of their group what they have written without discussing it. The best way to do this may be for each person to write her name on her work and circulate it around the group.

3. Students should read the instructions and the descriptions of artistic movements on page 47. Students should work on their own to try to match the description of each movement to the corresponding image on page 46. When students have finished matching on their own, they should compare their answers with other group members. If students have different answers, they should discuss why they made their choices and try to come to an agreement on the correct match. As students work, you may wish to circulate and help if necessary.

Answers:

a. Severini   b. Malevich

c. Magritte   d. Warhol

Page 47

4. Students should give reasons for connecting the picture to the movement.

Sample Answers:

The Futurists were fascinated with the modern age—speed and movement. In this work by Severini, the surface of the painting is broken up to portray the noise and movement of shooting.

Suprematists were revolutionaries who rejected art that looked like something from the real world. The image on page 46 is unlike anything one would see in the real world. Therefore, it reflects the revolutionary ideas of the artists at that time.

Surrealist art is concerned with dreams and the unconscious. Magritte's painting portrays something that is impossible in real life, yet is painted very realistically. It is like a dream in real life. The

picture might represent a man's two selves or, because his face is not shown, someone who is not easily known, even to himself.

Pop artists emphasized the everyday images that surrounded them. They depicted these images as they saw them. Marilyn Monroe was a famous movie star in daily life. Her image reflects what was valued at that time, a famous, sexy, blond actress.

B. Who Will You Be Listening To?

Students should read the introduction to the listening on their own. Tell students that the word *Luba* is the name of a tribe. At this point, you might want to remind students that visiting museums can provide great practice for them. Most museums in major cities provide tours on audiotape describing their art collections. Whether they are in an English-speaking country or not, museums usually offer an English version of the taped tours.

C. Looking, Listening and Notetaking

1. Students should follow instructions and write descriptions of both works of art.

Page 48

2. Students should listen and take notes in the appropriate space. You may want to refresh students' memories by asking for a volunteer to give an explanation of the artistic and social contexts. This will help students to focus before starting. Once the listening is over, students should compare notes. You can either circulate to check their work or go over the answers with the class as a whole.

Answers:

Luba Chief's Stool
Social Context

The stool was used by the chief to assert his political role.

Artistic Context

To use a single piece of wood

Exaggerate the size of the head because the spirit dwells there and it is the most important part of the body

To play down the role of the fingers, toes, and feet

The women as conveyor of nature

The headdress conveys rank.

Cubist Painting

Social Context

Responding to the tradition of painting the human figure, but keeping in mind that photography and film were more objective and better able to represent nature as it is seen

Anticipated Einstein's theory of relativity by being aware that time can be experienced in different ways depending on a person's experience of it

Artistic Context

The artist is working with traditional forms but approaching them in a radical way.

Details are deemphasized, and the design is emphasized.

The use of shapes in harmony, in musical harmony with each other

3. Have students work in small groups to respond to these questions.

Page 49

D. Language—Visual Description

When you are sure that students have identified the verb usage and historical present, they can move on to exercise 1. When they are ready, they can move on to exercise 2, for which they create written descriptions of the images presented.

Sample answers:

Chuck Close

This artist uses his finger and a stamp pad to draw the picture. The details of the face are **played down**. The surface of the image is **broken up**, but the subject would still be recognizable to anyone who knew him.

Edvard Munch

This artist **emphasizes** the feeling of the night by making the area around the lovers' faces very dark. The faces themselves are much lighter and **emerge** from the darkness. Because of this, we get the impression that the lovers are intensely aware of each other.

Henry Pearson

This abstract painting consists of a series of rings that are **lined up** next to one another. Because of the way it is drawn, the relation between black and white is **emphasized** and the image creates the optical illusion that the surface is vibrating.

Page 50

Listening 3

A. Who Will You Be Listening To?

Ask the question to the class as a whole. Elicit student responses.

B. Before You Listen

Have students review the list of artists. They should look at each artist's work and discuss the pieces among themselves.

C. Notetaking

1. Students work in groups. Remind them that their goal is to record information in the form of notes. This is not a dictation. Pause between quotations to allow time for the groups to exchange information. Then, as a group, students should perform the matching activity.

2. Students work independently and then check their answers with their partners. Emphasize to students that this exercise is more of a guessing game than a test of their knowledge. Review the answers with the class. Once students understand the answers, have them discuss the topic once more.

Answers:

1-d, 2-f, 3-a, 4-b, 5-g, 6-e, 7-c

Page 51

Video

A. What Will You Be Watching?

Students should read the introduction to Reiko Tahara's film and the Listening/Watching Tip on their own. Remind students that their only task is to watch, listen, and think about their impressions. Emphasize that this is not a film that can be understood in the same way a documentary with a logical sequence would be understood. This is an art film, and students must try to understand what the film is making them feel. When the film is over, discuss the questions with the class as a whole. Encourage all students to share their impressions.

B. Identifying Themes

Students should work in groups. They should read the instructions and the themes listed on their own. They may want to discuss the options with their group before watching; this will help clarify the task for them. Students should then watch the video and check the main themes of the video in the spaces provided. They should check their work with their group and agree on the correct answers. You may wish to circulate and check their work.

Answers:

The conflict between tradition and modernization in Japan

Her own identity: self and other

The way Tahara's family deals with issues of tradition and modernization

C. Analysis and Synthesis

Students will discuss the ideas that have come up throughout the unit, as they relate to the video. They should together review the questions presented in 1–4 and answer them based on their opinions, the work they have done, and how they feel. They should discuss all responses as a group, though a consensus is not necessary. It is important that students draw on all that they have done and use the ideas and the language that have been provided to express their point of view.

Chapter 6:
Smarts

Page 52

Listening 1

A. Before You Listen

1. You should read the tapescripts in this chapter before beginning to teach it. The first two listenings will discuss the eight different types of intelligences to be discussed in this unit. The types of intelligences traditionally tested through standard I.Q. testing are mathematical and linguistic intelligence. In this introduction, students are asked to think about the validity of such testing. Students should work in groups to answer the questions. Allow groups time to discuss this introduction based on students' personal experiences.

   a. It is assumed that at least some students in each group will bring up the point that not all students who are successful in school are successful in life. Encourage students to give examples from their experiences.

   b. Students should again try to come up with examples to support their answers to this

question. There are no right or wrong answers, so students should be encouraged to explore and draw on their own observations and experiences and those of other group members.

Preparation Note

Tell students that the more they know about their own strengths and weaknesses by the end of this chapter, the more rewarding the project will be for them. Therefore, they should record personal strengths and weaknesses as they recognize them throughout the chapter.

2. Students should read the definition and discuss the questions below. They will probably recognize that most of the exams they have taken in the past were based on linguistic and mathematical intelligence. Circulate to make sure that students are coping with the definition and the questions.

3. **Answers:**

linguistic, logical/mathematical, musical, spatial, bodily/kinesthetic, intrapersonal, interpersonal

Page 53

4. Students should work in pairs. They should read and discuss the characteristics of linguistic and mathematical/logical intelligence listed in the boxes. After they have done this, it may be a good idea to check back with the class as a whole to ensure that students have begun to understand how several characteristics might be classified under one type of intelligence. The point is again made that these two types of intelligences are tested by I.Q. tests. You might want to ask them for an example to back up this statement. Students should be able to respond that I.Q. tests are usually made up of mathematical problems to solve, vocabulary words to define, and reading comprehension exercises. Ask students how linguistic intelligence might be important for learning a language such as English. Students should be able to look at the list and respond, for example, that a person with excellent verbal vocabulary and writing skills in his or her own native language is likely to cope well with writing and vocabulary skills in a foreign language.

   a. Students remain in pairs; however, they

should first work individually to find the characteristics on the lists that best describe them. Once they have done this, they can share their answers with their partner.

b. Students will likely differ in their opinions. They may not be able to see the possibility of a person who is not linguistically intelligent succeeding in school. However, they will probably answer yes to succeeding in learning English and in life. Encourage students to give examples. They may know a person who succeeded in learning English without formal instruction. Surely they will all know someone who is successful and happy in life, yet lacks the characteristics associated with linguistic intelligence.

c. Student responses will likely differ. Again, encourage students to bring their personal experiences to the discussion.

B. Who Will You Be Listening To?

Students should read the background information on Mara Krechevsky on their own. However, you may wish to go over some of the areas that Project Zero deals with. Ask students what *assessment* is and how it might relate to education. Assessment is evaluation, and the assessment or evaluation of students' progress is an important factor in education. You might also want to ask students what they think a curriculum that recognizes individual differences might be. Students should be able to respond that such a curriculum would include nontraditional ideas for teaching based on the various interests and strengths of individual students. Also, remind students that Howard Gardner is the man who was quoted on page 52. They may want to go back and read his quotation. These issues should encourage students to start thinking about the topic of the listening.

Page 54

C. Listening for a General Topic

Students should read the general topic statements before listening. When the listening is over, they may compare their answers with a partner, or you may wish to go over the answer with the class as a whole.

Answer: 1

D. Listening for Specific Information

1. Students should work in pairs and read the intelligences listed. They should then listen and number the intelligences in the blanks below in the order that they hear Mara Krechevsky discuss them. When the listening is over, have students check their answers.

Answers:

linguistic

mathematical/logical

musical

spatial

bodily/kinesthetic

intrapersonal

interpersonal

naturalistic

2. Students should read the instructions and definitions a–h before listening. Students should match each intelligence to its description on the right and write in the corresponding letter. When the listening is over, partners should discuss and agree on their answers. You may want to work with the class as a whole to check the answers. Each pair can offer one or more responses.

Answers:

1. h. linguistic
2. g. mathematical/logical
3. f. musical
4. a. spatial
5. c. bodily/kinesthetic
6. d. intrapersonal
7. e. interpersonal
8. b. naturalistic

Culture Note

Have the students read the Culture Note and discuss it with their partner. Ask them to compare the information in the Culture Note to their knowledge of the educational systems in their own countries.

Page 55

E. Vocabulary and Dictation

1. Tell students that you will dictate a series of sentences and phrases to them. Students should first review the vocabulary words and synonyms

in a–d with their partner. You may want to ask students if they can match two synonyms to each vocabulary word before listening and allow them to try before the dictation. Each vocabulary item will appear in one phrase or sentence in the dictation. Tell students that they should understand the meaning of each vocabulary item by listening to the context it is used in. When the dictation is finished, students should check their answers with a partner and work on any answers they have missed.

Dictation:

1. Traditionally people have thought of intelligence as being a single entity. . . .

2. In 1983 Howard Gardner came up with a different notion of what an intelligence is. He devised a theory called the theory of multiple intelligences.

3. He had a set of eight criteria that he used to determine whether or not an ability counted as an intelligence.

4. He looked at whether he could identify core capacities; he looked at what was valued in different cultures. And then based on these kinds of criteria he came up with a list of seven, and currently there are eight, intelligences.

2. Students should write what they hear and then check their work with their partner. They should agree on the correct wording before being provided with the answer.

Answers:

a. entity—thing, item

b. notion—belief, idea

c. devised—developed, invented

d. multiple—many, several

e. criteria—requirements, rules

f. determine—discover, find

g. core—central, basic

h. capacities—abilities, capabilities

i. valued—appreciated, respected

j. based—built, developed

k. currently—now, at the moment

Dictation:

He looked at whether he could identify core capacities; he looked at what was valued in different

cultures. And then based on these kinds of criteria he came up with a list of seven, and currently there are eight, intelligences.

Spatial/Visual Test Samples

Have the students read the Spatial/Visual Intelligence characteristics in the box (p. 57) and discuss the information with their partner. Remind them to note any characteristics that they feel they have. Students can then try the samples. Tell them that they should have fun with this but not to give the answers away before their partner has finished.

Answers:

The form on the bottom right corner matches the one on the left.

(B) and (C) are the same but are shown from a different angle.

Page 56

Listening 2

A. Before You Listen

Students should work in groups. They should first read the *New York Observer* editorial on their own. Encourage students to help each other with any difficulties in the reading. Students should then work together to discuss and answer questions 1–4. Circulate while students work. You may want to bring interesting responses to the attention of the class.

B. Who Will You Be Listening To?

Students should read this introduction to the speakers on their own. This discussion is an authentic "brainstorming" session between Victoria Kimborough and Marjorie Vai about a subject that they are genuinely interested in exploring in order to help ESL learners.

Have students read the Listening Strategy note. Emphasize that despite the length of this listening it is not excessively difficult because students will likely be familiar with the language used. Students should focus on their task, noting the suggestions that the speakers offer.

Page 57

C. Listening to a Brainstorming Session on Language Learning/Notetaking

1. Students should read the introduction to the listening task and the instructions on their own.

Have students read the seven intelligences listed to refresh their memories. You might want to ask students if they can predict any of the suggestions that might be talked about. For example, ask them what somebody with musical intelligence might do to improve his or her English. Students will likely suggest listening to songs in English. You should try to elicit only one or two examples of suggestions that might be discussed. Students will have the opportunity to come up with others after the listening.

Possible Responses:

Linguistic: All of the things that apply to them (linguistic intelligence) would apply to being a good language learner.

Mathematical/Logical: Look at the patterns of a language and see how they relate to each other. Pay attention to grammatical diagramming and paradigms in books, or put what you've learned into a diagram yourself. Fill in the blanks in patterns that weren't necessarily emphasized in class, or find a book that emphasizes patterns to use outside of class.

Spatial/Visual: Pictures would help. Watch television and connect words to what is going on, on television. Make images in your mind when trying to learn vocabulary words. Look at magazines and connect words with pictures, then create cards.

Musical: Work with songs and learn the language through songs. Put a rhythm and a beat to the words you are trying to learn. Many songs tell stories, and this provides a natural context for the language. Songs also have colloquialisms and idioms.

Physical/Bodily: Anything you are able to do while you're learning will help. Physical games and connecting gestures will help. Put the language that you are learning together with the body movement and expressions, and learn how people interact physically with each other in that culture. Use language to write plays and act them out.

Interpersonal: Take risks in an English-speaking country, talk to people, ask them questions, and find yourself in social situations. If you don't live in an English-speaking country, call an embassy and ask for information, or call your classmates and talk with them. Enjoy talking to other people.

Intrapersonal: Think about the way you are using

language, practice putting sentences together in your head, have imaginary conversations in your head. Plan what you're going to say before you say it. Keep a journal.

2. At the end of the listening, partners should compare answers and complete the chart.

Page 58

D. Language—Brainstorming/Discussing Possibilities

1. Students should read the introduction, along with the language under **Modals, Conditionals,** and **Phrases.** Students may discuss any questions they have about this information with a partner. You may wish to circulate and help students when necessary. To illustrate the point that the speakers infer and suggest, you may want to write a sentence from the listening on the board. For example: *And people who have the logical/mathematical intelligence might want to pay more attention to those grammatical diagrams. . . .* This will help students to focus on the listening task.

Remind students to read the intelligence boxes on this page. They will use them for the task they are working on. They should also note any characteristics that seem to fit their personal profile. This will be helpful later when they work on the project.

2. Students should listen and check off modals, conditionals, and phrases. Again, it is unlikely that students will get all of them, and you may wish to tell them that. When the listening is over, have partners compare their notes. Circulate to see what students were able to note. If you feel students would benefit, go over their results with the class as a whole.

Page 59

3. Students should work in groups. Have students read the instructions and begin this task by reviewing their notes on the intelligences on pages 54 and 57. Students' task is to brainstorm about things the person might do to benefit from their particular intelligence(s). Instruct students that they must first identify the particular characteristics of the person they are reading about and decide what kind of intelligence(s) the person has. They can refer to

the intelligence boxes that appear throughout the chapter to do this. Once this is agreed upon by the group, students should brainstorm to come up with ideas to help this person improve his or her English. Emphasize to students that they should refer to the modals, conditionals, and phrases on page 58 and use that language in their discussion.

Answers:

The following are some ideas that students may come up with. Accept any ideas that students can logically support.

1. Jan has linguistic intelligence since he has good language skills in Polish. He also has musical intelligence. Students may even argue that he has logical/mathematical intelligence because he has a growing manufacturing business. Since he does not have enough time to study English, but spends two hours a day in the car, he should use that time to improve his English. This can be done by listening to songs in English and trying to understand the words and the stories in the songs. By singing along, he can practice English pronunciation, rhythm, and intonation. He might also try to use ESL tapes for instruction in the car. He has good linguistic skill, so it is likely that he will be able to learn from an instructional cassette.

2. Miki has visual/spatial intelligence, logical/mathematical intelligence, and intrapersonal intelligence. Her intrapersonal intelligence should help her to understand her strengths and weaknesses. Therefore, she should be advised to consider how she might use her strengths to improve her English. Miki can use visual images to remember English vocabulary. She would also benefit from using grammatical diagrams and patterns. Since she has intrapersonal intelligence, she probably enjoys working alone. She should keep a journal of visual images, pictures, drawings, and grammatical diagrams and patterns that reflect the new language she is learning in class. This might help her to better learn what she is studying.

3. Yolanda has logical/mathematical intelligence, intrapersonal intelligence, and bodily/physical intelligence. She should seek English-speaking people to interact with in social situations. This

might include playing sports and doing other physical activities with English-speaking people, such as hiking or dancing. She will then have the opportunity to practice English in a social setting and to communicate using language generated by the physical activities she enjoys. She may also want to buy an English grammar book that provides her with diagrams for self-study. Though she will spend a limited amount of time on this, she may find the language she hears in social situations clearly mapped out for her in such a text.

Page 60

Listening 3

A. Who Will You Be Listening To?

Students should work in groups. They will hear three listenings. Before beginning this task, you might want to ask students how they think the intelligences they have been studying might relate to work. Allow students to express their ideas and then tell them that they will have the chance to discuss this subject further after the listening.

B. Listening for Specific Information/Notetaking

1. Students can take notes individually on what the speakers say about their strengths and how they relate to work.

2. Students should then compare their work with their group members and agree on the correct information for each speaker. You may want to circulate to be sure that each group has recorded accurate information.

Answers:

Karen

Strengths

Interpersonal intelligence—she likes working with people and sees herself as a leader.

Intrapersonal intelligence—she clearly likes to reflect.

Musical intelligence—she likes to express herself through performing.

How they relate to work

She needs a job that allows her to relate to other people, such as teaching. She also wants be able to help people through music and leadership.

George

Strengths

Interpersonal intelligence—he's comfortable with people, he's a good advisor, and he has several good friends.

Linguistic intelligence—he writes a lot, reads a lot, and often speaks to groups.

Visual/spatial intelligence—he works with artists and art directors and designers, and visits museums in his free time.

How they relate to work

He's a public relations professional, director of communications at a university, so he works with people a great deal. He works with artists and speaks to groups as part of his job.

Robert

Strengths

Intrapersonal intelligence—he has a strong need to be alone to work things out.

Visual/spatial intelligence—he is creative, and the visual affects everything he does.

Interpersonal intelligence—he doesn't express any particular strengths for this intelligence, but he says that all of them fit.

Mathematical/logical—he does a lot of administrative duties that are very logical.

How they relate to work

He has his own business, running a photography department at a university, and he is also a creative artist. He uses all of his strengths in his work.

C. Brainstorming—Working with Your Strengths

Students should work in small groups. They must first think of their personal strengths and skills. This should not be difficult since they were asked to consider them throughout the unit. Students should tell their group members what their strengths and skills are, and then, together with the group, come up with work situations that would match these characteristics. The group should focus on one person at a time and analyze the information they have been told by that person to come up with some suggestions.

Page 61

Project

A. What Will You Be Doing?

Students should read the introduction to the project on their own. This project is really a self-study. You may want to discuss the question in the box with the class as a whole: What if, all of a sudden, the entire world accepted this view of intelligence? Students may come up with ideas about changes in education and in the way people relate to and appreciate each other. The discussion should be open, allowing students to respond according to their personal perspectives on this topic.

B. Self-Assessment

Students should take time to reflect on their personal strengths and weaknesses. Hopefully, students will have recorded some of their self-assessment observations throughout the chapter. If not, the intelligence boxes that appear in the chapter can serve as a guide for them. Remind students of the importance of understanding their intelligences. Self-assessment allows them to explore their strengths and weaknesses. Once they have understood these aspects of themselves as learners, they can begin to address their language learning needs.

1. Once students have given careful thought to their strengths and weaknesses, they should record them on a piece of paper. By using two columns they can easily see strengths and weaknesses listed. They may find that they have, for example, characteristics of intrapersonal intelligence on both the strengths side and the weaknesses side. That's OK. Few people fit one category perfectly.

2. Students should now apply their strengths and weaknesses to language learning. Tell them to think about the aspects of language learning that come easily to them, and what's difficult for them. They can make two columns again for strengths and weaknesses. Here the students are being asked to apply specific characteristics of their intelligence(s) from the first list to language learning. Circulate to make sure that students are doing just that.

C. Brainstorming with a Group

Students should now work in small groups. Students

should take turns telling their group their language learning strengths and weaknesses. Group members should take notes on this information. They should then take turns suggesting ways that person can use his or her strengths to improve as an English language learner. The student who is receiving the advice should create a list of the suggestions offered. By the end of this discussion, each group member should have a list of activities that will help him or her with language learning.

D. Presentation

1. Each student should summarize what he or she has learned about their language learning needs.

2. Students should present their new approach to language learning to the class. Allow students to comment and ask questions after each presentation. Also, encourage students to add any ideas they have heard to their own list if these seem appropriate. This is a time for students to learn from one another. Presentations should also help students to realize that everybody has different strengths and weaknesses and that everybody has the ability to become a good language learner.

E. Applying This Knowledge to Other Things

You may want to do this activity as a class, or split students into new small groups. Students should extend what they have learned about themselves as language learners and apply this knowledge to other areas of their lives. They should discuss their ideas about how their intelligence(s) applies to their personal life, career plans, personal interests, etc.

Chapter 7:
Crime as Entertainment

Page 62

Listening 1

Write the chapter title, "Crime as Entertainment," on the board and elicit ideas from the students about what the title means. Once ideas have been heard, ask students to explain to you what *sensationalism* means. Their answers will help the discussion along, and this is a good vocabulary check as well. Ask students to give examples of

television shows, movies, books, etc. in which crime serves as entertainment.

A. Before You Listen

1. Students should work in small groups. Have students read the quotation and answer the question above.

2. Students should then go on to check the statements they agree with individually and then compare their answers with other group members. Then students should discuss the most violent movie they have ever seen. While students are having their discussion, you might circulate to help students if they seem to have difficulty with the meanings of any of the statements.

Page 63

B. Who Will You Be Listening To?

Students should work in small groups. They should read the background information on Robert Polito and then individually predict what he might say about crime in literature, writing one idea on a piece of paper. They can then take turns reading their ideas to other group members, or they can circulate the written ideas from member to member to read.

Page 64

C. Listening for a General Topic

Students should remain in their small groups. They should read the instructions and all three general topic choices before listening. After listening, students can compare answers. You may wish to circulate to ensure that each group has answered correctly.

Answer: 2

D. Listening for Specific Information

Students should now work in pairs. Direct students' attention to the outline below. Point out that there is information missing in this outline of Robert Polito's lecture. The missing information is above. Give students time to read the main ideas and supporting details, and to discuss with their partner where each sentence should be placed in the outline. They may want to note their answers before listening. Students should then listen for the information needed to complete the outline. After the listening, pairs can agree on the correct answers.

Answers:

II. People who criticize today's entertainment for its focus on violence and shock forget about the violence in great literature of the past.

    b. In Ancient Greece, Shakespeare's time, and on into today, murder has been the theme of much great literature.

III. Our interest in murder is quite serious.

    a. Murder forces us to look at our basic beliefs about how the world works, about justice, and about ourselves.

Page 65

E. Focus—Listening for Specific Information

Students should read the statements before listening. Have students listen and correct the statements. When they have finished, students should compare their answers with their partner.

Answers:

1. Detective fiction in America begins with the short stories of Edgar Allan Poe.

2. The crime novel *Wieland* was published in 1798.

3. The Globe Theater burned down when a cannonball landed on the roof.

4. Television crime shows and video games are forms of modern media.

5. Gangsta rap is a type of music.

F. Vocabulary and Dictation

1. Students should read the instructions and items a–c before the dictation. Tell students that there are two synonyms for each vocabulary item. They may be able to fill in some of the answers before listening. Students should listen to the dictation twice without interrupting. They should choose the correct synonyms for each vocabulary item based on the dictation. When they have finished, students should compare their answers with a partner. You may wish to circulate to check answers.

Dictation:

1. Detective fiction, as you know, begins with the short stories of Edgar Allan Poe in the middle of the nineteenth century.

2. A character hears voices telling him to kill his family.

3. Politicians and editorial writers like to condemn contemporary literature and film for its reliance on violence and shock.

4. Murder is still one of those events in which the universe appears to crack open and every crucial ethical, moral issue jumps out at you, impossible to ignore.

Answers:

a. fiction—invention, fantasy

    character—person, individual

b. condemn—criticize, attack

    contemporary—modern, new

    reliance—need, dependence

c. universe—cosmos, heavens

    crucial—important, significant

    ethical—moral, virtuous

    ignore—overlook, disregard

2. Students should listen to the dictation and write as much of it as possible. Tell them that they should not ask questions during the dictation. When you have finished dictating, students can check their work with a partner. If students cannot complete the dictation in pairs, they can join another pair and compare further. They should then have a completed version of the dictation. Allow students to check their work by looking at the actual dictation.

Dictation:

Murder has been the subject of so much great literature. . . . And I think the appeal really is ultimately quite serious. Murder is still one of those events in which the universe appears to crack open, and every crucial ethical, moral issue jumps out at you, impossible to ignore.

Page 66

Listening 2

A. Before You Listen

Students should read the History/Culture Note on the First Amendment and freedom of speech. Allow students time to read the questions before discussing them with the class. Students' responses to the questions will vary depending on their personal point of view, culture, and experiences. Encourage students to give examples, perhaps based on freedom of speech in their own countries. The last question relates to the work that the students will be doing in this chapter. Freedom of speech protects filmmakers' right to include violence in film despite possible effects this might have on society. This is true for all forms of entertainment in the United States.

1. Ask the class if anyone has seen *Natural Born Killers*. If someone has, ask him or her to describe the film in his or her own words. The class should then proceed to read the description of *Natural Born Killers* provided in the text. Students should read the ad for *Natural Born Killers* as well. Discuss the questions with the class as a whole. Students will likely express opposing opinions about this film and violent films in general. This will be a good lead-in to the controversy that follows on page 67.

Page 67

2. Students should work in pairs. They should first read the introduction to the article presented in *The Oxford American* magazine. When students have finished, instruct them to read the arguments made by John Grisham and Oliver Stone. They should discuss these arguments and make notes agreeing or disagreeing with each point made, in the spaces provided. If students cannot agree, that's fine. Have them listen to each other's point of view and then note what they feel appropriate in their book. Circulate as students work. The language presented in these arguments is not easy, and students may need your help as they work.

Page 68

B. Who Will You Be Listening To?
Have students read the background information on David Rogers and Robyn Vaccara on their own.

C. Listening for Main Ideas/Notetaking
1. When they have finished reading, students should listen to the conversation between David and Robyn and write down at least two points that each speaker makes.

Possible Answers:

David

It's . . . a good kind of escapism.

It can have a cathartic effect of just like cleansing out that violence that's inside of you.

You can't deny reality and the human character . . . we all have a dark side.

I believe in the First Amendment; people should be able to see or do whatever they want as long as it's not negatively impacting society.

Robyn

It's irresponsible to sensationalize crime.

Violence has a bad effect on us; it's everywhere (in media); we need more beauty in our lives.

There needs to be a balance.

There should not be a law against making these films . . . but at the same time . . . freedom means we have a responsibility to try to do something positive in our world.

2. Students should compare notes with their partner. As students listen the second time, they should add their own notes to the points made. After the listening, have students discuss their responses with their partner.

D. Recognizing Fillers in Spoken English
Have students read the Culture/Language Note on their own. You might want to ask the students if they recognized the fillers. Do they generally notice fillers in English that they hear in real situations? In their native language? What fillers do they use? Emphasize to students that fillers are not incorrect, but rather a part of normal colloquial English. They tend to differ depending on the age of the person speaking and the situation. It is likely that in a formal situation fewer fillers would be used. Play the tape again and instruct students to raise their hands each time they hear a filler.

E. The Language of Disagreeing
Students should work in small groups. Have students read the instructions on their own. You may want to go over the examples with the class as a whole to make sure that students understand the difference between language used to disagree directly and language used to disagree indirectly. Remind them that after completing the exercise, the group as a whole should discuss how each expression should be used.

Answers:

x	I agree, but
x	I don't know
xx	I disagree

x	I partly agree, but
x	I'm not so sure
xx	How can you feel that way when
x	I certainly understand, but
x	(But) by the same token . . .
x	(But) don't you think?
x	I wish I could agree with you, but
xx	But there needs to be
xx	(But) I think
xx	I don't think so
x	That may be true, but
xx	How can you say that!

Page 69

F. Debating an Issue

1. Students should be split into two large groups. Tell students that they will need the notes they created earlier in the chapter. Students should compare and discuss the notes that they made on page 68 with their group.

2. Have each group split. Half the students should work on preparing an argument for crime in entertainment and half against. Students should use the appropriate column below to prepare their arguments. They will probably need additional paper to write their supporting points. Tell students that they should refer to their work on the previous pages to gather support for their argument. They should also use the language of disagreement above when appropriate. Circulate to answer questions when necessary.

3. When the *for* and *against* groups have finished, each student should find a partner from his or her original group with an opposing argument. Instruct students to sit down with their partner and argue the point of view they have worked on. Remind students that the arguments should be serious but not aggressive. They should stick to their point and use language as a tool to support that point.

4. The class as a whole should discuss how effective the arguments were. Ask them for specific examples. Ask students if the exercise changed their opinion in any way. If so, ask how.

Page 70

Listening 3

A. Who Will You Be Listening To?

Have the students read the introduction to the speakers on their own. Ask students to predict what point of view each person might have on crime in entertainment in general.

B. Comparing Two Perspectives on an Issue/ Notetaking

1. Students should work in pairs. Have students read the instructions and the quotations on their own. Then students should try to predict what John Douglas and Laura Morgan might say in response to the questions. Students should discuss their predictions with their partner. They can guess from John Douglas's statement that he feels there is a reasonable explanation why people are attracted to violence. Laura Morgan, on the other hand, indicates that she is disturbed by this attraction to violence. Students should then listen and write down the points each of the speakers makes in the spaces provided.

2. When the listening is over, students should compare their notes with a partner. You may want to circulate to check students' work and then go over the answers with the class as a whole.

Answers:

John Douglas

People are so troubled by injustice in their daily walk, and by the incomprehensibility of violence, that they either want release from that uncertainty and fear or they want to blow away those things in a burst of violence. Either of these releases can be available through crime fiction.

Laura Morgan

Students are showing that they enjoy watching someone else being hurt. This may be because it is not them, they can be victorious, they can vicariously experience danger and death and survive, but it's frightening. It's like the old saying, if something bad happens to someone else, it's comedy; if it happens to you, it's tragedy.

C. Personal Perspective

Students should work in groups and discuss the questions. Remind students that there are no right or wrong answers. They should talk about their own feelings and point of view. They should try to analyze how they react to violence in entertainment.

Page 71

Video

A. What Will You Be Watching?

Before students read the introduction to the video, you might want to ask questions to elicit some information from them and be sure that all students understand the following issues: What is the death penalty? Why do people usually get the death penalty in the United States? What is Death Row? When these questions have been answered, students can go on to read the introduction to the video. Allow students time to discuss the information in pairs and to ask you questions if necessary. It is important that they understand the basic story before beginning the video.

B. Watching for Specific Information

1. Students should read the instructions and then read each of the facts listed below. They must put these events in the correct order while watching the first part of the crime video. Emphasize that when the facts are in the correct order, they will describe the crime. Students should compare their answers with their partner when the video is over. They should agree on the correct order. Circulate to make sure that each pair has the correct answers. *Note: the crime video is split into three parts, with pauses between each part.*

Answers:
2
4
3
1
6
5

2. Direct students' attention to the box at the right. The speakers in the video are listed in the order that they appear. Students will listen to the rest of the video and check each speaker who says something in favor of Peter. They should read the list once before listening. When they have finished, have students check their answers with their partner.

Answers:

Peter Miller

Geoffrey Scott

Peter Montgomery

Mrs. Montgomery

3. Students will watch the entire video again. Each student should choose one of the ten characters and take notes on that character. They should record what their character says, his or her point of view. Tell students that they will have the chance to watch the tape again and check their notes.

4. Play the tape for students a third time.

C. Role-Playing

Students should work in pairs. They will role-play the character who they took notes on. One student should take on the role of a reporter, asking questions about the crime. The other student should tell the story from the point of view of his or her character. When they have finished, they should switch roles. Each student should get the opportunity to tell the story from his or her character's point of view while the other acts like a reporter.

D. Analysis and Synthesis

When students finish their role-plays, they should discuss the remaining question with their partner. You might want to then get a class consensus on the guilt or innocence of Peter Montgomery.

Chapter 8:

Work in the 21st Century

Note: At the end of this chapter there is a student project. You should look at the project now so that you can begin to prepare your students for it. Students should have several days to prepare since it involves interviewing outside of the classroom. Let them know when they should begin interviewing, and what day the project will be due.

Pages 72–73

Listening 1

A. Before You Listen

1. Direct the students' attention to the cartoon. Elicit some responses from them. Then, as

students answer the questions, you may want to list these responses on the blackboard.

2–5. Students should be placed in small groups. Give each group one of the questions to discuss. Be aware that this activity is likely to take a considerable amount of class time. Students should be told that they will need to report a summary of their discussion to the class. Since there are visuals that the students will need to interpret, be sure that you circulate from group to group making sure students are on the right track. After each group has explored its assigned question, a class discussion can take place during which students learn new information from their peers.

B. Who Will You Be Listening To?
Have students read about Vivian Eyre. Students may be particularly interested in Eyre's work with women in the workplace. Ask students if there are similar organizations in their countries.

Page 74
C. Listening for a General Topic
Students should read the instructions and the possible topics before listening.

Answer: 1

D. Listening for Main Ideas/Notetaking
1. After reading the instructions and the Listening/Notetaking Tip, ask students if they can remember the changes that Vivian Eyre discussed in the listening. Have students read the first main idea before the listening. Students may fill out the actual main ideas individually and then compare their notes with a partner.

Answers:
1. 33% of the workforce will be minorities, with major growth in Asian and Hispanic communities.
2. Globalization of business . . . business is going to need to expand to foreign markets.
3. Technology will be a part of every worker's job, regardless of the job, regardless of the level within the company.

2. Students should read the instructions and do this exercise in pairs.

Answers:
a. 2
b. 3
c. 3
d. 2
e. 1

E. Listening for Specific Information/Making Inferences
Students should work in pairs. Have students read the Listening Note. Emphasize that their answers should be based *only* on what Vivian Eyre has said. They should *not* guess what she thinks here. Point out that these are not Vivian Eyre's exact words.

Answers:
1. X
2. X
3. ?
4. ✔
5. ✔
6. ?

Have students discuss their answers with a partner.

Page 75
F. Vocabulary and Dictation
1. Tell students that you will read the sentences at a normal pace. Students should not ask you to repeat the sentences during this exercise. Students should read the items before your dictation begins. Tell students that they should listen for the vocabulary words in the exercises and try to understand their meanings from the context of the sentence read to them. Students should check their answers with their partner.

Dictation:
1. 33% of the workforce will be minorities, with major growth in Asian and Hispanic communities.
2. Business, and what that means is that business is going to need to expand to foreign markets.
3. This means that I have to regularly evaluate: "What are my strengths? What are my liabilities?" and to be able to build on my strengths and minimize my liabilities.

4. Every new entrant into the workplace can expect to have ten jobs by the time he or she retires.

5. These future jobs are going to require more skills. Skills in technology, in reading, in math, and in critical thinking.

Answers:

1. f
2. d
3. a
4. b
5. e
6. c

2. Students should do this exercise with a partner.

Answers:

1. evaluate, critical
2. retire
3. liability
4. expand
5. minority

3. Instruct students that you will read the dictation sentences at a normal pace. They should not interrupt you to ask for repetition. Assure them that they will have the opportunity to complete whatever they missed after the dictation. Students should check their answers in pairs. If you find that students are not able to get complete answers in pairs, you may want to put them into small groups and have them fill in missing words together until the dictation sentences are complete.

Dictation

What we learned from the Hudson Report is that by the year 2000, every new entrant into the workplace can expect to have ten jobs by the time he or she retires. These future jobs are going to require more skills. Skills in technology, in reading, in math and in critical thinking. So people who are going to be successful are going to need to be lifelong learners.

4. Students should work with a partner and read the instructions on their own.

Answers:

1. g

2. d
3. a
4. b
5. e
6. c
7. f

G. Critical Thinking and Analysis

Students should work in groups. They should read the quotation together and decide on its meaning before discussing their opinions. The quotation may be difficult for them, but as a group they should come to a correct understanding of its meaning. Circulate and make sure that they are on the right track. You may want to give students a time limit for this task.

Page 76

Listening 2

A. Before You Listen

1. Again, students should work through the instructions in their groups. However, you should circulate to make sure that they understand the introduction to this exercise. Each group should discuss the importance of the points listed. You also have the option of assigning only one point to each group and asking them to report their findings to the class. Be sure to direct the students' attention to the Culture Note. Give examples of university internship programs or other internships with which you are familiar.

2. Again, students should work in groups. You may wish to change the groups so that students work with different classmates. Students should discuss questions a–e. Circulate to make sure that students understand the questions and the chart. When appropriate to a specific question, ask students to draw from their knowledge of work in their countries. The chart illustrates that there is growth in the job market for highly educated people, and a decrease in jobs available to people who have not gone on to higher education.

B. Who Will You Be Listening To?

Students should read the introduction to the second listening with Vivian Eyre. Be sure to direct their attention to the Listening Strategy. You may want the class to discuss some of the predictions they can make about this listening.

Page 77

C. Notetaking and Summarizing

1–3. Students should work in pairs. Have students read the instructions on their own. Be sure that they take notes on a separate piece of paper the first time they listen. They should discuss their work between listening. Note the language Vivian Eyre uses to introduce each point: *First of all, Second, Third, Fourth, Finally.* You may find that students disagree on the last point because they may not recognize that the word *finally* introduces point five. This is a good opportunity to make students aware of such cues.

Answers:

1. Really continue your education; a high school degree is no longer going to be enough for even entry-level positions.

2. Find a teacher who can really teach you business skills.

3. Take charge of your career by asking yourself, "Will this new position teach me anything new?"

4. Learn about the company's culture.

5. Cultivate courage within, to persevere in the face of obstacles.

D. Making Inferences

Students should work in pairs. Emphasize that in this exercise they are going to use their knowledge of Vivian Eyre to *guess* how she might react. Compare this to the exercise on page 74, where they were told not to guess but rather to base their answers on what she actually said.

Answers:

1. ?
2. ✔
3. X
4. X
5. ✔
6. ?
7. ✔
8. ✔
9. ?

10. ✔
11. X
12. ✔

Page 78

E. Problem Solving and Giving Advice

Students should work in pairs. You may give each pair a chance to develop each counseling situation. Alternatively, you may wish to assign each pair only one situation. After students have worked on their situations, they can role-play them for the class. The rest of the class can discuss whether they agree or disagree with the advice given, or whether Vivian Eyre would agree or disagree with the advice given. If possible, these role-plays can be videotaped. Students can later watch themselves and evaluate their work.

Page 79

Students can work in pairs to complete this crossword puzzle. Go over the Note with the students. It may be easiest to actually do a couple of the items with students to be sure they understand how to complete the crossword puzzle. Advise them that they should skip items that are too difficult and go on to others. When pairs have done all that they can, have students form groups to go over answers. It is likely that someone in the group will have the correct answer to each item.

Answers:

Across

1. success
4. charts
8. pair
9. i.e.
10. apply
12. it
13. set
14. pen
15. ET
16. global village
20. EC
21. mom
22. biases
24. NA
25. ITP
26. tip
27. loan

28. co
30. ma
31. economy
35. some
36. am
38. gossip
40. prep
41. ivy
42. net
43. in
44. vent
46. event
47. overcome
48. on

Down

1. so
2. changeable
3. spy
4. critical
5. am
6. tie
7. set
11. pro
13. stamina
14. problem
15. even
17. business
18. got
19. employment
23. ETA
28. compete
29. one
30. my
32. coin
33. market
34. lover
37. memo
38. give
39. sync
43. inc
45. to

Page 80

Listening 3

A. Who Will You Be Listening To?
Explain to students that these three speakers are relatively young (under 35). Two are American, and Marcello is Italian and therefore speaks English

with an accent.

B. Notetaking
1. Students should take notes for each speaker. You may want to play the listening more than once depending on how students do.

Answers:

Refer to the tapescripts.

2. Have students check their answers with each other before listening for a second time.

C. Analysis
1. Students should continue to work in pairs and discuss each speaker and whether or not the speaker's plan illustrates some of the advice that Vivian Eyre gives. They should write their conclusions in the spaces provided.

2. Students should then answer the last question and discuss the answer with their partner.

D. Practical Applications
Students should discuss their career plans with a partner and answer the questions. You may want to give students a time limit for this exercise.

Page 81

Project
Students will interview people outside of the classroom. You might want to give students suggestions on where to find these people. If you feel it is possible, suggest that students go to a park or a store and interview absolute strangers. This will require more confidence in the language than interviewing a friend or an acquaintance. However, make this decision based on your students, their schedules, and the surrounding environment. Have the students read the Culture Note. This should make them feel more confident about asking people about their jobs.

A. Planning an Interview
1. Place the students in groups of three, or allow them to form their own groups of three. Have them read the topics and circulate to make sure that they understand each topic.

2. Once students have chosen their interview topics, they should choose appropriate questions from the list of issues provided. Encourage students to create additional questions. You may

choose to tell them that they must each add one original question to their list.

B. Conducting the Interview

Students should be given a deadline for interviewing two or three people. If you are teaching in an English-speaking environment, you might want to tell students that the interviews must be conducted in English.

C. Summarizing

Students should work together in their original groups and discuss their findings. A final summary should be written and reported to the entire class. An alternative to this is to have students report their findings individually at the front of the class. If you choose to do this, you should still allow students to practice by discussing their findings with their groups beforehand. If possible, these final reports can be videotaped for student self-assessment.

Chapter 9:
The Dreaming Self

Page 82

Notes on Freud and the unconscious: Freud was one of the first academic thinkers to concentrate on the unconscious in his studies and practice. The unconscious in psychology is considered to be the part of our mind that contains memories, thoughts, and desires that we are not aware of in our normal conscious state. Freud was one of the first to try to describe how the unconscious functions and to develop ways to interpret the functions of the unconscious. Since he viewed dreams as meaningful messages from the unconscious, the analysis of dreams was one way Freud believed he could do this. He tried to translate dreams into a language that we could understand.

Listening 1

Elicit student responses to the prompt questions listed above under *All of us dream . . . all the time. . . . Why?* (See p. 83.) You should try to get a few responses for every question. If after hearing some student responses, you find that all of the students want to respond to all of the questions, allow them to tell each other their responses in pairs.

   Students should read the Preparation Note.

They will need a description of one of their dreams for the final project. Encourage them to record the images from at least one dream between now and the final project. You should look ahead and estimate when the final project will be done in your class so that students know how much time they have. Tell students to pay special attention to any symbols from the chapter that may appear in their dreams.

A. Before You Listen

1. Have students work in groups to discuss their feelings about dreams and what they mean. Students can also discuss beliefs about dreams that are common in their cultures.

2. Have students read the passage and the Calvino quotation and then discuss, as a group, three important ideas that they learned.

Page 83

Read the Culture Note to the students or have them read it on their own. You may want to ask students some questions for discussion:

* What American films have you seen that depict characters in psychotherapy? (Woody Allen films, which tend to be popular in Europe, often depict psychotherapy sessions.)

* Is psychotherapy popular in your country?

* What do people in your country generally think about people who are undergoing psychotherapy?

3. This exercise should be done individually. You may check answers with the class as a whole or have students check answers in pairs as you circulate to help with any problems. Students should be able to guess answers since the symbols are clearly related to their meanings.

Answers:

a. 2
b. 4
c. 5
d. 1
e. 3

B. Who Will You Be Listening To?

By now, students should know what a psychotherapist is. Have them discuss Patricia

Simko's courses and what they think they might cover. This will help them focus for the listening.

Page 84

C. Listening for a General Topic

Students should read all three general topic choices before listening. You may want to have them check their answers with a partner after listening.

Answer: 2

D. Listening for Specific Information

Students should work in pairs. Explain to students that to skim when listening, they must know which information they need to listen for. In this case they will listen for the information in sentences 1–9. After the listening, pairs can combine to check answers while you circulate to help.

Answers:

1. Everybody
2. direct
3. difficult
4. creation
5. unconscious
6. gift
7. honest
8. conscious
9. tool

E. Listening for Details

1. Students should work in pairs. Circulate to check their work. If you find that they are having trouble, you may want to create small groups so that students can discuss what they remember and help each other complete the exercise.

2. When students have finished, they should listen and check their answers. Partners should agree on the answers after the listening. You can go over the answers as a class.

Answers:

a. dream
b. unconscious
c. unconscious
d. conscious
e. unconscious
f. dreams
g. conscious
h. Dreams

Page 85

F. Vocabulary and Dictation

1. Students should read the instructions and the matching lists before the dictation. They should also be encouraged to answer what they can before the dictation. Partners can discuss their answers before listening to the dictation. Remind students they should not ask you to repeat anything during the dictation. Partners should check their answers when you are done dictating.

Dictation:

1. Dreams are important in our psychic life, and they've always been important in the history of human consciousness.

2. It's difficult to really gain access to the unconscious mind.

3. The unconscious mind is also a storehouse for limitless interactions and the repository of information that we've had forever.

4. Our dreams bypass our conscious brains. In so doing they also bypass all the tricks of our conscious brain.

5. As that inner life comes to correspond with our outer life, we can join forces with our unconscious in moving forward in our lives.

Answers:

1. f
2. e
3. b
4. g
5. d
6. h
7. c
8. a

2. This time you will be reading an entire passage. Remind them not to interrupt during the dictation. After the dictation, students should check their answers in pairs and try to fill in any information that they missed. If you find that the exercise is difficult for students, create small groups. Together, students should be able to complete the passage. You may wish to

photocopy the passage and give it to students so that they can correct spelling, punctuation, etc.

Dictation:

Our dreams never fool us; they will tell us what we think . . . what we really believe . . . what we wish for . . . what we hope for . . . what we dread most, and in so doing they give us a picture of our struggles . . . of our inner life. As that inner life comes to correspond with our outer life, we can join forces with our unconscious in moving forward in our lives. And our dreams can also help us take this next step in resolving problems.

G. Analysis and Synthesis

1. Students should work together in small groups and discuss the introductory question together. Circulate and encourage students to give examples.

2. Students should then read the situations one at a time and discuss them. You may want to assign a different situation to each group. When a group has finished discussing one situation, assign another. Students should discuss the closing questions in groups. You may extend this exercise by having the class as a whole share conclusions about the role that the unconscious mind played in these people's situations.

Page 86

Listening 2

A. Before You Listen

1. Have students read the quotation from Freud and ask them to paraphrase it for you. Possible response: *By understanding dreams we can understand our unconscious mind.*

2. You may want to create new small groups for this exercise. Have students read the introduction to the six things that Freud believed about dreams. They should work in their groups to complete the six points. Students should use the vocabulary items listed to fill in the blanks. Each vocabulary item is used once. Have the class compare answers.

Answers:

a. unconscious

b. desires

c. socially

d. symbols

e. personality

f. analyzed

B. Who Will You Be Listening To?

Students should read the introduction to the listening and the account of the dream. Tell students to ask you questions about any unfamiliar vocabulary in Jane's description of her dream. *Curb, blocking,* and *putter* may need explanation.

Page 87

C. Listening to a Process

Students should work in pairs. Each partner can write in answers separately during the listenings and then compare with his or her partner after each listening. Students will listen twice. The first time they will fill in the *steps*. The second time they should fill in the *details*. When pairs have finished comparing answers, you may have students work with a new partner to further compare answers and fill in missing points while you circulate to check their work. Alternatively, you can go over the answers with the class as a whole.

Answers:

Steps

1. Tell the story.

2. Speak about the day's events.

3. Describe characters.

4. Describe feelings.

5. Examine symbols.

6. Speak about the meaning to her inner self.

Details:

1. Jane is stuck . . . can't move forward; her co-workers are blocking her. But even when they disappear, she still can't make progress.

2. Jane had been at work and hadn't been able to attend an important conference that she had been looking forward to because two other employees needed help. Her boss had told her to stay at her desk and help them.

3. Jane and two co-workers. . . .

4. Jane felt anxious when her progress was blocked, and she was frustrated when she couldn't get her car to go forward.

5. People. Her co-workers, two women, remind Jane of her sisters, who used to tease her and

make her do chores she didn't want to do. She never felt she could get out on her own.

Objects. Her car represents progress, her energy, her forward motion in life or in a job.

6. When Jane speaks as the car, she feels blocked. The other car is bigger, and she can't fight it. She feels weak and inadequate. All she can do is wait. When the other car moves, she still can't get going.

    This dream gets to the heart of Jane's uneasiness with competition and with rivalry. Now she feels blocked by competitive co-workers who don't care about her situation. In early life it was her sisters who kept her from making progress.

Page 88

D. Language—Describing a Process

Give students some time to read the dream symbols listed on the side of the page. Remind them to think about whether or not these symbols have appeared in any of their recent dreams. This will he helpful for the project.

1. Now have students read the introduction to the markers. Ask them to discuss examples of when they heard these terms in the listening. They should go on to read the other terms listed for describing a process. Circulate and help students with any questions they may have as they discuss these terms. Once questions have been answered, students should be ready to go on to the next step.

2. Students should read the instructions. Go over the instructions with the class as a whole once students have finished reading them on their own.

Page 89

Students should have fun with this page. They may read the feminine and masculine symbols in pairs, or you may choose to discuss them as a class. Encourage students to discuss the meanings of the symbols and why each is either masculine or feminine. Have students help each other with any difficult vocabulary before stepping in to help. Again, remind students that they should keep these symbols in mind when describing their own dreams for the final project.

Page 90

Listening 3

A. Who Will You Be Listening To?

Students should read this introduction and then go back through the chapter and read about all of the symbols presented. This will help refresh their memories before the listening.

B. Notetaking

1. Students should work in pairs. Have students read the introduction to Bill's dreams before listening. Students should fill out the chart individually while listening and then check their work with a partner. You may want to circulate to be sure that students got enough information. If they did not, then reviewing the answers as a class should help students fill in missing information.

Possible Answers:

Symbols

Test. Performing in front of an audience is a kind of test. It raises the same kind of anxiety and fear of failure.

Boat voyage (students may bring up drowning).

Descriptions

Bill is being made to perform in a theater, but he feels unprepared. He is on stage and the performance is about to begin when he looks out and sees a dark, empty theater.

Bill is sailing to a beautiful place when a storm hits and breaks the sails of his ship. He may be afraid of drowning. The storm passes, and he is able to make a temporary sail. In the end he sails to a beautiful island with exquisite fruit.

2. Students should listen twice. Students will take notes individually again and then compare their notes with a partner. Since some students may need to use this dream for their final project, advise them not to discuss its meaning in great detail. You may go over the answers with the class or circulate to make sure that students got enough information.

Answers:

Symbols

House

Fire

Descriptions

Robyn is upstairs in her grandmother's house. She can see the house and the things in it clearly. Her grandmother is looking for something, and Robyn tells her mother that her grandmother is looking for the things that they moved. She then leaves the house and goes to a wooded area, where she sees her relatives socializing around a fire and waiting for her.

Page 91

Project—Analyzing Your Dreams

A. What Will You Be Doing?

Explain to students that they can analyze one of their own dreams, someone else's, or Robyn's dream.

B. Following the Steps in a Process

Students should work together in small groups for this project. By now, students should have done steps 1 and 2 at home. If they have not, have them work on another student's dream or have them pick a dream from Listening 3 to analyze. Each student should tell his or her dream according to step 3. Tell other students that they should listen carefully because they will need to help analyze the dream. They may even want to take notes. After a student tells his or her dream, then that student should go through steps 4–8 together with the group members. Whereas the student telling the dream is responsible for describing feelings, the other students should contribute to analyzing the information. This should be done in the form of discussion. The goal is to agree on an analysis of the dream. A nice follow-up activity is for each group to choose a dream to present to the class.

Photo/Art Credits

p. 3: Reprinted by permission of HarperCollins Publishers, Inc.

p. 4 b & t: Reprinted with permission from Parade Magazine and Eddie Adams © 1991 and 1995. All rights reserved.

p. 6, 8 , 9 & 11 : Courtesy of Horatio Alger Association

p. 12, mr & tr: Michael Ochs Archives/Venice,CA

p. 12, bl: *Cross Road Blues,* words and music by Robert Johnson, basic transcription by Charles LaVere. Copyright © (1978) 1990, 1991 King of Spades Music. All Rights Reserved. Used by Permission.

p. 12, br: Reuters/Corbis-Bettmann

p. 13: *Robert Johnson photo booth self portrait,* early 1930's copyright © 1986 Delta Haze Corporation All Rights Reserved. Used by Permission.

p. 14, l: Corbis-Bettmann

p. 14, r: Bjorg

p. 16, l: Michael Ochs Archives, Venice CA

p. 16, r: © Larry Hulst/Michael Ochs Archives/Venice, CA

p. 17: Thomas Pollock

p. 18, all: UPI/Corbis-Bettmann

p. 19: Jon Sievert, Michael Ochs Archives/Venice, CA

p. 20, t: Springer/Corbis-Bettmann

p. 20, b: © Peter Sherman/Michael Ochs Archives/Venice, CA

p. 22: Courtesy of the New School of Social Research, New York, NY

p. 23, b: Courtesy of the New School of Social Research, New York, NY

p. 23, t: Joseph Schuyler

p. 25, t: Courtesy of the New School of Social Research, New York, NY

p. 25, b: Joseph Schuyler

p. 26, t & b: Courtesy of Mutfak Rehberi, Istanbul

p. 28, m: Linda Harris

p. 29, tl: Courtesy of the New School of Social Research, New York, NY

p. 30: Thomas Pollock

p. 33: Peter Kuper, Inc. New York, NY

p. 34: Thomas Pollock

p. 37: Laima Druskis Photography

p. 37, r: Courtesy of the New School of Social Research, New York, NY

p. 39: ©1995 Mike Ramirez and Copley News Service. Reprinted with permission.

p. 43, bl: Harry Heleotis

p. 45, b: J. Berndt/Stock Boston

p. 47: Reprinted by permission of BasicBooks, a division of HarperCollins Publishers, Inc.

p. 52: Copyright © 1983 by Howard Gardner. Reprinted by permission of BasicBooks, a division of HarperCollins Publishers, Inc.

p. 53: Jonathan Stark

p. 55: Copyright © 1983 by Howard Gardner. Reprinted by permission of BasicBooks, a division of HarperCollins Publishers, Inc.

p. 56: Thomas Pollock

p. 60: Thomas Pollock

p. 62, t: F.S. Shooting Star

p. 62, b: Giraudon/Art Resource, NY

p. 63, tl & tr: Corbis-Bettmann

p. 63, b: Courtesy, the New School of Social Research, New York, NY

p. 65: TM & © Marvel Characters, Inc. All rights reserved.

p. 66: Warner Brothers/Shooting Star

p. 67: Cover courtesy of *The Oxford American.* Cover illustration © Marshall Arisman

p. 69: TM & © Marvel Characters, Inc. All rights reserved.

p. 70: Thomas Pollack

p.72, t: NYT Permissions

p. 72, b: © Jimmy Margulies. Reprinted with special permission of North American Syndicate.

p. 73, t: Courtesy of The Hudson Institute, Indianapolis IN

p. 73, m: Reprinted from the October 17, 1994 issue of *Business Week* by permission. © 1994 McGraw-Hill Companies.

p. 73, b: Courtesy of the New School of Social Research, New York, NY

p. 82: Corbis-Bettmann

p. 83: Thomas Pollock

p. 90, b & t: Thomas Pollock

Illustrations

Ruth Flanigan, pp: 52, t; 53, tr & br; 57; 58; 59; 83, t; 88; 89